Masculinity in Fiction and Film

CONTINUUM LITERARY STUDIES SERIES

Also available in the series:

Character and Satire in Postwar Fiction by Ian Gregson
Fictions of Globalization by James Annesley
Joyce and Company by David Pierce
Women's Fiction 1945–2000 by Deborah Philips

Forthcoming titles:

Beckett's Books by Matthew Feldman
English Fiction in the 1930s by Chris Hopkins
Novels of the Contemporary Extreme edited by Alain-Phillipe Durand and
   Naomi Mandel
London Narratives by Lawrence Phillips

MASCULINITY IN FICTION AND FILM

Representing Men in Popular Genres 1945–2000

Brian Baker

continuum

Continuum International Publishing Group
The Tower Building, 11 York Road, London SE1 7NX
80 Maiden Lane, Suite 704, New York, NY 10038

www.continuumbooks.com

First published 2006
Reprinted 2007
Paperback edition 2008

British Library Cataloguing-in-Publication Data
A catalogue record for this book is available from the British Library.

ISBN-10: 0-8264-8652-5 (hardback)
        1-8470-6262-8 (paperback)
ISBN-13: 978-0-8264-8652-3 (hardback)
        978-1-8470-6262-8 (paperback)

Library of Congress Cataloging-in-Publication Data
A catalog record for this book is available from the Library of Congress.

Typeset by Aarontype Limited, Easton, Bristol
Printed and bound in Great Britain by Biddles Ltd., King's Lynn, Norfolk

Contents

Acknowledgements

I would like to thank my colleagues in the Department of English at the University of Chester for providing study leave in 2004, which allowed me to develop this long-standing project into a book and to write crucial chapters. The staff at the libraries of the University of Chester and the University of Liverpool have been diligent and accommodating in helping source critical material. I would also like to thank Anna Sandeman and Rebecca Simmonds at Continuum for their understanding and support.

Particular thanks must go to Ashley Chantler, who read several drafts of work included here and always responded with positive and detailed comments. I would also like to express my gratitude to Arthur Bradley, friend and erstwhile colleague, for his consistent support and encouragement for my work. Early versions of chapters and other work towards this book were delivered at conferences held at the University of East Anglia, John Moores University, St Anne's College Oxford, and Edge Hill College, and in seminars held at the University of Chester and the North East Wales Institute of Higher Education, Wrexham. My thanks to all who responded to my papers and gave food for thought. More general thanks go to Simon Lee, Ed Hill, Sebastian Groes, David James, John Bleasdale, Eliot Atkins, Joel Petrie and Alison Platt for encouragement and discussion of some of the films and novels in this book at different periods of my life. My thanks also to students at the University of Chester, upon whom some of the ideas and issues were tested, for their generous and positive responses. Finally, my love and thanks go to Deniz, who put up with this project for five years and saw things through to the very end, reading and proofing just days before our baby was due.

While all books are, of necessity, collaborative projects in the broadest sense – and without the input of those named above, this book would not have taken the form it has – I must stress that any errors or omissions herein are my own.

Introduction

What this book is about

Although this book is entitled *Masculinity in Fiction and Film: Representing Men in Popular Genres 1945–2000*, it is, of necessity, selective. My argument in this book concerns the ways in which representations of masculinity have been bound up, in popular generic fiction and film, with the ideological imperatives of the American (and British) nation-state since the end of World War 2. Many of these imperatives are themselves bound up with the Cold War, but the scope of this book ranges beyond the strictly geo-political (and genres which explicitly engage with the Cold War, such as espionage fiction). Though the masculinities discussed herein are selective, not comprehensive, they have been chosen to be in some sense typical of crucial historical and cultural moments: the late-1950s and early-1960s; the early-1970s; the 1990s. It is in these moments, this book argues, that key films encode the critical connection between the ideology of the nation-state and the ideologically sanctioned (what I will call, following Steven Cohan, the 'hegemonic') form of masculinity at the time. These popular fictions and films negotiate, or more properly renegotiate, forms of masculinity that express something about the cultural, social and political formations of their period of production, and taken together, form a kind of loose history of both representations of masculinity in Anglo-American texts and in the postwar period as a whole.

This book is published into a burgeoning critical field of studies of masculinities. Critical texts such as Berthold Schoene-Harwood's *Writing Men* (2000) for twentieth-century British fiction, Lee Clark Mitchell's *Westerns: Making the Man in Fiction and Film* (1996) for masculinities in a particular genre, and more general texts like Peter Middleton's *The Inward Gaze* (1992) and John Beynon's *Masculinities and Culture* (2002) indicate the growing importance of masculinity as a field of investigation in both fiction and film. In retrospect it seems like the period from 1992 to 1994 was a kind of 'origin point' for the study of screen masculinities. Several books were published on masculinities in film, indicating a critical reconsideration of gender and masculinity on screen, perhaps responding to the increased visibility of the male body in American and British culture. Among them were Kaja Silverman's *Male Subjectivity at the Margins* (1992), Yvonne Tasker's *Spectacular Bodies* (1993), Susan Jeffords's *Hard Bodies* (1994), and the collections *Screening the Male* (Cohan and Hark 1993) and *The Sexual Subject* (Caughie *et al.* 1992).

The majority of this book concentrates on screen masculinities, though the reader will find considerable material on fiction. The tradition of theorization of gender in screen theory has been through Lacanian models since Laura Mulvey's famous and discipline-transforming 'Visual Pleasure and Narrative Cinema' (1975) suggested that the camera in classical Hollywood cinema regulates the look of the audience, constituting an identification with a male gaze. An active/passive binary mapped onto masculine and feminine subject positions results in gendered spectator-ship. The male looks, and the female is looked upon; this leads to the objectification and fetishization of the female body, and the negation of female pleasure. Steve Neale's 'Masculinity as Spectacle' (1983) has been almost as influential, and explored the spectatorial paradigm of the Mulvey article to open a space for the investigation of screen masculinities. I will work with these models, necessarily, but my own approach is historicist rather than psychoanalytical.

I use the plural of 'masculinities' throughout this book to indicate that there is not one single 'masculinity' analysed here, but a range of different representations of masculinity. In analysing masculinities in film, I have particularly found models worthy of emulation in Steven Cohan's *Masked Men* (1997) and Robert Corber's *In the Name of National Security* (1993), which look at Hollywood cinema in the 15 years following World War 2. Both of these texts take a historicizing and contextual approach to understanding film texts that I have sought to marry to close analytical attention to the films themselves. Cohan, in his article 'The Spy in the Gray Flannel Suit' (1995) and in *Masked Men*, uses Judith Butler's conception of gender as performance (in *Gender Trouble* (1990)) to analyse Cary Grant's performance in Hitchcock's *North by Northwest*, and a variety of other films and star personae. Butler's performative notion of subjectivity is vital to Cohan's, and my, argument. He explains its critical consequences thus:

> From this perspective, 'masculinity' does not refer to a male nature but instead imitates a dominant regulatory fiction authorizing the continued representation of certain types of gender performances for men (like the breadwinner), marginalizing others (like the momma's boy), and forbidding still others (like the homosexual). (Cohan 1995: 57)

Cohan argues that a 'hegemonic masculinity' (the male 'breadwinner' in the 1950s) organizes a range of subordinate masculinities in relation to this dominant term. I have found this model persuasive and very useful for my own investigations in this book. The forms of masculinity I analyse are as follows: in Chapter 1, in relation to science fiction, the 'organization man' and the 'citizen-soldier'; in Chapters 2 and 3 (on British and American espionage fictions, respectively), the 'soldier/spy' and the 'double agent'; in Chapter 4, on masculinity in 'crisis', I analyse the 'psycho' and the 'man in the grey flannel suit'. Chapters 5 and 6 consider the 'rogue cop' and its variants; Chapter 7 the 'superannuated shootist' in Westerns; and Chapter 8 the 'cowboy' and the 'astronaut'. In this book I am not concerned with analysing what masculinity *is*; rather, I investigate a range of fictional and filmic texts to try to reveal how the cultural production of masculinities is central to the ideological structures of the contemporary nation-state.

This book explicitly connects representations of masculinity to the ideological imperatives underpinning the nation-state, taking a cross-generic (and interdisciplinary) approach to a *political* understanding of the connection between masculinity, citizenship, law, community, and violence. *Masculinity in Fiction and Film* takes a broad, multi-genre, interdisciplinary approach to the study of masculinities in fiction and film, largely considering popular texts that have remained within the realm of popular consumption, and that have generated relatively little critical interest. This book determinedly concentrates on popular fictions. By this I mean literary and filmic texts that are produced by mass entertainment industries (such as Hollywood or mainstream imprints); that are generic texts, related to some of the dominant genres of the twentieth century; and that are texts where the ideological structures that frame the ways in which gender is represented are visible just below the surface. The ideological study of popular fictions has a worthy critical heritage, and the reader will find the crucial name of Tony Bennett among the critical texts I cite; this is also connected to the study of popular culture, not to decry its commercialized crassness, but to investigate the investment that readers have in popular fictions, and also the investment the ideological structures of the British and American nation-states have in the production of their own popular cultures and fictions. In this context, it would be correct to mention Raymond Williams and Richard Hoggart, and the Birmingham Centre for Cultural Studies (now closed) as antecedents.

How this book is organized

This book is organized in several ways. Firstly, it takes a broadly chronological structure in which to study representations of masculinity in genre fictions, and how they connected to the ideological imperatives of their time of production. Secondly, it emphasizes key spaces or places which stand in relation to the male subject: the dystopia, the West of the United States, the frontier (and New Frontier), and the cities of Berlin, San Francisco and Los Angeles. Thirdly, it attempts to trace the significance of different representations of masculinity with regard to genre fictions, which, it is argued, are particularly invested with ideological or mythic significance with regard to the nation-state: the Western, espionage fiction, dystopian science fiction and crime narratives.

The book falls into two connected parts. The first four chapters are organized around the theme of fractured subjectivity; each chapter investigates a progressively more splintered, paranoid and schizoid masculine subjectivity, resulting in the psychosis of characters such as Patrick Bateman in *American Psycho* (1999), whose culturally induced fragmentation releases a hellish (and hallucinatory) violence. Generically, these chapters concentrate on science fiction, the fantastic and espionage fictions. The second part (also of four chapters) considers fictions where masculinity is stitched into an ideological narrative of the nation-state (and state power). These chapters investigate crime/detective/police procedural fictions, the Western, and finally return to science fiction in end-of-the-Cold War films such as *Star Trek VI* (1991) and *Space Cowboys* (2000). These four chapters are thematically connected by the recurrent motif of ageing or old age, and both a manifestation of, as well as a critique of, a nostalgic vision of 'heroic' masculinity.

The chronology of the book begins in the mid-1950s. According to Steven Cohan, in *Masked Men* (1997), the figure of the 'breadwinner' is the hegemonic term by which representations of masculinity are regulated in 50s America, all other types of masculinity being arrayed in relation to this central term. I argue that in the 1950s, anxieties concerning social and economic organization are arranged around the term of masculinity: the 'organization man' or the 'man in the grey flannel suit', the breadwinner whose economic success was at once the index of a 'new' masculine order of success, yet also the indicator of a problematic 'de-masculinization' in a corporate world which reduced the possibilities for 'heroic' action. The necessity for unreconstructed heroism (in the form of the 'soldier' masculinity supplanted by the 'breadwinner' type after World War 2) is the basis for a reconstruction of masculinity in two science fiction novels of the mid- to late-1950s: Pohl and Kornbluth's *Gladiator-at-Law* (1955) and Robert Heinlein's *Starship Troopers* (1959). Where the first is set in a near-future dystopia, and figures social reorganization through the restitution of 'gladiatorial' male subjectivity, *Starship Troopers'* Cold War-inflected scenario imagines the need for the citizen-soldier to defeat the interplanetary Other/enemy, the 'Bugs'. Both also encode the necessity of heroic action (legitimated violence) and heroic sacrifice as ideological underpinnings of the renewal of the nation-state.

This motif is analysed further in the more explicit Cold War fictions of the British spy genre. While James Bond represents the imagination of the unconflicted 'warrior' male subject needed to fight the Cold War, John Le Carré's novels investigate the fractured and fragmented subjectivities of those who conduct the Cold War's secret conflicts, most particularly in the form of the 'double agent'. Berlin is the topographical analogue of this split subjectivity/split state. Ian McEwan's *The Innocent* (1990) uses the espionage genre to rethink masculinity at the end of the Cold War, setting its narrative in 1955; James Ellroy's 'secret history' of the post-World War 2 United States, *American Tabloid* (1995) and *The Cold Six Thousand* (2001), again rewrites the Cold War from the point of view of FBI and CIA operatives. Where McEwan follows Le Carré in his narrative of betrayal and psychological fragmentation, Ellroy reinvests the masculine agent with near-heroic potency, remaking history as the product of the machinations of a tiny male elite. Ellroy's espionage fiction is of the paranoid strain inaugurated by Richard Condon's *The Manchurian Candidate* (1960, film 1962), which forges a powerful narrative out of Korean War brainwashing anxieties and Cold War invasion narratives. In Frankenheimer's film the soldier becomes the double agent, whose revolt against his conditioning eventually leads to a double parricide/matricide.

The figure of the 'Spy in the grey flannel suit' is central to Cohan's *Masked Men*, who takes the psychoanalytic reading of *North by Northwest* of Raymond Bellour and contextualizes his argument through the dominant 'performance' ethic for 50s masculinity (an argument inflected by Judith Butler's work on performativity and gender). Like Robert Corber in *In the Name of National Security*, Cohan reads the masculine maturation of Roger Thornhill as an acculturation into the ideological imperatives of the Cold War; to be an adult is to be a soldier/spy citizen. Several novels and films in the mid- to late-1990s return to the figure of the 'man in the grey flannel suit' to express recurring anxieties about the 'crisis in masculinity' diagnosed by several social texts of the last decade. As in the 1950s, an increasingly commodified and consumerist organization in life leads, in the films *Falling Down* (1991), *Fight Club* (1999) and *American Psycho* (1999), to a fragmentation of the (white) male psyche and a violent, quasi-psychotic reaction against the conditions of contemporary life.

The police thriller, the Western and space programme-based science fiction are the focus of the second half of the book; each demonstrates the connection of the ideology of the nation-state with popular fictions. The 'old age' Westerns *The Man Who Shot Liberty Valance* (1962) and *Ride the High Country* (1962) encode a tension between the necessity for the male 'frontiersman' (and his violent, individualistic ethos) for forging the development of the American nation-state – represented in the Western as the 'taming of the frontier' – and the necessity of his exclusion from the *polis* which he helps to bring into being. This had been a common theme of the Western before 1962, but few films had explicitly focused upon the trials of old age, and encode a nostalgia for the untroubled heroism of the gunfighter masculinity. *The Man Who Shot Liberty Valance* and *Ride the High Country* inaugurate a sequence of elegiac, 'old age Westerns' (such as *The Wild Bunch*, *The Shootist* and *Unforgiven*), in which the ageing stars of the Western are restyled as old men who face a heroic 'last showdown', keeping their honour while stepping off the stage of history. The tension between the frontier and 'civilization', between the individualistic frontiersmen and the needs of social and civic community, recurs throughout the second half of the book.

Typically, the texts analysed – from *Dirty Harry* (1971) to *LA Confidential* (1997), from *Ride the High Country* (1962) to *Space Cowboys* (2000) – inhabit and replicate the tension between the necessity for law to organize a democratic, civic society, and the extra-legal violence which the law both excludes and relies upon to discipline the community. These texts also nostalgically commemorate a Cold War, heroic masculinity: James Ellroy's 'LA Quartet' and Walter Mosley's detective novels are set in the late-1940s and 1950s; the 'rogue cop' films (symbolized by Eastwood's Harry Callahan) revisit the masculine individualism of the classical Western; and *Space Cowboys* and *Armageddon* (1998) explicitly look back to the 'Right Stuff' era of space exploration to imagine a space for heroic male action.

Finally, although this book is certainly about masculinities, and is about representation in fiction and film, I intend it to also act as a kind of discursive cultural history. Throughout, I have tried to historicize my discussion wherever possible. Where masculinity was once a monolithic and unexplored subject in relation to gender studies, I hope here to use it as a lens to focus a discussion of what Raymond Williams called the 'structures of feeling' of the second half of the twentieth century.

CHAPTER ONE

Cold Warriors

Postwar hegemonic masculinity

The men who fought World War 2 in Europe and in the Pacific have recently been valorized as the 'greatest generation', which is in fact the title of a book on the subject by the American journalist Tom Brokaw. The same ideological value embodies such films as Spielberg's *Saving Private Ryan* (1998). Nostalgic and sentimental, this rewriting of postwar masculinity masks the very real anxieties that accompanied the return of the wartime heroes. Many of these men returned to their wives or families changed, unable and unwilling to communicate what they had seen and experienced. Susan Faludi, in her book *Stiffed* (1999), which charts the 'crisis in masculinity' that seems (or seemed, in the late-90s) to afflict contemporary American society, writes:

> They were just fathers in the era after the war, living in brand-new suburbs with wives and children they barely knew, working at brand-new jobs on brand-new corporate 'campuses', miles from their brand-new aluminium-sided houses. Which is to say that the life of the postwar father was altogether too newly out of the box for him to understand it, much less explain it to his son.
> Many of these fathers were veterans of World War II or Korea, but their bloody paths to virility were not ones they sought to pass on, or even usually to discuss. (Faludi 1999: 5)

While Faludi locates the crisis in contemporary masculinity in a failure of fatherhood, this passage indicates that the postwar American life constructed for the GIs' return was, in fact, a major factor in their own alienation and dislocation. The repetition of 'brand-new' indicates both the elevation of modernity in the postwar American economic boom to a lifestyle aspiration, but also the way in which the returning soldiers were corralled by a new economic and cultural system designed to enforce their domesticity. Not all men followed this path, of course: the 'GI Bill' enabled a generation of working-class and underprivileged young men to go to college, often the first time anyone in their families had done so. Faludi herself notes that 'what gets left out of the contemporary nostalgia of baby-boom men for their World War II father ... is what their fathers did *after* the war' (Faludi 1999: 35–6, Faludi's emphasis). Two of the main anxieties surrounding masculinity in the immediate postwar era are: firstly, to do with the idea of the 'damaged soldier', the man so inured to war that he transports violence and aggression back into the peacetime world; and secondly, that the kind of relationships that were forged between men in combat may have disrupted not only the domestic or familial normative, but hetero-sexuality itself.

Studs Terkel, the American oral historian, has spent a large part of his life talking to 'ordinary Americans' and listening to their stories, understanding the experience of the twentieth-century United States not through official history but through the recollection and recounting of diverse lives. On his book on World War 2 (notably titled *My American Century*), Terkel spoke to Peggy Terry, a 'mountain woman' from Kentucky who lived in Chicago. Married before the war, she recounted how her experiences were 'the beginning of my seeing things' (Terkel 1998: 193). Her husband became a paratrooper, and fought in North Africa and Europe. She said:

> Until the war he never drank. He never even smoked. When he came back he was an absolute drunkard. And he used to have the most awful nightmares. He'd get up in the middle of the night and start screaming. I'd just sit for hours and hold him while he just shook. We'd go to the movies, and if they'd have films with lots of shooting in it, he'd just start to shake and have to get up and leave. He started slapping me around and slapped the kids around. He became a brute. … It seems so obvious to say – wars brutalize people. It brutalized him. (Terkel 1998: 193)

Peggy Terry's experience indicates the disruption to ideals of masculinity suffered in the postwar period, and the very real social problems caused by war. The damaged soldier recurs in the representations of masculinity in the immediate postwar period, and the period of his prominence can be bookended by two films, *The Blue Dahlia* (1946) starring Alan Ladd, and *In a Lonely Place* (1950) starring Humphrey Bogart. In *The Blue Dahlia*, Ladd's character Johnny Morrison and two of his wartime 'buddies' return to the States, and to California. One of his friends, Buzz (William Bendix), has been wounded in the war, and has a metal plate inserted in his skull. Early on in the film, as the three sit in a bar while Morrison considers how to stage his return to his wife (which he seems anxious about), a juke-box plays in the background. The music pounding in his head, Buzz picks a fight with a fellow patron and it is not until his friends explain his violence, by revealing his identity as a veteran, that the confrontation subsides. As the narrative unfolds, we come to realize the importance of this episode. Morrison returns to find his wife has become a 'fast' woman, having an affair and partying with an assortment of hedonistic and unpleasant types. His wife is murdered, and Morrison becomes the prime suspect. However, the audience suspects that it is Buzz who is the murderer, in one of his violent fits. The narrative resolves this particular conundrum by revealing the killer to be a sleazy house detective, and places Morrison in a secure heterosexual relationship with Joyce Harwood, played by Veronica Lake, but the film clearly enunciates cultural anxieties about both the returning soldier and the importance of the wartime-buddy relationship between men. Ladd and Lake's images can be found as an intertextual reference in Curtis Hanson's film of *LA Confidential*, the focus of Chapter 6 of this book.

In a Lonely Place stars Humphrey Bogart as a screenwriter, living in Hollywood. After he takes home a hat-check girl, she leaves and is murdered. Across the courtyard lives Laurel, played by Gloria Grahame, one of the key femmes fatales of the postwar period. (She also stars in Fritz Lang's *The Big Heat* (1953), which also narrates the problematic status of the postwar male, this time in the figure of the rogue cop.) Although she only sees Bogart at the window, she provides him with an alibi, and soon a romance develops. As the film progresses, however, her doubts begin to surface. Bogart's character, Dix Steele, is, as his name suggests, a 'man's man', a wartime hero who brawls in bars on a regular basis (a bit like Bogart himself). Not only is he sexually attractive, he is also charismatic for his male associates. One of the policemen assigned to the murder case is an old war-buddy, Brub Nicolai (Frank Lovejoy), whose admiration of Dix is plain; 'He's an exciting guy' he says, after a dinner-party where Dix's storytelling powers almost lead Brub to accidentally strangle his own wife (the fate, not coincidentally, of the hat-check girl). Laurel eventually suspects Dix and plans to leave him: when he discovers her plan, he tries to strangle her, and is only interrupted by a phone call that pronounces his innocence of the murder. It is, of course, far too late. Steven Cohan, in his excellent investigation into 1950s screen masculinities *Masked Men* (1997), suggests that 'Whether or not he turns out to be a murderer, [Dix's] masculinity is shown to be dangerous to domestic life and heterosexual coupling' (Cohan 1997: 100).

The attractiveness of Dix to his wartime buddy implicitly compromises and destabilizes the heterosexual orientation of the postwar male. The emphasis on the 'buddy' relationship is indicated by another of Studs Terkel's interviewees, E. B. 'Sledgehammer' Sledge. 'Sledgehammer' (whose name seemingly brooks no homosexual connotations) says: 'the only thing that kept you going was your faith in your buddies. It wasn't just a case of friendship. ... You couldn't let 'em down. It was stronger than flag and country' (Terkel 1998: 197). The intensity of the 'buddy' bond seems to go beyond the normative markers of male friendship, and it is unsurprising that anxieties about the experiences of enlisted men were also sexual: that, in the words of Gore Vidal (who was there), 'perfectly "normal" young men, placed outside the usual round of family and work, will run riot with each other' (Vidal 1996: 102). Here I want to introduce a term favoured by the literary critic Eve Kosofsky Sedgwick, which she uses in her book *Between Men* (1985). The word is 'homosocial'.

'Homosocial' is a word occasionally used in history and the social sciences, where it describes social bonds between persons of the same sex; it is a neologism, obviously formed by analogy with 'homosexual', and just as obviously meant to be distinguished from 'homosexuality'. In fact, it is applied to such activities as 'male bonding', which may, as in our society, be characterized by intense homophobia, fear and hatred of homosexuality. To draw the 'homosocial' back into the orbit of 'desire', of the potentially erotic, then, is to hypothesize the potential unbrokenness of a continuum between homosocial and homosexual – a continuum whose visibility, for men, in our society, is radically disrupted. (Sedgwick 1985: 1–2)

The possibility of such a 'continuum' is what provokes such anxiety in postwar America: that the rigorously repressed element of desire in male homosocial relationships may have manifested itself in wartime. This fear was exacerbated by the publication of the first volume of the Kinsey Report in 1948 (on men), which, in the words of Steven Cohan, showed that '[a]mong other moral and legal transgressions, they masturbated, had homosexual encounters, were promiscuous before marriage, [and] adulterous afterward' (Cohan 1997: 58). The Kinsey Report became something of a *cause célèbre* and a nationwide bestseller, and suggested that homosexual acts were much more widespread than anyone had believed. Robert Corber, in his book on gender and the Cold War, *In the Name of National Security*, suggests that it 'seemed to confirm psychoanalytical theories that stressed the instability of sexual identities' (Corber 1993: 63). Gore Vidal's understanding of gender – 'the dumb neologisms, homo-sexual and hetero-sexual, are adjectives that describe acts but never people' (Vidal 1999: 721) – is perhaps a product of his experience of the fluidity of both sexuality and gender roles in the war years. For Vidal, the 'buddy' and the sexual partner become indistinguishable, and the Kinsey Report suggests that Vidal's experiences were not anomalous.

To counter both the possibility of male violence or homosexuality, and the disruption to the familial and economic structures of capitalist America, masculinity had to be redefined in the postwar period. The ideological work of this redefinition was partly carried out by representations of men in film and popular fictions. It is particularly in film noir, according to Steven Cohan, that such renegotiations can be discerned. He writes:

> Though a product of postwar Hollywood and responsive to demobilization in its own war, film noir still represents masculinity in the militant terms of a war culture, opposing both femininity and domesticity to specific standards of 'tough' male prowess (e.g., physical obligations, social mobility), which it plots through a thriller narrative. (Cohan 1997: 42)

'Hegemonic' masculinity, the term used by Cohan to characterize certain representations of masculinity found throughout the 1950s, 'articulates various social relations of power as an issue of gender normality' (Cohan 1997: 35). It appears to accommodate other forms of masculinity, including 'young', 'effeminate' and 'homosexual', but subordinates them into a power hierarchy, with the 'hegemonic' variant at the top (Cohan 1997: 35–8).

Hegemonic masculinity in the 1950s in the USA, argues Cohan, is the figure of the 'man in the grey flannel suit', the corporate male breadwinner whose hegemony is ideologically connected both to the dominance of a professional elite (as in C. Wright Mills's *The Power Elite* of 1956) and to culturally reproduced ideologies of economic performance and responsibility. We will return to versions of the 'man in the grey flannel suit' in Chapter 4. Masculinity is then a ' "regulatory fiction" of normality' (Cohan 1997: 24), not a biologically or naturally occurring role, and this model (influenced by the work of Judith Butler) can become, in Cohan's hands, a provocative and very useful analytical tool.

In his book on the 1950s American film, *Seeing Is Believing*, Peter Biskind notes the importance of domesticity in adjusting the returning GI to the demands of postwar life. He writes:

> The millions of American men who were coming back from Europe and the Pacific in 1945 found, to the surprise of many, that man's place was in the home. Home was more than a pipe, slippers, and a warm bed. For one thing, it was the seat of the family, the domestic version of the group so favoured by pluralists. 'Whether you are a man or a woman,' as *The Woman's Guide to Better Living* put it, 'the family is the unit to which you genuinely belong'. (Biskind 2001: 250–1)

Cohan calls this the 'domestic mystique', a knowing inversion of the 'feminine mystique' identified by Betty Friedan in the late-1950s. As the 1950s drew on, American society had begun to renegotiate 'hegemonic masculinity' in favour of the domestic, validating marriage and responsibility, and marginalizing or demonizing other variants of masculinity. Cohan argues:

> Domesticity pervaded the entire culture as the standard of normality, not just the middle class, resulting in a new definition of the family's role that crossed social divisions, and it extended to men as well as women, as indicated by the male's position in the family as its moral and psychological leader. (Cohan 1997: 50)

The Baby Boom, so often (and rightly) seen as a cultural means by which patriarchal American society removed women from the workplace and reinserted them into the domestic sphere, also operates as a way in which masculinity could be redefined, and to eliminate the possibility of non-normative behaviour among the postwar generation.

The Organization Man

In the 1950s, several celebrated texts analysed the rise of the culture of corporations and the construction of the so-called 'organization man', the rise of mass culture and television enforcing a conformity of social desires and behaviours. The domination of a bureaucratized, highly organized and regulated life was predicted by James Burnham in *The Managerial Revolution* (1941), whose vision that 'the world political system will coalesce into *three* primary super-states' (Burnham 1972: 176) had a large impact upon George Orwell and *Nineteen Eighty-Four*'s Oceania, Eurasia and Eastasia. Burnham's prediction of the 'managerial society' was characterized by 'governmental (state) ownership and control of the major instruments of production' (Burnham 1972: 118). No longer owned by a bourgeoisie, as in Marx's nineteenth-century analyses, production becomes controlled by state managers, the bureaucrats becoming the ruling class. Burnham also outlined the ideology of the managers: 'the more effective prosecution of war, and the support of the power and privilege of a new ruling class' (Burnham 1972: 137). This form of domination is enabled and maintained by technology, particularly communications and transportation, again foreshadowing the ubiquity of the telescreens in *Nineteen Eighty-Four* and television itself in the American dystopian science fiction of the 1950s and 1960s.

As Aldous Huxley, in *Brave New World Revisited*, a text of commentaries on how his dystopian novel now related to the world of the 1950s, suggested: '[t]hat we are being propelled in the direction of Brave New World is obvious' (Huxley 1994: 34). In a fairly pessimistic series of analyses, Huxley investigated the ways in which *Brave New World* had anticipated some of the techniques of control and the tendencies towards oppressive organization in American society. He wrote:

> Civilization is, among other things, the process by which primitive packs are transformed into an analogue, crude and mechanical, of the social insects' organic communities. At the present time the pressures of overpopulation and technological change are accelerating this process. ... However hard they try, men cannot create a social organism, they can only create an organization. In the process of trying to create an organism they will merely create a totalitarian despotism. (Huxley 1994: 33)

In Huxley's analyses as in the dystopian science fiction of the 1950s, too much order is the problem. The metaphor of the hive, used here by Huxley, is a common dystopian image of the city, a spatial image of a society which prizes communitarian ideals over individual freedom. This is an anxiety common to many texts of social theory in the 1950s. The destruction, or perhaps superseding of the individual (and necessary erasure of the mythos, peculiarly American, of individualism and struggle) was the theme of David Riesman's *The Lonely Crowd* (1950), and William H. Whyte's *The Organization Man* (1956), which attempted to describe a transformation in the motivation and behaviour of the (male) individual in immediately postwar America. Riesman analysed a change in the way conformity is constructed. He described the typical person of the American 1950s as 'other-directed', whose conformity is less to the values of parents but to the desires and preferences of the social or peer group, and who experienced fear of transgression as a constant anxiety. *The Lonely Crowd* suggested that this

indicated a change from a myth of individual freedom and entrepreneur-
ship, which legitimated the forms of earlier American capitalism, to a myth
of belongingness which was required in a more bureaucratic, corporate
postwar society.

William H. Whyte perceived that the Protestant Ethic of individualism
and work was disappearing under pressure from the needs of big business;
he saw it being replaced by a 'social ethic': 'that contemporary body of
thought which makes morally legitimate the pressures of society against
the individual' (Whyte 1956: 7). Huxley, in *Brave New World Revisited*, cites
Whyte's analysis approvingly. Both Whyte and Riesman analysed the
pressures towards conformity and 'belongingness' in order for people to
succeed in society, what amounts to the suppression of individuality in
exchange for material wealth. Whyte wrote that 'the dominant ideological
drift in organization life is toward (1) idolatry of the system and (2) the
misuse of science to achieve this' (Whyte 1956: 171). He advocated a 'fight'
against the organization, *for* the individual. David Savran, in *Taking It Like
A Man* (1998), suggests that anxieties about the 'organization man' in the
1950s indicate 'a retreat from the more independent- and entrepreneurial-
minded masculinities that preceded it' (Savran 1998: 47). Changes in social
organization are inextricably bound up, then, with forms of hegemonic
masculinity.

The liberal self

Richard Corber has suggested that such an emphasis on individuation
and selfhood was part of a move towards a Cold War (anti-Communist)
liberal consensus: 'Cold War liberals were able to determine the way in
which Americans thought and lived their relations to the world by limiting
the fund of interpretative possibilities available to them for understanding their lived experience. ... [I]n doing so, they gained control over
the production of the postwar subject' (Corber 1993: 3). Anxieties about
male subjectivity were reflected in the deliberate construction of a postwar
liberal consensus which emphasized a heterosexual and familial normative.
Influenced by this cultural movement, Pohl and Kornbluth's *Gladiator-at-
Law* (1955) narrates the construction of both male friendship groups and
heterosexual (i.e. procreative) couples as an attempt to recover male identity in a less anxious form.

This anxiety about male subjectivity and sexuality was partly created
by the Kinsey Report. Corber argues that 'Kinsey's findings that the sexual
identities of most Americans were fluid and unstable only reinforced fears
that homosexuals and lesbians had infiltrated the federal government and
threatened to subvert it from within' (Corber 1993: 63). Homosexuality
and Communism were implicitly linked as the 'enemy within'; the regulation of sexual behaviour was complementary and directly produced by the
emergence of the national security state, 'which insured that Americans

scrutinized themselves for any indication of sexual and/or political deviance that might call into question their loyalty to the nation' (Corber 1993: 10). The liberal consensus, which undermined or negated Marxian critique, also served to impose a sexual normativeness.

Underlying this regulation of behaviour, Barbara Ehrenreich suggests, 'was, of course, contempt for women; in psycho-math, "I am not a man" = "I am a woman", which, in turn, equated failure, immaturity, mental illness and all the rest' (Ehrenreich 1983: 26). Ehrenreich, in her text *The Hearts of Men*, analyses a fear of homosexuality in postwar American culture. She suggests that the 'irresponsible' male, or the social or economic 'failure', was stigmatized and placed in a position of Other to a naturalized heterosexual, monogamous, conformist masculine ideal. She suggests that the following equation formed a matrix of fear and control which regulated both the ways in which homosexual men thought about and represented themselves, and also the behaviour patterns of heterosexual men: '*I am a failure = I am castrated = I am not a man = I am a woman = I am a homosexual*' (Ehrenreich 1983: 25). Homosexuals, communists, and women: the construction of these Others to a heterosexual male normativeness, itself characterized by Sedgwick's 'homosociality', becomes an ossification of social and sexual formations, closing down what Corber describes as the 'emergence [in the 1950s] of an increasingly heterogeneous and antagonistic social field in which the proliferation of differences threatened to lead to a generalized crisis of identities' (Corber 1993: 7).

Pohl and Kornbluth's *Gladiator-at-Law*

Frederik Pohl and Cyril Kornbluth's 1955 text, *Gladiator-at-Law*, has received nothing like the critical attention bestowed on another of their collaborations, *The Space Merchants* (1953). This somewhat forgotten text constructs the male subject as a fragile and anxious entity, which is reconstructed through codes of aggressive and combative behaviour: the 'Gladiator' of the title. Pohl and Kornbluth were both a part of the 'Futurians' group of science fiction writers of the 1940s, some of whom, like Pohl, came directly out of leftist politics of the 1930s, a politics characterized by the broad anti-fascist umbrella of the Popular Front period. Pohl describes in his autobiography his time with the Young Communist League, and his subsequent suspicion of, and departure from it. The United States of the 1940s and 1950s saw a movement away from the politics of the Communist-influenced left towards a centrist and 'liberal' consensus. Christopher Brookeman, in his *American Culture and Society since the 1930s* (1984), describes 'that disenchantment with communism and explicit ideological commitment that became a hallmark of the 1940s and 1950s' (Brookeman 1984: 2). Perhaps under the pressures of the House Un-American Activities Committee (HUAC), active in this period though only gaining notoriety in the McCarthyite early-50s, and the burgeoning dictates of a nascent Cold War and National Security State, socialism itself was identified with Stalinist totalitarianism. Brookeman writes that:

> [t]he problems of sustaining ideological positions and loyalties within the contradictions of world history led many American writers and intellectuals to seek what Arthur M. Schlesinger called the 'vital center', a core of agreed basic democratic values that could act as a focus of critical enquiry, not subject to the sudden ravages of history, revolution and ideological schisms. (Brookeman 1984: 3)

Many of the writers of dystopias of the 1950s reflect this move in imagining an oppressive state organization of life, one which is opposed by the dystopian protagonist and the idealized/utopian space in the text he strives to find. The reliance upon individual rebellion perhaps betrays a suspicion of all organized political movements or ideological positions. They are in some sense reliant upon a discovery (through alienation from the system) of an autonomous self and an expression of a universalized human desire, experience or trait which opposes the pressures towards conformity and control in a bureaucratized American 1950s.

Frederik Pohl and Cyril Kornbluth's *Gladiator-at-Law* (1955) exhibits a retreat into heroic patterns of male behaviour as a way out of male anxiety and perceived societal powerlessness. Most of Pohl's dystopian texts are narratively structured by the reconciliation of a formerly estranged heterosexual couple. Kathy and Mitchell Courtenay in *The Space Merchants* (1953), Helena and Ross in *Search the Sky* (1953), Mitzi Ku and Tennison Tarb in the belated 'sequel' to *The Space Merchants*, *The Merchants' War* (1984), Norma Lavin and Charles Mundin in *Gladiator-at-Law*: in all of these cases, narrative closure is effected by the device of the restitution of the heterosexual normative. In *Gladiator-at-Law*, this restitution is complemented by the reconfiguration of the male subject along 'gladiatorial' lines. Elsewhere, Pohl (and Kornbluth), while attempting to satirize patriarchy through inversion, in particular in *Search the Sky*, are caught in a system of representation of women which only allows them to be seen to caricature male behaviour when in control. The texts unfortunately repeat sexist codes while attempting to satirize them. Tom Moylan offers the same analysis with reference to *Gladiator-at-Law*:

> the role of women ... is more problematic. Norma, the feminist, and Ginny, the shrewish wife, are both transformed by their men in traditional sex-role development; at this level, the novel still participates in the sexist ideology of the very postwar American society it attacks. (Moylan 1979: 897)

While offering a fairly sophisticated critique of economic and political formations, Pohl and Kornbluth's dystopias exhibit an unacknowledged reliance on the sexual and gender normatives of the day.

The dystopian text typically imagines a male subject whose identity and individuality forces him into a trajectory of alienation from a conformist society and state, and it is possible to read the individualistic male subject as a necessary construction when opposed to invasive systems of power and control. The trajectory of estrangement from the dystopian system of Mitchell Courtenay, the former 'Star Class copysmith' in *The Space Merchants*, plays out as a domestic drama. Mitchell fails to win the woman he loves because he is symbolically already married, to the system of exploitation; and he is overly dependent on the praise and leadership of a father-figure, Fowler Schocken. His alienation from the system is prompted partly by his love for his wife Kathy; his ultimate escape from the dystopian structures of Earth is figured as a restoration of the happy marriage, the heterosexual couple as a zone of freedom. (This motif is repeated in the 'reich der zwei' inclinations of the double agent's wife, Sarah Castle, in Graham Greene's *The Human Factor* (1978) that will be considered in the next chapter.) The resolution of the narrative as a reconstitution of the heterosexual couple is echoed in *Search the Sky*, where the space-travelling quester Ross accumulates companions, one of whom is his partner-to-be, Helena. In that text, in which the group visits a series of dystopian worlds, one such world encountered is a matriarchal society. The satirical inversion here consists of the women being in control and displaying the most malign features of (American) patriarchy in an estranged and caricatured manner. Ross must negotiate a position of powerlessness and social exclusion, feeling uncomfortable with the frankly assessing gaze of powerful women. This world, like the others the group encounters, proves to be a societal dead end, because the dominance of the women is assumed to create an inevitable stultifying of technological and economic development. The matriarchal society is also predicated on female sexual promiscuity (particularly queasily imagined) with a concomitant denigration of the heterosexual pair. In *Search the Sky*, the matriarchy is malign, from which the questers must make their (relieved) escape.

   Gladiator-at-Law imagines a near-future dystopian world of corporate business, in which an oppressed underclass are controlled by a plutocratic capitalist elite, some of whose members rebel (in the paradigm of the dystopian narrative) and cause the downfall of the system. The usual tripartite social division of the dystopian state (typically Orwell's Inner Party, Outer Party and Proles) here depicts a 'Captain of Industry' class; a middle bureaucratic level based on corporations and a system of tied housing, controlled by 'G.M.L. Homes'; and an underclass, who live in a ghetto called 'Belly Rave'. Essentially, *Gladiator-at-Law* is the narrative of a small group of dystopian malcontents, taken from every part of the social structure, who confront, undermine and eventually destroy an exploitative and malign economic system. Charles Mundin helps Don and Norma Lavin, the dispossessed scions of a deceased 'Captain of Industry', to wrest control of their rightful inheritance from corporate mandarins. A subplot describes the fall and rise of Norvell Bligh, a middle-manager of spectacular gladiatorial games who is undone by the machinations of others.

Gladiator-at-Law begins with a courtroom scene, where Charles Mundin, a low-level lawyer subsisting on the crumbs that fall from the high table of office, confronts a mechanized system of justice. Mundin attempts (unsuccessfully) to defend a lawbreaker. There is a system of class and privilege among the lawyers: Mundin (from the 'John Marshall Law School') has little chance against the institutionalized power and status of the 'Harvard grandee' he faces.

> Not for them the golden showers that fell when you pleaded before human judges and human juries, human surrogates and human commissions. For them – the jury box and the trivia of the criminal law. (Pohl and Kornbluth 1973: 7)

The class stratification of the legal profession is mirrored by a two-tier legal system: for the upper classes, Harvard grandee pleading before human judge and jury; for the lower classes, a mechanical and mechanized system of justice, a 'jury box' which sifts the evidence and pronounces sentence. There is no camaraderie between professional colleagues, only games of power: the Harvard Grandee patronizes (and thereby humiliates) his 'inferior' colleague. This pattern is repeated throughout the text. Mundin helped a friend, William Choate IV, through the same law school: Mundin does not belong to one of the 'great hereditary corporation-practices' (Pohl and Kornbluth 1973: 7), and his 'friend' Choate, who is in a position of eminence through familial connections, fears that Mundin will approach him asking for favours. Such a thing is taboo in the codes of business life, and becomes a sign of absent mutual support. The hereditary principle – a usurpation of which is, paradoxically, the locus of the 'restoration' narrative of Don and Norma Lavin – signifies the rigid stratification of the social system in *Gladiator-at-Law* and also, particularly ironically in this context, its injustice.

Gladiator-at-Law constructs, initially, a set of false or betraying friendships between the male protagonists and their acquaintances, and 'inverted' or 'false' relationships between men and women. The gladiatorial male subject defines (is defined by) a feared Other, a sexual rival or object; attempted subjection of this Other is accompanied by fear that the Self may in fact *be* that Other. Male social groups in *Gladiator-at-Law* then consist of atomized and anxious male subjects who are unable to express desire other than in terms of domination of the Other. Homosocial relationships are figured as zones of competition: the 'Gladiator' of the title applies not only to the battle of the individual against (or within) the economic system, but also the conflict waged between male subject and male subject. Masculine subjectivity is gladiatorial, combative. Typical are the 'Captains of Industry' whom Mundin encounters in the G. M. L. Homes boardroom. These are males without solidarity, without friendship, without loyalty: it is a group of social flux, with power-alliances changing when one or several identify a possibility of advantage over their colleagues.

Norvell Bligh's trajectory from hen-pecked bureaucrat, through cuckold, to self-sufficient (and physically capable) denizen of Belly Rave, the suburban 'ghetto' in the text, is exemplary. At the beginning of the text, Norvell Bligh's male acquaintances exploit or betray him: an underling plots Bligh's dismissal from his job, and his boss Candella's attitude towards him oscillates from superiority, to sycophancy, to avoidance, depending on Bligh's (apparent) relative position in the power-hierarchy. Bligh's 'friendship' with the unctuous Arnie Dworcas is most telling: this 'best friend' patronizes and belittles Bligh, and eventually shuns him when Bligh seeks his help. Bligh's fear of both his own impotence and his wife is a fear that he is not a warrior, but passive, weak, submissive rather than dominant. This narrative strand is then the recovery of 'gladiatorial' male subjectivity for Bligh, the reimposition of the 'Gladiator' Self and the concomitant subjection of the (feared, same) Other.

The positioning of the Self/Other binarism, aligned with man/woman, which structures the 'gladiatorial' male, is the same social matrix as that which 'guarantees' heterosexual marriage. Gayle Rubin, in her famous article 'The Traffic in Women', argues that 'individuals are engendered in order that marriage be guaranteed' (Rubin 1975: 180). Subjectivity itself, in this formulation, is constructed in order to buttress gender inequality through marriage. The Bligh familial unit is one constructed by implicit power-relations. Bligh's wife Virginia – a name whose symbolic connotations demonstrate both his sexual impotence and his powerlessness – was a widow with an adolescent daughter when they married: she comes with both a sexual history and the means with which to judge Bligh, and therefore a position of power within the marriage. In the first scenes between the two, she is dominant; her daughter remains their only child, suggesting that Bligh has been made impotent by the presence of a dominant wife. The words 'castrator mines' and 'eunuch' appear (Pohl and Kornbluth 1973: 27), reinforcing this pattern of signification. *Gladiator-at-Law* suggests that Virginia is only a 'bitch' because Bligh is unable to be a 'real man', one that corresponds to the codes of the heroic male or the machismo of the corporate war. Virginia shouts at him: 'Call yourself a husband! You can't even take care of a family!' (Pohl and Kornbluth 1973: 62). When the Blighs are first removed to Belly Rave, Virginia waves around a pistol, a symbolic demonstration of her power and Norvell's impotence, for it is she who wields the phallus. Sexual impotence is linked to economic failure: Bligh takes the passive position in both worlds.

This is an equation made throughout the text. Bligh is dominated by his wife because he fears losing his job, and tensions at work are transmitted to the domestic zone. It becomes apparent that her reaction is also generated by fear: she has come from Belly Rave (a history she had previously hidden from Bligh) and fears falling back into poverty, into the mass. Once this occurs, however, she becomes resolute and fearless. Once in Belly Rave, Bligh also undergoes a trajectory of recovery, of physical and sexual power. The inverted power relationship between Bligh and Virginia (Bligh as passive, 'feminized' male Other to Virginia's dominant Self) of course does not transgress that very binary, and the text narrates the reinversion of the binary so each takes the 'natural' position. This is done by violence and by male sexual power. The Blighs are at first aided by the streetwise character Shep, who then conducts an unseen but implied affair with Virginia. The gift of a pair of cuckold's horns is the catalyst for Bligh's transformation: he threatens, 'if I see any more monkey business between that hairy ape Shep and you, there is going to be trouble. I'm warning you!' (Pohl and Kornbluth 1973: 99–100). To become 'master in his own house' he must first offer the threat of physical violence and then deploy it: Shep 'had an accident with a lead pipe' (Pohl and Kornbluth 1973: 133). Thus his sexual territory is marked, and his recovery of 'gladiatorial' male subjectivity begins.

This is complemented by his engagement as helper (and later, minder) of Mundin and the Lavins. In this narrative, he is able to gain a measure of revenge for his dismissal by his former employer Candella, and his false friend Arnie Dworcas, through his alignment with the Lavins and their corporate power bloc. Again, in the case of Dworcas, once Bligh has manipulated his former friend, he beats him up: an act of violence is a symbolic regeneration or restitution of masculinity. Ultimately, his stepdaughter Alexandra is subtracted from the dysfunctional Bligh family unit and is replaced by a child of his own. Even then, when told of the birth, Mundin first suspects that the parentage may not be Bligh's.

> Bligh grinned. 'Oh, nothing like that', he said cheerfully. 'The kid's mine. First thing I did was drag her to an immunochemist and get that settled. Good thing; I would have broken her back.' (Pohl and Kornbluth 1973: 138)

Sexual potency is then buttressed by a (convincing) display of a potentiality for violence. Bligh, by the end of the text, is 'man enough' to have a child of his own, and is the dominant partner in his marriage. Virginia has been returned to the normative heterosexual, male order: a role of subservient wife to the potent, 'Gladiator' male.

The narrative of *Gladiator-at-Law* reincorporates the recalcitrant female into the position of passive Other to the male warrior subject. Norma Lavin is first described as 'mannish': 'no lipstick, cropped hair, green slacks, a loose plaid shirt' (Pohl and Kornbluth 1973: 20). She also refuses the title 'Miss', and prefers to be known by the name 'Lavin' only – an assumption of a 'masculine' form of address. Mundin, reacting to this transgression of normative gender roles, says: 'Okay. Lavin, or Spike, or Butch, or whatever you want me to call you' (Pohl and Kornbluth 1973: 21). Mundin's reaction, therefore, is to imply that Norma Lavin is a lesbian, in a markedly aggressive and hostile tone. Mundin's hysteria over Norma's attempted self-definition and his name-calling is the panic-reaction of a fragile male subject faced with an Other who not does respond in the correct (passive) manner. She threatens to abrogate the code of societal and sexual normativeness, and Mundin can only see the transgression of the one order as transgression of the other, reacting accordingly.

Norma is kidnapped by the plutocratic elite who control G. M. L. Homes, but then released by Mundin's intervention (who thereby becomes the 'gladiator' of the title): in Richard Erlich's terms, who analyses *Gladiator-at-Law* in terms of quest-romance motifs, Mundin's quest is to save his future bride (and rightful heir to the kingdom) from those who are ruling falsely in her stead. In one of the few articles to focus on *Gladiator-at-Law*, Richard Erlich, in 'A Womb with a View', attempts to read the text as a quest romance. This has a problematic reliance upon myths of the male Hero and tends to reproduce the construction of the individualistic, heterosexual male subject which ideologically underpins the novel. Erlich suggests that in *Gladiator-at-Law* 'Mundin and Norvell Bligh ... divide between them the role of the Hero in attempting to redeem it' (Erlich 1981: 35). The method of his analysis dislocates any possibility of engagement with the problem of masculinity, and the role of the male in *Gladiator-at-Law*. The heroic male is restored to a central position in society by the end of the text, and the society itself is constructed on the primacy of the heterosexual couple. Richard Erlich's description, of the problem of the dystopian protagonist in terms of relationship to the Mother, unfortunately perpetuates rather than helps tackle the issue. He writes:

> As we find with much sf and dystopian literature, what first appears to be protective and nurturing containment turns out to be imprisonment. A womb with a view may be pleasant, but one must leave the womb if one is to go from foetus to infant and on into adulthood. In terms of archetypes, the Great Mother is always dual in her nature: she is both the Nurturing Mother and the Terrible Mother, the protecting womb and the bowels of Leviathan. (Erlich 1981: 36)

This kind of analysis reveals the limitations of the mythic type of criticism which, ironically, prevailed during the 1950s, and which sustained the focus on individual experience and selfhood which characterized the postwar, liberal critical consensus. The 'liberal turn' predominates in the work produced by the American literary academy in the early postwar years (famously exemplified by the work of Lionel Trilling). Another critic from this time, Leslie Fiedler, was more concerned with gender and particularly masculinity in American fiction. Fiedler was a key figure in the critical and cultural debates of the 1950s and 1960s, and his thesis in *Love and Death in the American Novel* was that

> the typical male protagonist of our fiction has been a man on the run, harried into the forest and out to sea, down to the river or into combat – anywhere to avoid 'civilization', which is to say, the confrontation of a man and a woman which leads to the fall to sex, marriage, and responsibility. (Fiedler 1967: 26)

For Fiedler, the retreat of the male into wilderness, heroic or mythic behaviour, and the company of other men, for him the archetypal pattern of American literature (largely the Gothic strand), was an expression of the avoidance of maturity in the American male subject. He wrote:

> It is maturity above all other things that the American writer fears, and marriage seems to him its essential sign. For marriage stands traditionally not only for a reconciliation with the divided self, a truce between head and heart, but also for a compromise with society, an acceptance of responsibility and drudgery and dullness. (Fiedler 1967: 338)

The male retreats from relations with women but is unable to embrace homosexuality either: a double bind. The American male protagonist then has recourse to a sublimated homosexual feeling with other like men, what Sedgwick calls 'homosociality'. The continuum between homosexuality and homosociality is 'radically disrupted', the element of desire repressed, excised, remaining unacknowledged. Male subjectivity within these groups is figured as overtly (even parodically) masculine, or macho, and is reliant upon heroic, mythic and individualistic ideals of behaviour, character and sexual potency. The heroic is patterned upon a version of male subjectivity dependent upon the violent conquering of the feminine Other in order to buttress the construction of the masculine Self.

Perhaps it is little wonder, then, that Pohl and Kornbluth turn to such types in the construction of the dystopian narrative of *Gladiator-at-Law*. After Norma is rescued by Mundin, she speaks 'not so mannishly', 'weeping on his chest, sobbing' (Pohl and Kornbluth 1973: 109–10). From being proactive, she becomes the rescued victim; from being the equal or superior to her brother, she becomes Mundin's inferior; from a rational and intelligent being to one of uncontrolled emotion. She also becomes an object of sexual desire for the male, complaining that Hubble 'can't keep his damned hands to himself' (Pohl and Kornbluth 1973: 150). Ultimately she also berates 'Mundin, with his infuriating, aggravating way of treating me as if I were *not* a woman' (Pohl and Kornbluth 1973: 154). Norma must become the Normative, the passive Other and sexual partner of a dominant male. She comes to define herself by another's conception of her (a 'woman' in contradistinction to Mundin's view of her as not-'woman'); the irony, for the intended male reader, is that Norma had previously attempted to define herself and refused the title 'Miss'. The text suggests that the 'liberated' Norma only seeks independence and power because she lacks a spouse: heterosexual love defuses feminism, and female power. The same equation we saw made in the narrative of Bligh and Virginia.

Barbara Ehrenreich, again in *The Hearts of Men*, suggests that the suppression of women in the immediate postwar period is a direct manifestation of both the conformist culture of the period and bureaucratic, corporate capitalism:

the less sophisticated grey flannel rebel needed a scapegoat, and if the corporate captains were out of the bounds of legitimate criticism in Cold War America, there was always another more accessible villain – woman. (Ehrenreich 1983:36)

Note again the figure of the 'man in the grey flannel suit', which we will return to in Chapter 4. The protagonists of Pohl and Kornbluth's dystopias then represent the figures of a masculine subjectivity, undermined by economic and social powerlessness, transposing these feelings of impotence onto sexual relations and engendering a mythic conception of sexual potency. *Gladiator-at-Law* offers the possibility that the world of the heroic is not lost, and that it could be recovered in mid-twentieth-century America. There is little heroic about the bureaucrat: the corporate warrior, the dystopian rebel and the sexual athlete represent fantasies of action and potency for the male science fiction devotee. The dystopian narrative, of the rebellious and individualistic protagonist resisting the conformist dictates of the state, all too easily reproduces ideological structures the text attempts to critique. In *Gladiator-at-Law*, as in *The Space Merchants*, the male protagonist regains his primacy within the regulating structure of heterosexual desire and the legal sanction of marriage. Frederik Pohl and Cyril Kornbluth, while offering satire and criticism of the postwar United States, exhibit the implicit sexism of the period and fail to escape either the constraining conventions of the science fiction market or the cultural assumptions of the time.

Towards the citizen-soldier

Gladiator-at-Law was published in 1955. It is, definitively, a mid-1950s text in its satire and its sexual and gender politics. By 1959, when Robert A. Heinlein published *Starship Troopers* in book form, the cultural and political landscape had changed. From the middle of the Eisenhower presidency (a decade of consumerism, corporate capitalism and the reign of 'normalcy') to the end is a change from male anxieties produced by settlement and social comfort to one where the Civil Rights movement in the South, and Cold War abroad, was beginning to make manifest the fracture lines in US society, fractures that would become all too evident in the 1960s. In 1959, both Democrat and Republican parties were beginning to gear up for the next year's Presidential campaign. In his long-gestating political campaign to gain advantage over the incumbent Republicans (Eisenhower's Vice President, Richard Nixon, was his heir-apparent and eventual losing candidate in 1960) Senator John F. Kennedy ratcheted up the Cold War rhetoric, making speeches about a so-called 'missile gap' between Soviet and American nuclear arsenals which would leave the US vulnerable to pre-emptive strike. As we will see during the rest of this chapter (and in Chapter 8), the end of the 1950s and beginning of the 1960s is a time of increasingly active militarism in terms of rhetoric and foreign intervention.

This process, however, had begun much earlier. C. Wright Mills, in *The Power Elite* (1956), suggested that a mass society had been deliberately created in the United States in order to circumvent democratic scrutiny and perpetuate the power and control systems of the military, corporate giants, and the 'political directorate' (which are not elected representatives). *The Power Elite* analysed the 'military definition of world reality' since World War 2, the way in which the economic and political life of the postwar United States became militarized:

> The terms in which [the American elite] have defined international reality are predominantly military. As a result, in the higher circles there has been a replacement of diplomacy in any historically recognized sense by calculations of war potential and the military seriousness of war threats. (Mills 1956: 184)

He also states: 'war or a high state of war preparedness is felt to be the normal and seemingly permanent condition of the United States' (Mills 1956: 184). The American postwar prosperity was inextricably linked to military spending. As he left office in 1960, even President Eisenhower – a former Commander-in-Chief of the US Army – was forced to sound a warning against this trend, in which he made famous the phrase 'the military-industrial complex' (Mills defines this as 'the coincidence of interest between those who control the major means of production and those who control the newly enlarged means of violence' (Mills 1956: 276)). According to Mills's analysis, the Cold War becomes an alibi for enlarged military budgets and powers, rather than simply the structure of super-power conflict: economic, political and cultural discourse is shaped by the needs and designs of the military.

This increasing militarism, however, was accompanied by an increase in anxiety, particularly after the war in Korea (1950–53), in which the US Army fought under a United Nations flag largely against Chinese troops. The apparent weakness of the performance of the American soldier, just five years after triumph in Europe and Pacific theatres in World War 2, was a cause of much concern. Eugene Kinkead, a journalist, and William E. Mayer, who was a psychiatrist in the US Army, produced what Peter Karsten, writing in 1966, called 'harbingers of doom' (Karsten 1966: 34). Kinkead, in his *In Every War But One* (1959), suggested a 'new softness' had entered American masculinity in the postwar years causing the American soldier to perform in Korea less than honourably. Mayer, who testified before the Senate Armed Services Committee in 1962, suggested that there had been a high rate of collaboration by captured US soldiers with the Chinese enemy. (A key text dealing with this issue, *The Manchurian Candidate*, will be considered in Chapter 3.) Mayer, suggested Karsten, 'calls for a return to the "old-fashioned, basic ideas," to keep the flame of '76, dangerously flickering low, alive' (Karsten 1966: 34). Karsten punctures the rhetoric offered by both Kinkead and Mayer, which proposed 'that the G.I. in Korea fell "far short of the historical American standards of honor, character, loyalty, courage and personal integrity"' (Karsten 1966: 35). Karsten suggests that the US soldier in Korea was not deficient, but was being judged by a nostalgia-imbued set of standards which glosses over the true record on American military performance. 'On the whole our ancestors-at-arms conducted themselves tolerably well,' writes Karsten, 'But the record is far from spotless. The nostalgia for past warriors is, therefore, unwarranted' (Karsten 1966: 38).

The source of this nostalgia is indicated in Karsten's sardonic phrase quoted above: 'the flame of '76, flickering dangerously low'. This refers, of course, to 1776, the American Revolutionary War, or War of Independence, and the democratic, or at least self-determining, impulses (famously 'No Taxation Without Representation!') that precipitated it. Karsten is sceptical about the myths surrounding the Revolution, and particularly the figure of the militia-man who figures large in this narrative. 'The Minute Man,' argues Karsten, 'mythical hero of the Revolution, was largely just that – a myth existing principally in the pages of true-blue textbooks and the speeches of incumbent Congressmen' (Karsten 1966: 35). This myth has, itself, a long history. Karsten, in a later article, points out that compulsory service in militias was held to be a social good in American republican writings of the later eighteenth century, but 'responsible men [of the time] should respond to their sense of obligation in order to protect "their private property and political rights"' (Karsten 2001: par. 4). Gore Vidal, probably the most acerbic of all commentators on American history and myth, also argues that '[t]he Inventors of the United States ... were hostile to the idea of democracy and believed profoundly in the sacredness of property' (Vidal 1994b: 644). The franchise, Vidal argues, was limited early in the American Republic in order to prevent what the Founders or Inventors considered to be the dangerous instability of democracy. Vidal cites the example of the revolt of Daniel Shays, with former soldiers in the Revolutionary War, who were protesting about the doubling of property qualifications for voting rights after the end of the war: 'Shays's Rebellion was quickly put down' (Vidal 1994b: 650). Little wonder, then, at the fear of standing armies among ruling elites in the eighteenth and nineteenth centuries.

The militia-man, then, the ideal of the soldier-citizen, virtuous, honourable and loyal, is exposed by Vidal to be troubling in actuality even in the immediate aftermath of Independence; therefore, it is no surprise that the citizen-soldier would enter so quickly into ideology and myth. Karsten, in 2001, acknowledges the importance of the militia-man in 'denying the British from effectively regaining the loyalty of such regions as they passed through or temporarily occupied' (Karsten 2001: par. 7), but notes that there was a marked 'reluctance of most youth to volunteer out of a sense of patriotism or political obligation' for the majority of the history of the United States (Karsten 2001: par. 9). The Jeffersonian ideal of 'a society of honest yeoman' without strong government or a standing army gave way to the needs of the growing American nation-state (Vidal 1994c: 907). To try to ensure the 'loyalty' of American youth (the lack of which was bemoaned by Kinkead in 1959), Karsten argues, early republican essayists proposed a society that

> expects military service from youth who would (by the 1890s) 'pledge allegiance' in publicly funded schools and enjoy other such free social benefits, as well as more general advantages like the rule of law, prosperity, and the prestige of citizenship in 'The Great Republic,' and the capacity to elect their own lawmakers, the franchise (by the age of 18 in 1971 for all, earlier for some). (Karsten 2001: par. 4)

Karsten connects military service to citizenship and to the franchise in a way which echoes the rhetoric of Heinlein's *Starship Troopers* perfectly. Rather than being an obligation to the state, military service becomes part of an ideological project to forge the ideal citizen.

Heinlein's novel is, in a sense, the product of a time when debates about citizenship and military service were becoming increasingly important in a Cold War that seemed to be hotting up. I would argue that it is no coincidence that John F. Kennedy wins the 1960 Presidential election using the 'missile gap' to create an atmosphere of urgent military vulnerability and the necessity of strong (even heroic) action, and the writings of such commentators as Kinkead and Mayer. Both forms of rhetoric call for a kind of renewal that would have seemed impossible under the stewardship of Eisenhower. The language that Kennedy uses in his Inauguration speech in 1961 explicitly connects the ideals of the Revolution to a current wish for change:

> We observe today not a victory of party but a celebration of freedom – symbolizing an end as well as a beginning – signifying renewal as well as change. ... [T]he same revolutionary beliefs for which our forebears fought are still at issue around the globe – the belief that the rights of man come not from the generosity of the state but from the hand of God. We dare not forget today that we are the heirs of that first revolution. Let the word go forth from this time and place, to friend and foe alike, that the torch has been passed to a new generation of Americans – born in this century, tempered by war, disciplined by a hard and bitter peace, proud of our ancient heritage. ... Let every nation know, whether it wishes us well or ill, that we shall pay any price, bear any burden, meet any hardship, support any friend, oppose any foe to assure the survival and the success of liberty.

The language here rings out; it is a clarion-call. It connects the Kennedy Presidency with the ideals of the Revolution and emphasizes military experience; this 'renewal' brings to leadership a citizen-soldier, loyal to the Republic, loyal to the imperatives of the military and state, an active agent rather than a passive participant. It also distinguishes Kennedy (who had famously commanded a Navy PT boat during World War 2) from Eisenhower, a very different kind of citizen-soldier. Eliot A. Cohen, writing of

General (and later Secretary of State) Colin Powell, suggests this kind of citizen-soldier 'reflects a yearning for the Cincinnatus-type – paternal but folksy, sturdily reassuring, and easily imagined in a variety of civilian settings, including the Oval Office' (Cohen 2001: par. 11). Cohen could very easily have been writing of the image of the cosy, golf-playing Eisenhower, whose television election spots famously included the slogan 'I Like Ike'. If Americans were in any doubt that Kennedy calls, in 1961, for a renewal of the role of the citizen, his defining and famous phrase: 'And so, my fellow Americans: ask not what your country can do for you – ask what you can do for your country' calls for the kind of participant 'loyalty' that is, as we have seen, such a part of the rhetoric of the citizen and citizen-soldier in American culture. The renewal of the citizen is itself a renewal of the state.

This renewal, of course, is couched in military terms; there can be little doubt that 'pay any price, bear any burden' refers to a renewed commitment to foreign intervention. The citizen-soldier is crucial in forging a connection between Americans and the nation-state, for the construction of the American subject is inextricably bound up with obligations to, and rights conferred by, the state. (Note how Kennedy obscures this connection in his Inaugural speech by insisting that rights are the gift of God – not the state.) Eliot Cohen argues that 'the true army of citizen-soldiers represents the state' (Cohen 2001: par. 4), but one could go further and suggest that the citizen army in fact becomes a legitimizing instrument of state power: the army acts not in the name of the state but in the name of the citizens who form its body. The army then becomes a kind of substitute *polis*: Cohen goes on to suggest that 'the idea of military service as the great leveller is part of its charm in a democratic age' (Cohen 2001: par. 4). The fundamental connection between army and state is at the centre of Philip Bobbitt's *The Shield of Achilles* (2003), which suggests a sequential development in the form and role of the state that is dependent upon changing military imperatives. 'The modern state', he argues,

> came into existence when it proved necessary to organize a constitutional order that could wage war more effectively than the feudal and mercantile orders it replaced. The emergence of a new form of the State and the decay of the old one is part of a process that goes back to the very beginning of the modern state, perhaps to the beginning of civil society itself. That process takes place in the fusing of the inner and outer dominions of authority: law and strategy. (Bobbitt 2003:xxv)

Bobbitt overturns the commonplace verities of the relationship between civil society and the military. Rather than an army being an instrument of the state, for purposes of defence or aggression, he argues that the development of the two are intertwined, or even that military imperatives predominate. He suggests a sequential development of the state in which two key events in American history signal a change in the form of the state.

The American Revolution inaugurates the 'State-Nation', which he defines as 'a state that mobilizes a nation – a national, ethnocultural group – to act on behalf of the State. It can thus call on the revenues of all society, and on the human talent of all persons. But such a state does not exist to serve or take direction from the nation, as does the nation-state' (Bobbitt 2003: 146). It therefore corresponds to the non- or even anti-democratic principles Gore Vidal sees at work in the construction of the Republic. Whereas the state-nation 'was responsible *for* the nation, [the nation providing] the raw material with which the state-nation powered the engines of state aggrandizement' (Bobbitt 2003: 178), the nation-state – brought into being in Bobbitt's schema by the 1861 US Civil War – is responsible *to* the nation. The state-nation forges the identity of the nation, while the nation-state betters the welfare of its citizens. Vidal sees American history in very similar terms: he writes that '[b]etween Lincoln and Grant the original American republic was jettisoned. From the many states they forged one union, a centralized nation-state devoted to the acquisition of wealth and territory by any means' (Vidal 1994a: 721). It is only at the end of the twentieth century, suggests Bobbitt, with the end of the Cold War and collapse of the Soviet Union and Communist Bloc, that the time of the nation-state comes to an end.

The nation-state, the ideological construction of the ideal citizen and subject, the imperatives of authority and law identified by Bobbitt: all of these concerns are central to the argument of this book. The late-twentieth century, which this book concentrates on, is where the nation-state is at its height and, according to Bobbitt's schema, arrives at its dissolution. The representations of masculinity in popular cultural forms, this book argues, both reveal the ideological constructions of the national subject and also reveal anxieties and fracture-lines within these ideologies. In Pohl and Kornbluth's *Gladiator-at-Law*, as we have seen, a mid-1950s American culture, anxious about the increasing over-organization of life, produces a dystopian satire which relies upon a rather retrograde sense of heroic masculine individualism in order to imagine some kind of resisting subject. Heinlein's *Starship Troopers* even more explicitly engages with the remodelling of the subject along the lines of an ideal citizen-soldier in a time of renewal and change.

Starship Troopers and the citizen-soldier

Alasdair Spark, in an essay which maps out the connection between *Starship Troopers* and the citizen-soldier, suggests that 'the trademark of all Heinlein's novels is a concern with citizenship and proper order, and Heinlein's opinions really belong to a "native and proud of it" school' (Spark 1990: 136). *Starship Troopers* has something of a troubling reputation; I. Q. Hunter's judgement, that the text offers a 'crypto-fascist utopia' full of 'liberal-baiting views', is the critical commonplace (Hunter 1999: 183).

A summary of the narrative gives the same impression. The novel is narrated by Juan Rico who, on something of a whim, decides to enter Federal Service and becomes part of the MI, the Mobile Infantry. Large sections of the novel are taken up with his training and then combat as the MI fight first the 'Skinnies' and then the 'Bugs', two alien species. Seemingly equally large sections of the text are given over to right-wing mouthpieces, such as the teacher Mr Dubois, who give long (and unchallenged) lectures on the rights and responsibilities of the citizen, the relationship of violence to law and the state, and the necessity for civic discipline. The MI troopers are undoubtedly heroic; but as I will show, there are tensions and ambiguities in the text, particularly surrounding gender, which place the text firmly in the debates and discourses of the late-1950s.

The narrative of training and successful combat is a staple of generic war films and fictions. Spark argues that the 'Mobile Infantry are exactly such [citizen-soldiers]', but in *Starship Troopers*, to become a proper soldier, the armed forces must also construct a form of proper masculinity. Like *Gladiator-at-Law*, narrative resolution comes in the novel through the construction or restitution of a 'tough' masculinity, self-sufficient and capable of violence; but here, gender relations are not organized through the restoration of a 'normative' heterosexual couple, but the reorganization of the relationship between father and son. When Juan brings up the idea of Federal Service, his father asks 'Son, are you out of your mind?', and instead proposes a future: that of the organization man:

> When you graduate, you're going to study business at Harvard; you know that. After that, you will go on to the Sorbonne and you'll travel a bit along with it, meet some of our distributors, find out how business is done elsewhere. Then you'll come home and go to work. ... [Y]ou'll be an executive before you catch your breath, because I'm not getting any younger and the quicker you can pick up the load, the better. (Heinlein 1970: 25)

Although his father 'sympathizes' with the desire to go into Federal Service, he dangles a holiday on Mars to try to seal the deal. Once Juan enlists, 'Father stormed at me then quit speaking to me; Mother took to her bed' (Heinlein 1970: 34). Juan is ostracized, it transpires, not because he has made the wrong decision, but because his father cannot understand or embrace the 'rightness' of what Juan has done. When the Bugs later destroy Buenos Aires, Juan's visiting mother is also killed, giving him the rationale to continue with his difficult training and obviating some of his own misgivings. (In Paul Verhoeven's 1997 film version of *Starship Troopers*, Buenos Aires is 'home'; in one of the most critically noted devices of the novel, it is only revealed at the end that Juan's native language is actually Tagalog, making him a Filipino. Juan's ethnicity had previously gone completely unremarked all through the text, a highly unusual feature for a science fiction novel published in 1959.)

Throughout the text, Juan adopts substitute father-figures to provide him with the kind of authoritative discourse and subject-position that is required of the ideal citizen-soldier. The first is Dubois, the teacher of 'History and Moral Philosophy', who outlines some of the key issues to do with violence, authority and citizenship. Secondly, Juan's training Sergeant Zim offers him a model of 'tough', hardened masculinity that corresponds to the soldier ideal. Most importantly, towards the end of the novel, when Juan becomes a sergeant himself and then a career officer, Juan's own father joins the MI to serve as a sergeant in his son's own company. The scene in the text where he accidentally meets his father, who is on his way to his first posting, outlines the crucial change in their relationship, and in Juan's subjectivity: literally, the son becomes the father to the man, as he becomes a father-figure to his own father. 'He would be better off in the Roughnecks than in any other outfit. All my friends ... they'd take care of him, keep him alive' (Heinlein 1970: 143). Becoming a soldier, is, for Juan's father, an opportunity to recant his previous 'irresponsibility'. He confesses: 'At least half of my anger at you was sheer resentment ... that you had actually done something that I knew, buried deep in my heart, I should have done' (Heinlein 1970: 145).

Crucially, however, this encounter reveals the essential fact of masculine subjectivity at the heart of the citizen-soldier. Just before they part, Juan's father says, 'I had to prove to myself that I was a man. Not just a producing-consuming economic animal ... but a *man*' (Heinlen 1970: 146). Crucially, this masculine subject has everything to do with gender and little to do with biology. Shortly after his interview with his father, Juan meets up again with Carmen Ibanez, a high-school friend who had become a pilot. Commenting on her uniform, Juan muses: 'It made Carmen look distinguished, gave her dignity, and for the first time I realized that she really was an officer and a fighting man – as well as a very pretty girl' (Heinlein 1970: 149). In his article on *Starship Troopers*, Everett Carl Dolman remarks upon this passage as revealing that 'Heinlein is an oblivious sexist. ... He is not, as are most chauvinists, aware of his insulting behaviour, and believes he is being complimentary rather than insulting' (Dolman 1997: 205). While not necessarily disagreeing with this, surely the more important issue is that Juan sees absolutely no contradiction between the fact of Carmen's biology ('a very pretty girl') and her subjectivity as a citizen-soldier ('an officer and a fighting man'). This passage could not expose the cultural constructions of masculinity in the text any more clearly: you do not have to be of the male sex to be a 'man'. Masculinity is performative, an ideological construction. Dolman also suggests, in the same point, that Heinlein 'admires the special abilities of women and profoundly believes they should be fully and equably integrated into society' (Dolman 1997: 205), which is arguably true of the Federal Service in *Starship Troopers*. In Heinlein's novel (unlike Verhoeven's film adaptation) there are no female MI troopers; and in both novel and film, physically and mentally women are much better suited to being a spaceship pilot than men. If there is equality, it is of a form that is biologically determined: a female 'fighting man' is suited to a different (if equal) role to her male counterpart.

The construction of masculinity as a kind of performative role is also highlighted by the uniform that Juan must learn to wear as an MI trooper, and which makes the MI different to other kinds of armed forces personnel: the powered MI suit. The suit is a form of exoskeleton, a mixture of spacesuit and weapon that entirely encases, and gives enormous power to, its wearer. The highly exciting and very cinematic opening to Heinlein's *Starship Troopers* (strangely ignored by Verhoeven) concentrates on Juan's participation in a raid on the home plant of the Skinnies, an alien species who will eventually become allies with humans against the Bugs. The sequence offers a fantasy of physical power and destruction not unlike that offered by superhero texts: 'Twice jumping blind over buildings, I landed right in the middle of a group of [Skinnies] – jumped at once while fanning wildly around me with a hand flamer' (Heinlein 1970: 18). The death and destruction visited upon the city by the MI troopers gives place to intoxicating (and, as quoted above, breathless) descriptions of quasi-heroic action, representing Juan's excited consciousness as he bounds around (and over) the city. The suit itself, and Juan's training in it, forms the bulk of Chapter 7 of the book. The suit is described thus:

> Suited up, you look like a big steel gorilla, armed with gorilla-sized weapons. . . . Two thousand pounds of it, maybe, in full kit – yet the very first time you are fitted into one you can immediately walk, run, jump, lie down, pick up an egg without breaking it . . . and jump right over the house next door and come down to a feather landing.
> The secret lies in negative feedback and amplification. (Heinlein 1970: 88)

It is not unlike Buzz Lightyear's suit in *Toy Story* and *Toy Story 2*, which we will return to in Chapter 8. Operating the suit becomes unconscious: 'you just wear it and it takes orders directly from your muscles and does for you what your muscles are trying to do' (Heinlein 1970: 89). The suit then becomes an extension not only of the body, but an extension of the will.

The MI suit protects against Skinnies and Bugs (alien hordes or floods), but also signifies an anxious regime which rigidly reinforces difference and protects against sexual activity. The Juan of the novel is not a sexualized being, and idealizes women as a rationale for fighting: to protect them. Indeed the troopship *Rodger Young* is rigidly demarcated in terms of space and sexual difference. 'Bulkhead 30' is guarded by sentries day and night, and prevents traffic between male and female quarters. Boundaries that protect also reinforce sexual difference, as had the 'gladiatorial' masculine subjectivity of Pohl and Kornbluth's *Gladiator-at-Law*. The MI troopers are not only ideal citizen-soldiers but are also (it seems) celibate, or perhaps, one might say, immaculate.

The imagery surrounding the MI suit provides some unlooked-for ammunition for charges that Heinlein was creating a 'crypto-fascist utopia'. Rather than echoing the American 'Minute Man' version of the citizen-soldier, Heinlein unconsciously echoes the imagination of German *Freikorps* militia-men of the early-1920s, ex-soldiers who went on to form the core of the SA, the paramilitary force of the Nazi party. Klaus Theweleit's *Männer-fantasien* [*Male Fantasies*] (1987 and 1989) analyses the diaries and journals of these militia-men to discover a recurrent pattern of imagining which figures the male body as an armoured entity, protected against the floods of sexual desire, femininity and Communism, all of which are identified with each other. The male body in these diaries is consistently figured as a machine of war which gains pleasurable release when 'the totality-machine and its components explode in battle' (Theweleit 1989: 155). The armoured body attempts to 'pursue, to dam in, and to subdue any force that threatens to transform him back into the horribly disorganised jumble of flesh, hair, skin, bones, intestines and feelings that calls itself human – the human being of old' (Theweleit 1989: 160).

The male 'hard body' or armoured body, however, is an anxious body, its display of musculature paradoxically both disguising and revealing its fragility. Theweleit suggests that '[the male] is afraid of falling back into a state of intermingling with the opposite sex – a state in which his own power would dissipate' (Theweleit 1987: 321), a fear not dispelled by the armour. Bodily boundaries therefore have to be constantly reasserted. Scott Bukatman, in *Terminal Identity: The Virtual Subject in Postmodern Science Fiction* (1993), makes the connection between the armoured body of the *Freikorps* imaginary and the cyborg of science fiction explicit: he suggests that 'the armoured body of the cyborg (the Real Man) represents a fantasied state of masculine invulnerability that carries disturbing echoes of the misogyny of German fascism' (Bukatman 1993: 315).

The MI suit is an instrument of (troubling) fantasy; but, as the novel makes clear just a few pages later, it is an instrument that can imprison the wearer. After 'cheating' during an exercise, Juan finds the power to his suit cut in mid-jump; 'I grounded and there I stuck, squatting, held upright by gyros but unable to move. You do not repeat *not* move when surrounded by a ton of metal with your power dead' (Heinlein 1970: 92). For his infraction, Juan is punished. This takes the form of 'administrative punishment', which is military code for flogging. Previously, the recruits had been called to witness such an event. Juan faints whilst watching the strokes of the whip. When his turn comes, he notes: 'Now here is a very odd thing: A flogging isn't as hard to *take* as it is to *watch*' (Heinlein 1970: 93). The public nature of the punishment is vital: it has more effect on the spectators than it has upon those who are actually punished. In Verhoeven's film, the male body of Casper Van Dien as 'Johnnie Rico' is put on display in this scene, available as a (sadistically erotic) spectacle for the viewer. Roz Kaveney suggests that 'the widespread use of flogging as a military punishment in [Heinlein's] armed forces is represented as a ritual of bonding as much as one of punishment' (Kaveney 2005: 14). While the creation of a certain kind of social bond is clearly crucial to these scenes, I would argue rather that the emphasis is, in Michel Foucault's terms, on discipline rather than on punishment.

In *Discipline and Punish* (1975), Foucault distinguishes between a system of social control (it may be non-judicial or para-legal) which relies on the spectacle of punishment – 'men will remember public execution, the pillory, torture and pain duly observed' (Foucault 1991: 34) – and one which relies upon the internalization of prohibitions on behaviour which make a system of explicit punishment redundant. Curiously, Foucault uses the figure of the soldier in the late-eighteenth century to characterize the 'disciplined' body: 'the machine required can be constructed; posture is gradually corrected; a calculated restraint runs slowly through each part of the body, mastering it, making it pliable, ready at all times, turning into the automatism of habit' (Foucault 1991: 135). The institution of the army – like other disciplinary institutions that Foucault analyses, such as the prison or the asylum – produces the disciplinary subject. Just as Foucault uses such institutions as a paradigm for a mode of social control as a whole, a hint in *Starship Troopers* suggests that the same pertains for its world. 'I had never seen a flogging. Back home,' says Juan, 'while they do it in public of course, they do it in back of the Federal building' (Heinlein 1970: 67). While his father had warned him off the spectacle, another index of his failure as a citizen (or *man*), clearly the spectacle of punishment as a disciplinary device is crucial to the workings of civil, as well as military, society.

If this were not hint enough, the discourse of the 'History and Moral Philosophy' teacher, Dubois, makes the necessity of discipline explicit. In dialogue with Juan, they discuss the house-training of a puppy. To train the dog, one must discipline him: 'You scold him so that he knows he's in trouble, you rub his nose in it so that he will know what trouble you mean, you paddle him so that he darn well won't do it again – and you do it right away!' Juan says (Heinlein 1970: 100). The 'paddling' is the crucial act here, which leads Dubois to lecture on the failings of a twentieth-century system which rejected physical punishment of children and youth: '[T]he time-tested method of instilling social virtue and respect for law in the minds of the young ... was too simple for [child psychologists], apparently, since anybody could do it, using only the patience and firmness needed in training a puppy' (Heinlein 1970: 102). The invective against 'liberals' and 'professionals' is all too familiar. The equation between dogs and humans – that neither has a 'moral instinct' and must be disciplined to acquire one – reveals the human to be without agency, malleable, programmable – the ultimate meaning of the MI suit. The MI trooper, like his suit, is programmed to obey commands. What has happened to the fleshly body within?

The New Frontier

The connection between *Starship Troopers* and a debate about the relationship between citizen and state is, hopefully, now clear. Something else connects this text with the Kennedy administration and its emphases: the 'space race'. In his cultural history of what he calls the 'American Rocket State', *The Final Frontier* (1988), Dale Carter entitles his chapter on the Kennedy era 'Starship Troopers', though he mentions Heinlein's novel nowhere else. We will investigate NASA fictions in more detail in Chapter 8, but here we should note the tension between technology and heroic agency that forms a part of Norman Mailer's *Of a Fire on the Moon* (1970) and Tom Wolfe's *The Right Stuff* (1980): that the Mercury and Apollo astronauts were (or were not) more than just 'spam in a can'. As Debra Benita Shaw has noted, '[t]he Mercury astronauts could be said to wear their space vehicles in the same way as the Starship Trooper wears his suit. Both are technological extensions of the body that wholly define the public identity of their operators' (Shaw 2003: par. 12). In this sense, Heinlein's novel anticipates Kennedy's coming rhetoric of the 'New Frontier' and the problematic male subjects (citizen-soldiers/astronauts) who would be the 'pioneers'. The astronaut, like the MI trooper, is not only a functioning extension of the state and its imperatives, but he is also meant to embody the ideal virtues of its citizens.

The rhetoric of the frontier, which we will investigate in greater detail in Chapter 7, is clearly crucial to science fictions that involve contact (and warfare) with alien species. Alasdair Spark suggested that Heinlein should be considered a 'Social Darwinist, whose ideal society is one in which the individual is free to rise to his "natural" level of power, wealth, and authority' (Spark 1990: 136). The same may be said of the model of competition, between humans and Bugs as competing colonists, that Heinlein employs macrocosmically in *Starship Troopers*. Victory, in the MI troopers' war, will produce the colonial hegemon. Ziauddin Sardar has suggested that 'Wherever we look, the colonising, imperial mission of science fiction is hard to miss. Space, the final frontier, is the recurrent frontier on which Western thought has been constructed and operated throughout history, or time' (Sardar 2002: 16). Domination is legitimated through the pseudo-Darwinist competition for resources. Politically, this is legitimated through the novel by yet another authority/father-figure, Major Reid, who operates as a similar mouthpiece to Dubois. Underpinning the authority of the state, he argues, is force: the law is secured by violence. (We will return to this theme in Chapter 5.)

> To vote is to wield authority; it is the supreme authority from which all other authority derives – such as mine to make your lives miserable once a day. *Force*, if you will! – the franchise is force, naked and raw, the Power of the Rods and the Ax. Whether it is exerted by ten men or ten billion, political authority is *force*. (Heinlein 1970: 155)

(The bundle of Rods is another symbol of fascism, itself appropriated from the Roman republic.) The intertwining of military and state, force and franchise, corresponds to Philip Bobbitt's assertion that the state operates through 'strategy and law'. For Heinlein and Bobbitt, the two are inextricable. In his film version of *Starship Troopers*, Paul Verhoeven manipulates this speech for satirical effect: 'force, my friends, is violence, the supreme authority from which all other authority derives', put into the mouth of the character of Rasczak (Michael Ironside, who performs the roles of both the teacher Dubois and the original leader of the Roughnecks). Where Heinlein made the franchise the prime authority (made so by elective citizenship), Verhoeven exposes what he sees as the legitimation of military aggression in this rhetoric. Indeed, his cynicism about the construction of a military state approaches that of C. Wright Mills: he said, at the time of the film's production, 'The US is desperate to find a new enemy. ... Alien sci-fi gives us a terrifying enemy that is politically correct' (quoted in Hunter 1999: 187). The threatening Other is a necessary legitimation of the militarized nation-state.

Although *Starship Troopers* is clearly a Cold War text, deploying what David Seed has called the 'Communists-as-bugs trope' (Seed 1999: 30) common to science fiction of the 1950s, Verhoeven's film version emphasizes Western intertexts rather than either the war film or the Cold War. Arriving on a disputed planet, Rasczak, Rico and the Roughnecks seek out a human outpost that has lost contact with the fleet. The landscape they march through is red desert; in the visual rhetoric of the Western, this is Indian country. They come across the fort to find it overrun and all its inhabitants slaughtered. I. Q. Hunter is surely correct in identifying Verhoeven's *Starship Troopers* as a 'parody of Heinlein's novel [and] a wicked deconstruction of the xenophobic militarism of both 1950s sci-fi and the war film' (Hunter 1999: 189), but here, his identification of the 'Bugs as Indians fighting off genocidal colonists' is more pertinent (Hunter 1999: 188). One of the most spectacular images in the film is when the Bugs emerge to surround the fort: the mixture of alien Other, flood or tide, and imagery from countless Westerns is telling. The MI troopers, like the *Freikorps* militia-men, must withstand the 'red tide'. Even if the film is camp and overblown, which it certainly is, Verhoeven is intent on exposing the underpinnings of militarism in narratives of the frontier, and how the price of 'colonialism' and 'expansion' is often death and destruction on horribly vast scales. The citizen-soldier, the Starship Trooper, becomes a troubling presence, whose violent means are not obscured by ideologically sanctioned ends. We will return to the Western (and its ideological uses), the frontier and the American nation-state, later in this book; but first we will turn to other fictions of the Cold War.

CHAPTER TWO

Soldier, Spy

In Britain as in the United States, the re-assimilation of the soldier male into postwar society, and the creation of what Steven Cohan has called the 'domestic mystique' to reinsert masculinity into the realm of home and hearth, are key concerns for an analysis of masculinity in the 1950s. As Lynne Segal notes, this ideological renegotiation of masculinity itself led to the creation of 'two opposed faces of masculinity' in the 1950s (Segal 1997: 20). Segal suggests: 'There was the family man, content with house and garden. And there was the old wartime hero, who put "freedom" before family and loved ones' (Segal 1997: 21). This contradiction, a conflict at the heart of constructions of masculinity, was reflected in a series of texts expressing anxiety about the masculine role in the 1950s. Segal cites Helen Hacker's 1957 paper 'The New Burdens of Masculinity', in which men 'were expected to be more patient, understanding and gentle in their dealings with others, and yet "with regard to women they must still be sturdy oaks"' (Segal 1997: 21). This conflicted or 'split' masculinity is at the heart of this chapter, and underlines the fractured masculinity of Leonard Marnham in Ian McEwan's *The Innocent* (1990), which will be its central focus.

In Richard Hoggart's *The Uses of Literacy* (1957), which investigated changes to the British working classes (in fact, the working classes of northern England: Hunslet in Leeds, Ancoats in Manchester, and districts of Sheffield and Hull), the same dual masculinity is in evidence, although for the working-class men Hoggart describes, the normative is closer to the independent, wartime 'sturdy oak' than the sensitive postwar male. The chapter 'Landscape with Figures – A Setting' investigates gender and the domestic world, including material on 'There's No Place Like Home', 'Mother' and 'Father'. Hoggart's portrayal of working-class masculinity is a traditional one: men are bound to the world of work, and though 'father is a part of the inner life of the home, not someone who spends most of his time miles away to keep the establishment going', adolescent sons soon learn that ' "it's different for men" ', which is reinforced by their transition to 'the real world of work and men's pleasures' (Hoggart 1958: 40, 56, 57). Women's expectations and evaluation of their husbands are organized around the phrase 'he treats me alright': in one sense this indicates she is given a fair amount of the wage-packet, but it also signifies a lack of pre-disposition towards violence. Hoggart crucially (if unconsciously) indicates a conflict at the heart of this conception of masculinity, one that attempts to conflate economic success (or survival) with a 'crudeness in personal relations and expression': 'the man who is able to growl', suggests Hoggart, 'is also able to defend; he has something of the cock about him' (Hoggart 1958: 54). Traditional successful working-class masculinity, in Hoggart's analysis, is situated in the role of the economic 'protector', a 'roughness' and 'hardness' which endures and provides, but which also embodies the potentiality for violence against wife and children. The violator co-exists with the protector.

The attempted renegotiation of masculinity in the 1950s finds an ironic counterpoint in the institution of National Service, a two-year conscription of all British young men, which operated between 1948 (which fixed a limit to the length of conscripted service, succeeding wartime regulations) and 1963. This institution can be read as a rite of passage between adolescence and maturity (National Servicemen were conscripted at age 18, *before* they were able to vote at 21), a means of interpellating an adult masculine subjectivity which does indeed internalize the ideological imperatives of the state. The soldier becomes the embodiment of the need for the state to construct a 'rough' or violent masculinity in the 'defence' or 'protection' of England/Britain, and the waging of the Cold War. We find here echoes of the American 'citizen-soldier' we encountered in Chapter 1. National Service introduced many young men in Britain in the 1950s to what the novelist B. S. Johnson, in the collection of writings by National Servicemen, *All Bull*, called

> a system of basic training designed to suppress individuality, restrict freedom in every possible way, instil instinctive obedience without question of any kind, increase physical fitness, and generally so depress the conscript into a common mould that he would instantly serve the forces' purposes in anything that it asked him to do: to the point of killing human beings, or offering to be killed. (Johnson 1973: 5)

The masculine subjectivity of the soldier is predicated, ironically, in the suppression of individuality in favour of obedience to the needs of the group, a reflection of the communal or even 'communist' ideologies that the Cold War sought to demonize and confront. This motif of 'becoming the other', having to use the methods of tyranny to fight tyranny, is a central ideological incoherence in Cold War fictions, and I will return to it later. The soldier-ideal was, however, fraught with frustration and disappointment: in a Cold War, the training for killing becomes training for nothing at all. As Segal suggests, 'one "problem" for some of these young male conscripts, therefore, was that they were unlikely to realise their sexualised fantasies of military glory' (Segal 1997: 19). Segal emphasizes the construction of masculinity in the conscript soldier-male as a masculinity defined by its denigration of, and opposition to, 'feminine' attributes. Trevor Royle, author of the 2002 text on National Servicemen, *National Service: The Best Years of Their Lives*, noted that 'effeminacy was the ultimate soldier's crime', and another serviceman recalled that homosocial culture of the conscript was oriented around 'an overt disdain for anything that might appear soft or wet' (Segal 1997: 20); that is to say, feminine.

The postwar generation of men, with no war to fight (unlike their fathers), brought their 'tough' masculinity back into the realm of the social and domestic. The masculinity of the postwar British male found its characteristic embodiment in the figure of the 'Angry Young Man', who seemed to rebel against the traditional forms of social organization and the 'phoniness' of postwar life. However, the reaction of the sons of the wartime generation is to restate a 'hard' masculinity along the lines of the soldier-subject. Constructions of British masculinity in the 1950s, the 'two faces' suggested by Segal, are marked by the mid-decade phenomenon of the 'Angry Young Man', and also by the 'soldier-subject' of National Service. This is exposed in the language of Joe Lampton, the protagonist of John Braine's *Room at the Top* (1957), who describes his social ambitions in terms of a military campaign:

> I was like an officer fresh from training-school, unable for the moment to translate the untidiness of fear and cordite and corpses into the obvious and irresistible method of attack. I was going to take the position, though, I was sure of that. I was moving into the attack, and no one had better try to stop me. General Joe Lampton, you might say, had opened hostilities. (Braine 1991: 30)

The university-educated rebels (or 'dissentients' of Kenneth Allsop's phrase) of Kingsley Amis's *Lucky Jim* (1953) or John Osborne's *Look Back in Anger* (1956), or the working-class heroes of *Saturday Night and Sunday Morning* (1958) and *Room at the Top* (1957) share 'an aggressive, misogynist masculinity' (Segal 1997: 13) which defines its own independence and 'toughness' in relationship to a feminizing (or emasculating) authority – in the shape of the boss, the government, or the wife/girlfriend. We can find the same process, of Othering the feminine/feminizing the Other to define the masculine, in the discourse of the National Servicemen. John Osborne, writing on Tennessee Williams, betrayed the misogynist violence at the heart of the 'Angry Young Man': 'The female must come toppling down to where she should be – on her back. The American male must take his revenge sometime' (Segal 1997: 14–15). His revenge, suggests Segal, 'is rape' (Segal 1997: 15). The violator is here revealed beneath the surface of the 'tough' protector. Jimmy Porter, who launches violent tirades against his psychologically oppressed wife, the 'hero' of Osborne's *Look Back in Anger*, is the dramatized version of Osborne's attitude. Taken to task by Kenneth Allsop in his 1958 critique, *The Angry Decade*, the 'anger' of Jimmy Porter is another restatement of violent, 'tough' masculinity, but one, Allsop suggests, which is a retreat from political and social maturity:

> The Jimmy Porters are not interested in mankind's political dilemmas such as the ideological and economic contest between East and West, and even their concern with the deeper plight of the pervading loss of spiritual direction is

utterly introspective. Their anger is a sort of neurological masturbation, deriving from the very problems they cannot bring themselves to confront. (Allsop 1958: 28)

Allsop argues that Porter's 'anger' is a symptom of 'a general conviction that certain man-made problems that man is facing are beyond the capacity of man to solve', those problems largely being the 'ideological and economic contest between East and West' (Allsop 1958: 29). At the heart of Allsop's critique is a diagnosis of a 'nostalgia' built in to both the culture of the 1950s, and Jimmy Porter's own masculine subjectivity. Allsop confesses that

I personally have, and I believe a great many men and women in my age group have, an intense nostalgic longing for the security and the innocence that seems to have been present in Britain before the 1914 war. (Allsop 1958: 26)

This longing for 'security and ... innocence' (note the use of that word) is an ideological construction which conflates Imperial nostalgia and Cold War anxiety, the sense that, in Churchill's phrase quoted as an epigraph to *The Innocent*, Britain 'should have no money and no strength and we should lie between the two great powers of the USA and USSR'. This 'loss of strength' is figured as passivity, and recalls Osborne's phrase of women lying on their backs. The anxiety here is over a loss of manliness, a loss of the soldierly prowess which made Britain 'Great': Britain becomes 'emasculated' or feminized by the dominance of the superpowers. 'Jimmy's secret regret', argues Allsop, 'is that everything *isn't* the same [as it used to be in the Edwardian era]'; and Jimmy's 'secret hero is Colonel Redfearn [his father-in-law] and all the self-discipline, certainty and courteous gentleness that he despises *forte*, and *pianissimo*, yearns for' (Allsop 1958: 117). This 'innocence' is, as Jimmy Porter suggests, 'phoney' (a key word of the 1950s), and obscures the Imperial history of dispossession, colonization and war that produced the 'Long Edwardian afternoon' (let alone the class conflict and war anxiety which threatened to fracture Britain before 1914). It is, of course, vital that McEwan sets the espionage narrative of *The Innocent* in 1955, before the catastrophic British intervention at Suez, and the symbolic death of late-Imperial dreams of 'Great Power' status. As Kiernan Ryan says of *The Innocent*, 'the novel's title acquires its pathos from a tragic sense of the end of innocence both for an individual and the country he stands for, as each stumbles into an era of lost simplicities' (Ryan 1994: 56). The nostalgia for the Edwardian period − the *belle époque* 'age of innocence' − is also a longing for the unconflicted masculinity of the soldier-subject, and innocence that masks a history of violence, dominance and conflict: literal and symbolic rape.

This nostalgia for the 'soldier-subject' is part of the reorganization of masculine subjectivity in the British 1950s. As I suggested above, the incoherence of this ideological renegotiation rests upon the incompatibility of the 'rugged individualism' of the soldier-subject with the needs of social stability in peacetime, as well as the needs of state institutions (particularly the Army) for obedient subjects. As Hoggart indicated in his portrayal of working-class masculinity, the 'protector' (or economically successful) element of masculinity is co-present with the 'violator' element (which visits domestic violence on wife and children). In fact, the 'violator' is the supplement and guarantor of the 'protector'. As an expression of hegemonic masculinity, then, the traditional male or what I am calling the 'soldier-subject' contains within it the force of its own rupture: the potentiality for unrestrained (and not socially sanctioned) violence always exceeds the limits of the 'soldier-subject' as a hegemonic term. We will see a similar tension between violence and law, between the hegemonic masculine subject and an excessive 'toughness' that guarantees it, in 'rogue cop' texts in Chapters 5 and 6.

The phrase 'hegemonic masculinity' I am deploying in the usage of Steven Cohan in *Masked Men* (1997). 'Hegemonic' masculinity is a ' "regulatory fiction" of normality' which 'articulates various social relations of power as an issue of gender normality' (Cohan 1997: 24, 35). It appears to accommodate other forms of masculinity, including 'young', 'effeminate' and 'homosexual', but subordinates them into a power hierarchy, with the 'hegemonic' variant at the top (Cohan 1997: 35–8). My contention is that the 'soldier-subject' forms the hegemonic term in articulations of masculinity in Britain in the 1950s, a status which can be anecdotally supported by the predominance of World War 2-set films in the postwar British film industry and the centrality and importance of the experience of the soldier in them. Andrew Spicer, in *Typical Men*, suggests that many of these armed-services films were organized around the relationship between 'cadet' and an older hegemonic male who embodied 'the modern no-nonsense professional and the traditional British hero, the saintly father and the virile tough guy', the relationship representing 'a powerful generational continuity of masculine styles and values' (Spicer 2003: 38).

The interpellation of the 'soldier-subject' in British National Service in the 1950s was emphasized in homosocial rituals (male bonding, drinking, womanizing) which 'othered' the feminine ('soft and wet') in favour of a 'tough' masculinity. In the same way, debates over homosexuality in the 1950s indicate an anxiety about the constitution of masculinity and the extent to which the 'feminine' in men could be made Other, and repressed. The Wolfenden Report of 1957 (which led to the legalization of homosexuality some ten years later) represents not an 'advance' in the rights of a group of men, but in Michel Foucault's sense in his *The History of Sexuality* (1990), the codification of the sexual category of 'homosexual' within the law (and therefore stricter regulation of homosexuality in public *and* private), and a locating of 'homosexual behaviour' within what John Hill has called a 'general framework of moral censure' (Hill 1986: 19). The Wolfenden Report codifies the articulation of a heterosexual, married and socially stable male along the lines of the traditional 'hard' masculinity of the 'soldier-subject', while regulating subordinated masculinities such as the homosexual within legal and moral frameworks.

A socially acceptable and fantasy representation of the hegemonic soldier-subject can be found in the figure of James Bond, the 'secret agent'. Bond is, clearly, a nostalgic figure in British culture, whose hyper-competent masculinity is a comforting fantasy of covert Great Power status. The screen Bond, whose class and national significations have been somewhat obscured (and made more universally acceptable) by casting and by the tuxedo-uniform he wears, is a much less troubled figure than Ian Fleming's original creation. Indeed, both Andrew Spicer, who connects Bond to 'the unwavering patriotism of the traditional British gentleman hero and the guiltless sexual philandering of the international playboy who em-bodied the "swinging" sixties' (Spicer 2003: 75), and Michael Denning, who analyses even Fleming's Bond in terms of a 'heroic tourism' and 'the discourse of consumer society' (Denning 1987: 104), place Bond as a transitional figure between masculinities of the 1950s and the 1960s. Bond's consumerism is inflected with a residual imperialism. In their response to Denning's thesis, Tony Bennett and Janet Woollacott make the con-nection explicit:

> The Bond novels construct imperialist and racist ideologies by means of a narrative code of tourism through which the strange and exotic locations of peripheral societies are represented as the object of Bond's Western, metro-politan look. (Bennett and Woollacott 1990: 440)

As Bennett and Woollacott also stress, the 'look' is also a gendered one: Bond is figured as something of a sexual predator, and women are rendered as quasi-pornographic objects of desire. In the figure of James Bond, then, British masculinity finds a rather retrograde fantasy-figure of sexual and political potency.

An anxiety-ridden representation of a disruptive 'double' masculinity can be found in Fleming's *From Russia with Love* (1957). This novel begins with the figure of Donovan 'Red' Grant, also known as Krassno Granitski, a Soviet assassin. Grant's body is seen through the eyes of a female mas-seuse. It was 'the finest body she had ever seen', 'formidable' with 'fantastic muscles' (Fleming 2004: 6, 9); yet, there is something repulsive about it, 'somehow bestial. No, reptilian' (Fleming 2004: 7). The physicality of Grant's body is emphasized to such an extent that eroticism topples over into revulsion. What Fleming is indicating here is that Grant's body is a symbolic body: excessively muscled, dangerous, even murderous, it represents the kind of fleshly armature that we saw represented as the fascist body in Chapter 1. Grant's body, like Heinlein's MI suit, is also an ideological body: it represents, and serves as an instrument of, the malign will of the Soviet secret apparatus. In a rather curious narrative turn, Fleming reveals that Donovan is actually Northern Irish, and had been on National Service, but posted to Berlin, the site of so many British espionage fictions, that he decided to defect to the Russians. He has three names, and a 'split' (and psychotic) subjectivity. Grant is an inflated and parodic version of the double agent, whose ideologically constructed British subjectivity collapses in the face of his psychosis. (Grant, it is revealed, is particularly dangerous at the full moon, intimations of lycanthropy tipping the narrative into the realm of horror fiction. He is an interesting early variant on the 'psycho', who we will return to in Chapter 4.) Ultimately, Bond defeats Grant, but not before Grant has assumed the very 'gentleman' persona (a disguise to encourage Bond to let his guard down and again indicating the instability of his identity) that Bond superseded in British spy fiction.

Bond's rise to prominence can be traced to a British culture in the late-1950s which, after the 'failure' at Suez, could no longer hold on to concrete and practical ideas of retaining what was left of Empire, but which found it very difficult to let those ideological fantasies (of power, security or domination) go completely. British spy fictions have a long connection with Imperial dreams and anxieties. Erskine Childers' *The Riddle of the Sands* (1903), which depicts two 'gentleman amateur' spies foiling a German invasion fleet in the inlets and sandbanks of the coast of Holland, is a crucial early espionage text that is related to the raft of 'invasion' narratives that were produced in Britain in the later nineteenth century. More important here, though, is Rudyard Kipling's *Kim* (1901). Set in India, *Kim* narrates the coming-of-age of one Kim O'Hara, the son of an Irish soldier and a nursemaid but raised by a 'half-caste' woman, who is first discovered as 'the little friend of all the world', living off his wits (extremely successfully) on the streets of Lahore. He takes up with a lama and departs on a spiritual quest, at the same time entering into the Raj's world of espionage. In a sense, Kim's journey to maturity is the construction of a British masculine subjectivity that fully accepts the ideological imperatives of British domination in India, and who is therefore prepared to work secretly for that end. Kim, curiously, is the model for Roger Thornhill and his own path to the development of a Cold War maturity in Hitchcock's *North by Northwest* (1959), a film that we shall return to in Chapter 4.

The first page of *Kim* states that

> Kim was English. Though he was burned black as any native; though he spoke the vernacular by preference, and his mother-tongue in an uncertain singsong; though he consorted on terms of perfect equality with the small boys of the bazaar; Kim was white. (Kipling 1994: 7)

He is, therefore, at the beginning of the narrative, already capable of inhabiting several worlds or identities, even though Kipling takes pains to stress his fundamental Englishness (much obscured until much later in the novel). Edward Said, in very illuminating analyses of *Kim* in *Culture and Imperialism* (1993), twice describes the boy as 'chameleon-like': Kim is 'a great actor passing through many situations and at home in each' (Said 1993: 192). This capacity makes him ideally suited for a life in espionage. Said notes '[Kim's] quickness, his capacity for disguise and for getting into a situation as if it were native to him [and his] complex and chameleon-like character, who darts in and out of adventure, intrigue, episode' (Said 1993: 187). The sense of Kim as an 'actor', a 'chameleon', suggests that a 'spy' subjectivity is one that is in flux, capable of putting on masks or clothing in order to function most effectively.

Said, however, argues that this very ability, for the English boy to 'pass' undiscovered in the world of the 'native' Indian, represents a kind of Imperial fantasy, one of agency and domination. For the white male spy can pass as an Indian; but this never happens in reverse. The native cannot pass for white, and is always exposed. It is vital, then, that Kim is English; and Said suggests that beneath the disguises lies the construction of an uncompromised and unitary British Imperial subject: 'Kim must be given a station in life commensurate with his stubbornly fought-for identity [and] the fact that *he is Kim*' (Said 1993: 169). Unlike the 'double agent' to be considered shortly, or the 'hipster cop' that we will look at in Chapter 5, Kim's ability to move in two (or more) worlds does not result in psychological corrosion or self-destruction, perhaps because in Kipling, an Imperial ideology (which assumes British dominance) still underpins the narrative. By the time of the Cold War, these certainties had collapsed.

From the early 1950s, several scandals involving highly prominent 'traitors' had provided the popular backdrop for representations of British 'national interest' and 'national security'. Most prominent were Donald Maclean and Guy Burgess, two men recruited while at Cambridge by the KGB, who later achieved positions of power to provide the USSR with high-level information on the British security apparatus. The KGB's biggest coup was in recruiting 'Kim' Philby, who was actually head of the Russian section of the British SIS while reporting to the KGB. (Curiously, Philby was named after the boy-spy of *Kim*, who is also able to assume other identities in the service of what Kipling characterizes as the 'Great Game' of espionage.) John Atkins, in *The British Spy Novel* (1984), argues that 'all modern spy novels work under two shadows: those of Bond and Philby' (Atkins 1984: 123). What Atkins calls the 'Philby obsession' can be found in novels such as John Le Carré's *Tinker, Tailor, Soldier, Spy* (1974) and Graham Greene's *The Human Factor* (1978), both of which we shall consider here. Greene in fact knew Philby, and had 'been responsible in London … for counter-espionage in Portugal under Kim Philby' (Greene 1980: 297). While Greene suggests that he abandoned *The Human Factor* in the late-1960s 'mainly because of the Philby affair', as he 'disliked the idea of the novel being taken as a *roman à clef*' (Greene 1980: 298), clearly the narrative of the 'mole' or 'double agent' gains a much more pervasive cultural currency in Britain after Philby's defection in 1963. *The Human Factor* provides the link between Cold War espionage fictions and the vestiges of Empire: the protagonist, Castle, who has leaked documents to the Russians from his post in the African section of the secret service, does so because they had helped his black African wife Sarah (once his agent) to escape from Apartheid-era South Africa, when the British secret service did not. Castle acts as a double agent partly because of what he sees as British complicity in South Africa's then institutionalized and violent racism; as part of his current responsibilities, he is forced to liaise with Cornelius Muller, a white South African operative who had pursued Castle and Sarah in South Africa. Castle inhabits a 'liberal', white subjectivity that finds the traces of Imperial and racist discourse in the Cold War unbearable, much unlike the fantasy-figure of James Bond.

The betrayal in *The Human Factor* is of country, but his wife Sarah invokes a kind of higher loyalty that legitimates his behaviour. When Castle confesses that 'I became what they call a double agent, Sarah. I rate a lifetime in jail' (Greene 1978: 236) – in fact he is overestimating his worth here, as he finds out in Moscow that his actions covered a much more important double agent placed elsewhere – Sarah replies: 'We have our own country. You and I and Sam [their son]. You've never betrayed that country' (Greene 1978: 238). Greene, I think, does not intend the reader to take this assertion of innocence on face value: we have already seen the corrosive effects of his 'doubleness' on both Castle himself and his marriage to Sarah. The novel ends, in fact, on a very downbeat note, with the three separated, Sarah and Sam in Britain, Castle having defected to Moscow, with little chance of resolution.

The connection between betrayal in love and betrayal of country can also be found in John Le Carré's *Tinker, Tailor, Soldier, Spy*. The central character, George Smiley, is a small, rather rotund, quiet man, very different from the machismo of James Bond. Like Castle, he is something of an 'organization man'. As the narrative progresses (Smiley attempts to find the 'mole' in the British secret service known as the 'Circus'), it is revealed that Smiley's wife Ann is unfaithful, and has left Smiley after another of her affairs; Smiley also discovers that one of these affairs occurred with Bill Haydon, a dashing senior figure who is eventually revealed as 'Gerald', the mole. Michael Denning suggests that both Le Carré's and Greene's novels focus upon 'the antinomies of professional masculinity – the antinomies of public and private, love and loyalty' (Denning 1987: 130). While public and private masculinities are usually 'split', he argues, 'the world of the spy novel is precisely one where this split has not been made' (Denning 1987: 131). This split indicates doubling, that all subjectivities are double: 'Everybody in the world, so they say, has a double' says Castle in *The Human Factor* (Greene 1978: 290). The double agent, then, is not an anomalous version of Cold War masculinity, but a central one: a suggestion I will pursue further shortly.

The most notorious 'double agent' was Guy Burgess, whose homosexuality provided an important reinforcement of the connection between espionage and masculinity. Burgess's homosexuality was identified with his status as a 'traitor': non-normativeness with regard to sexual orientation was clearly mapped onto non-normativeness of political orientation: Burgess was doubly 'queer'. In *Tinker, Tailor* Bill Haydon is also bisexual; his 'closeness' to Jim Prideaux, an agent captured and shot in Czechoslovakia because of Haydon's actions, is later revealed as love: 'This man

[Haydon] was my friend', muses Smiley, 'and Ann's lover, Jim's friend and for all I know Jim's lover too; it was the treason, not the man, that belonged to the public domain' (Le Carré 1983: 297). Note here that Smiley makes a distinction between public and private: Denning's 'split' has now occurred. Jeremy Black, in *The Politics of James Bond*, makes a surprising and overt connection between Burgess and Bond:

> the repeatedly affirmed heterosexuality of Bond is a rejection of the ambiguity that Fleming saw in homosexuality, an ambiguity that was political as much as sexual. The homosexual traitor Guy Burgess was thus the antithesis of Bond. (Black 2001: 105−6)

As Black also notes, until the film *GoldenEye* (1995), Bond narratives did not feature traitors, only megalomaniac super-villains or the Soviet spy network. While the Bond narratives are insistent (to the point of caricature) on emphasizing the ideological (and sexual) boundaries between Self and Other, in the figure of the double agent or traitor, Berlin espionage fiction destabilizes both fixed identity and the boundaries between Self and Other, East and West, communist and capitalist, totalitarian and democratic. In the form of Burgess, such sexual and political 'immorality' undermines not only the moral framework of British society but also its security, its integrity and safety. In his 1988 teleplay, *An Englishman Abroad*, Alan Bennett offers a sensitive representation of Burgess in exile in Moscow. The play is based upon a historical incident in which the Australian actress, Coral Browne, while on tour in Moscow, was barged in upon by the inebriated Burgess, who then invited her for lunch, largely to ask her to take his measurements so she could send him a Savile Row suit. As its title suggests, *An Englishman Abroad* securely locates Burgess within the (class-based) identity of an 'Englishman', an identity largely denoted by the Savile Row suit. Bennett suggests that, though a 'traitor', Burgess's national identity, and even class subjectivity, is undamaged, unchanged. (The tailor has no qualms in preparing a suit for 'Mister Guy', nor moral sanction for Burgess's actions. His identity as an 'Englishman', therefore a legitimate customer, remains.)

This portrayal of Burgess as an irreducible 'Englishman' is worthy of investigation, for it marks the extent to which espionage fictions not only articulate the relationships between hegemonic and subordinate masculinities, but also suggests that espionage fictions indicate the ways in which plural (British) national and regional identities are collapsed onto the 'English' soldier-subject. 'The articulation between forms of masculinity and the state is an old story,' wrote Sallie Westwood in 1996, 'conjuring images of the military and tied to conceptions of the nation and national identities' (Westwood 1996: 21). She continues:

> These very visible signs of the relationship between masculinities, the state and the nation are organized around 'fictive ethnicities' … and racialized

conceptions of national identity – the 'freeborn English man', for example, who fights for Queen and Country. Although imperial in tone, it is a vision re-generated within the racial formation of the 1990s. (Westwood 1996: 21)

The figure of James Bond signifies that throughout the espionage genre one finds the collapse of the term 'English' (the category of nation, with its racialized conception of identity) onto 'British', the state in whose interests the spies of the Cold War worked (either for or against).

Leonard Marnham of McEwan's *The Innocent*, 'So English! So male!' (McEwan 2001: 223), like James Bond, George Smiley, or the narrator of Len Deighton's *Funeral in Berlin* of 1964 (who is called 'English' by his antagonist Colonel Stok), is particularly marked as English rather than British. The narrative of *The Innocent* is as follows. Marnham, a telecommunications engineer, is sent to Berlin in 1955, to help with a secret operation (based on the historical Operation Gold) that involves tunnelling under East German phone lines to intercept secret communications. Marnham meets and falls in love with Maria, a young German woman, but their relationship eventually disintegrates when Maria's ex-soldier husband Otto, who causes a violent confrontation with Marnham, is accidentally killed. Marnham is forced to dismember and try to dispose of the corpse; his guilt leads him eventually to betray the secret tunnel, where he has deposited some of the remains. Marnham leaves Berlin, but the novel ends in the late-1980s, with a possible reconciliation between the two former lovers. Marnham's reticence, his lack of confidence and class-based anxiety about social behaviour and relationships, his very 'innocence', is connoted as 'English', indicating a kind of ideological metonymy: his Tottenham-born, middle-class upbringing situates him as a kind of English (British) everyman. Like Bond or Smiley, Marnham represents the British state in his role as telecommunications engineer in Berlin, but also represents a form of English masculinity which is presumed to be natural (and stands for 'British') but is in fact an ideological and racial construct which obscures both the diversity of British regional and national identities, and also the growing plurality of ethnic identities in Britain which followed the 1950s. This, I would suggest, is consciously deployed by McEwan to bring the ideological underpinnings of 'Englishness' into play, just as his choice of the genre of espionage fiction necessarily brings ideology itself into the foreground of the novel's world and narrative. One of *The Innocent*'s most powerful insights is in the identification and exposure of the Cold War masculinity which Leonard Marnham inhabits.

It is curious how early in the sexual relationship between Marnham and Maria that McEwan enters a 'troubling', and eventually destructive, psychological undercurrent. Marnham appears to be the archetypical inexperienced English middle-class man: shy, sexually unaware and uncomfortable with his own body and desires, unconfident and awkward in both sexual and emotional relationships with women. This 'innocence', while attractive to Maria and marking Marnham's sexual and psychological difference (there seems little or no potentiality for violence in him, little or no trace of the 'traditional' male qualities located in Hoggart's working-class 'father'), is problematic. For it reveals not simply immaturity, but the possibility of the fragmentation of the desiring subject:

> These fantasies came a little closer each time, and each time they continued to proliferate, to take new forms. There were figures gathering at the edge of thought, now they were striding towards the centre, towards him. They were all versions of himself, and he knew he could not resist them. (McEwan 2001: 77)

This potential fragmentation, Marnham's desire being dislocated (or dismembered) into separate 'versions', is a bringing-forth of the ideological sub-strata of 'innocence': fantasies of domination and submission. This is revealed in the passivity of Marnham's own subject-position: 'he could not resist them'. A correlative of Marnham's submergence in fantasies of domination comes in his realization of Maria's own nationality, that 'she was a German', which provides him with the rationale for domination: 'she was his by right, by conquest, by right of unimaginable violence and heroism and sacrifice' (McEwan 2001: 77). Marnham's soldier-subjectivity is interpellated by a consciousness of Maria's German ('defeated') victim-subjectivity, couched in terms of national difference. In fact, Marnham is not revisiting the soldier-fantasy of British victory in Berlin, but proleptically and uncannily foreshadowing the narrated memory of the rape of a wounded German woman by a Red Army soldier, witnessed by Maria. In discovering the soldier within, explicitly signified in the phrase 'he was a soldier' (McEwan 2001: 78), Marnham is also uncovering the Cold War subjectivity of the warrior male, a subjectivity he shares (at least in his fantasies) with his antagonist and alter-ego, Otto. The 'innocent' here is not Marnham, but Maria: not the conquering soldier, but the female victim.

If Marnham enacts the 'rape' of emasculating/feminizing authority in the shape of a sexually active and experienced woman, he is repeating Lynne Segal's critique of the misogyny of the 'Angry Young Man'. He is also becoming Otto, Maria's 'war hero' husband who drunkenly returns to beat her and take money from her. Curiously, like the working-class women in Hoggart's *The Uses of Literacy*, Maria also seems to validate the masculine soldier-subject in the fatal scene between Maria, Marnham and Otto. When they return to Maria's flat after announcing their engagement, they find Otto claiming his right to the flat (if not to Maria herself). When Marnham reacts to his presence by giving her an ultimatum about Otto's role in her life, she responds:

> 'You want to throw him in the street, why don't you just do that? Do it! Why can't you just act? ... I've had men screaming at me, hitting me, trying to rape me. Now I want a man to look after me. I thought it was you. I thought you could do it. But no, you want to be jealous and scream and hit and rape like him and all the rest.' (McEwan 2001: 139)

This again probes the blurred boundary between 'tough', competent, 'protector' masculinity and its supplement, the violent and violating 'soldier-subject'. Maria, in extremis, seems to want one without the other, while Marnham, who has previously fantasized about breaking Otto's arm in a demonstration of physical and mental superiority, ends as neither, despite his desire to make sexual fantasy into the reality of rape. Marnham's physical incompetence in fact leads to the accidental death of Otto, whose skull is split by an iron cobbler's last.

The split subject

It is no coincidence that Marnham's subjectivity fragments to reveal the 'soldier within' in Berlin, the divided city. Berlin was the front line of the Cold War from 1945 to the destruction of the Wall in 1989, a city divided (like Europe) into East and West, a city split (like the Cold War masculine subject) into Self and Other. The transactions and spy games of Berlin, and the subjectivities of those who participate in them, encode Cold War ideologies but also manifest their conflicted and 'troubled' state, particularly in the figures of the 'spy', and the 'double agent'. It also is no coincidence, then, that the Bond films have assiduously avoided Berlin as a major location, and in the screen adaptation of the single Fleming narrative to be set in Berlin, *The Living Daylights* (filmed in 1987), the Berlin setting is relocated to Bratislava. The short story of the same name was written in 1962, the year after the erection of the barbed-wire barricades that were to become the Wall. Bond is sent to ensure the safe passage of a defector across the 'death strip' by Checkpoint Charlie (at Friedrichstrasse), by assassinating a Soviet sniper before (s)he kills the defector. Bond is not comfortable in Berlin: he 'had always found Berlin a glum, inimical city dry varnished on the Western side with a brittle veneer of gimcrack polish, rather like the chromium trim on American motor-cars' (Fleming 2002: 102). This aside indicates what is central to all Berlin narratives, including *The Innocent*: that the real 'enemy' may not be the East Germans, or even the Soviets, but 'our cousins' the Americans, whose presence in West Berlin clearly provokes Bond's repugnance. However, perhaps due to the proximity of Berlin's troubling moral and physical doubleness, Bond is uncomfortable with his mission. Waiting for the appointed time, Bond comes into conflict with his local 'handler' Captain Sender, who, like Lieutenant Lofting at the beginning of *The Innocent*, is an Englishman who plays by the rulebook.

> 'Look, my friend,' said Bond wearily, 'I've got to commit a murder tonight. Not you. Me. So be a good chap and stuff it, would you? You can tell Tanqueray anything you like when it's over. Think I like this job? Having a Double-O number and so on? I'd be quite happy for you to get me sacked from the Double-O section. Then I could settle down and make a snug nest of papers as an ordinary Staffer. Right?' (Fleming 2002: 113)

Bond's doubts, and his moral coding of his assassination as 'murder' (rather than an act in the national interest), does provide a rather more conflicted representation of the activities of the 'secret agent' than the Bond films usually allow for. However, Bond's derision at the 'snug nest' of the Staffer does seem to indicate that the life of the Double-O agent is more authentic (and more manly?) than his non-combatant opposite number. The end of the narrative shows Bond disobeying orders: realizing the Soviet sniper is a woman he has spotted on the street, who had produced a 'sharp pang of longing' in him (Fleming 2002: 108), he shoots the barrel of her gun rather than to kill. With a strange mixture of sentimentality and misogyny ('Poor little bitch!' (Fleming 2002: 118)), Bond both completes his mission and retains the 'tough' subjectivity which allows him to be an effective Cold Warrior. Not all espionage narratives are able to paper over the ideological cracks so blithely.

Bond's 'longing' of course does not inhibit him from performing his task: were he urgently required to kill the female sniper to protect the national interest, there is little doubt that he would do so. Throughout Cold War espionage fictions, the 'dangers' of emotional or sexual contact with the 'Other' are emphasized, a trope inherited by *The Innocent*. One finds a conflation of sexual 'deviance' or otherness with betrayal and danger in Grant and the lesbian spymaster Rosa Klebb in *From Russia with Love*, and also in Len Deighton's *Funeral in Berlin* (1964). The unnamed narrator of Deighton's espionage thriller affects an anti-authoritarian stance in keeping with his northern England (Burnley), grammar school, red-brick university background (identical to the Angry Young Men), although this identity as 'an insolent intractable hooligan' is a self-confessed 'illusion' (Deighton 2001: 203) and is mediated through his wartime Army experience. The convoluted narrative, whose analogy to a chess-game is indicated by chapter epigrams indicating chess moves (another version of Kipling's Great Game), is based upon a fraudulent handover of a key Soviet scientist in Berlin, arranged by the KGB officer Colonel Stok as part of his own 'defection' (also fraudulent). At the centre of this plot is one Johnnie Vulkan, a marginal figure in the Berlin espionage scene who is really Paul-Louis Broum, a wealthy concentration-camp inmate who murdered a guard and took his place in 1945, while the other guards were paid to look the other way. Vulkan has to find a way of proving his identity as Broum, in order to claim monies held in a Swiss bank account, then to prove his identity as Vulkan to avoid the fatal consequences of being Broum. In the scene where the 'handover' is made, the narrator exposes the 'truth' of Johnnie's identity:

> 'I'll tell you your trouble, Johnnie,' I said from a safe distance. 'You've become a professional phoney. You've become so good at pretending to be different that you have lost contact with your identity. You've learnt so much jargon that you don't know which side you're on. Every time you move through the frontier of space you slip through the frontier of time.' (Deighton 2001: 251–2)

Johnnie's 'phoney' subjectivity is the subjectivity of the double agent: multiple, fractured, with the possibility of an 'authentic' or 'real' identity lost in the strata of cover stories and 'fake' selves. In the Cold War's split city, the sense of a unified subject is fissured into an array of different and competing subjectivities. In John Le Carré's *The Spy Who Came in from the Cold* (1963) espionage fiction's performance-based articulation of subjectivity is taken still further. Alex Leamas, the protagonist of the narrative, has himself 'defected' to East Germany, but he is a double agent, intended (so Leamas thinks) to compromise the head of the GDR's intelligence service, Paul Mundt. While being debriefed, Leamas ponders the 'part' he plays:

> A man who lives a part, not to others but alone, is exposed to obvious psychological dangers. In itself, the practice of deception is not particularly exacting; it is a matter of experience, of professional expertise, it is a facility most of us can acquire. But while a confidence trickster, a play-actor or a gambler can return from his performance to the ranks of his admirers, the secret agent enjoys no such relief. ... Aware of the overwhelming temptations which assail a man permanently isolated in his deceit, Leamas resorted to the course which armed him best; even when he was alone, he compelled himself to live with the personality he had assumed. (Le Carré 1999: 133)

Leamas must do this as a form of 'self-defence', by which Le Carré means *defence against the self*: Leamas must constantly perform his identity to avoid betraying himself by some gesture that reveals the 'true' identity beneath. Although this seems to suggest that the secret agent can maintain the distinction between 'true' and 'fake' identities, the 'psychological dangers' alluded to in the first sentence indicate that the imperative of performance is bound up with the possibility of fissure and fracture.

As I suggested above, the hegemonic 'soldier-subject' contains within itself the elements of its own rupture: the 'violator' is the supplement and guarantor of the 'protector'. One can argue from this, then, that British hegemonic masculinity in the 1950s is already split, fissured, doubled. Berlin espionage fictions demonstrate the importance of this split subjectivity in the parallel, mirrored activities of West and East, of Self and Other. (It is no coincidence that Le Carré's next novel after *The Spy Who Came in from the Cold* was called *The Looking-Glass War*.) When the 'soldier-subject' enters Berlin, he is transformed into the 'double agent'. Leonard Marnham finds this out in *The Innocent*. Marnham's own betrayal of his country, when giving the 'secret' of Operation Gold to a Berlin operative in a café, is, of course, invalidated by the prior treachery of the historical George Blake, who appears in *The Innocent* as Marnham's neighbour. Marnham's betrayal is a personal one, of Maria and, in a sense, also to the possibility of his future happiness. Here we can detect clear echoes of Haydon and Prideaux in *Tinker, Tailor*, Castle and Sarah in *The Human Factor*, and Bernard Sampson and his wife in Deighton's *Berlin Game* (1983). The futility of his attempted intervention in the Cold War indicates his ongoing 'innocence': that individual action of that kind is able to make a substantive difference to much larger configurations of power and influence. However, his failure also indicates the ideological aporias of Cold War masculinity and its representation in espionage fiction: the 'rugged individualism' that forms a key ideological plank in 'capitalist liberal democracies', the fantasy world of James Bond, either must be suppressed, or is irrelevant, to the contestations of the Cold War.

Johnnie Vulkan is not the real cause of anxiety in Deighton's *Funeral in Berlin*, as he is a Berliner, not English. The most dangerous double agent in the narrative is revealed at the end in the figure of Hallam, an espionage mandarin who is implicated in the Vulkan operation. Hallam is characterized by a seedy effeminacy, and is, in a sense, a version of Burgess, but who betrays his country for money rather than political beliefs, and in the moral universe of Deighton's novel, receives his 'desserts' when immolated at the Bonfire Night party at which he attempts to kill the narrator. Hallam's betrayal, like Burgess's, is most problematic because it indicates that the enemy *is within*: that the Other is the Self, and that there is a continuum between the homosocial soldier-subject and the homosexual double agent. With a sense of irony, I would like to name this conflicted Cold War subject 'ein Berliner'.

The historical root of this phrase for Cold War purposes can be traced back to President Kennedy's June 1963 speech, given from the balcony of the Rathaus Schönberg, within sight of the Berlin Wall. In it, he spoke the sentence that perhaps has characterized the NATO democracies of Western Europe, their Cold War ideologies and their relationship to Berlin:

> Two thousand years ago the proudest boast was '*civis Romanus sum*'. Today, in the world of freedom, the proudest boast is *Ich bin ein Berliner*. (Hilton 2001: 363, n. 35)

Diethelm Prowe has analysed this to suggest that Kennedy's identification with the inhabitants of the split city was 'a call to Berliners to feel like special citizens of the Free World, "a vital part of the Free World and all its enterprises," as he had expressed it in ... August 1961', but also changed *ein Berliner* into a 'heroic Cold Warrior' (Prowe 1996: 185). What Kennedy did not say, of course, was '*Ich bin Westberliner*', but in the service of his Cold War rhetoric, this is what he really meant: the 'free', West(ern) Berlin, itself organized (or split) into sectors controlled by the British, French and Americans. His use of '*Berliner*' signifies that the true state of Berlin is the whole, unified city, not its current split form. Strangely, the split Berlin was in fact the last hurrah for British (and French) 'Great Power' status, although the dominant powers were always the United States and Soviet Union. Churchill's fear of British geopolitical weakness, expressed as an epigraph to *The Innocent*, finds its fantasy negation and true expression in Berlin.

In Len Deighton's later spy novel, *Berlin Game* (1983), the first in a trilogy, the central spy, Bernard Sampson, English but raised in Berlin (therefore a subject twice doubled), discovers that his own wife is the 'mole' in the British secret service. Dudley Jones pinpoints the connection between Berlin and the split subject:

> Berlin clearly appeals to Deighton because, as a divided city, it presents starkly the opposition between the communist and capitalist political systems and the Wall is a tangible and symbolic reminder of that opposition. But it goes beyond this – at least as far as the trilogy is concerned – because the internal divisions of the city reflect the divided self of the hero, Bernard Sampson. (Jones 1990: 105)

Jones suggests that Deighton's spy-world is a simpler one than the moral ambiguities of Le Carré's or Greene's fictions; for Deighton, 'East stands for evil and the West for good' (Jones 1990: 109). Accusations of political simple-mindedness do not mean that Deighton is incapable of recognizing a historically and culturally significant event, however. In the middle of the novel, Bernard travels to meet Frank Harrington, the Berlin station chief. Harrington says:

> 'You're *berlinerisch*, Bernard. You grew up in this funny old town. You were cycling through the streets and alleys before they built the Wall. You speak Berlin German as well as anyone I've met here. You go to ground like a native. That's why we can't bloody well find you when you decide you can't be bothered with us.'
> '*Ich bin ein Berliner*,' I said. It was a joke. A *Berliner* is a doughnut. The day after President Kennedy made his famous proclamation, Berlin cartoonists had a field day with talking doughnuts. (Deighton 1984: 102)

Despite Deighton's usual sardonic tone, the text clearly refers to the idea of the ideal agent, in the tradition of *Kim*: Sampson, 'like a native', can pass for German, though his loyalties and primary subjectivity remain British. Being '*berlinerisch*' is clearly problematic, however. It means that Sampson can operate outside regulations and official procedures, to exceed his role. Here, to be 'native' carries the connotations of 'going native': that the agent's loyalties may be ambiguous. The ideal spy very easily becomes the double agent.

My appropriation of 'ein Berliner' is a reappropriation, a reinscribing of the conflicted and double status of Berlin and the split subjectivity of the Cold Warrior. In asserting '*Ich bin ein Berliner*', Kennedy was unconsciously acknowledging that Berlin mirrored the split state of the 'West's' ideological foundations (by 'West' I mean the capitalist 'liberal democracies' of NATO, some of which were neither liberal nor democratic), and the morality of the Cold War itself. This is indicated in a speech by the 'spymaster' Control, made to Alex Leamas in *The Spy Who Came in from the Cold* before Leamas's 'defection'. Control says:

I would say that since the war, our methods – ours and those of the opposition – have become much the same. I mean, you can't be less ruthless than the opposition simply because your government's *policy* is benevolent, can you now? (Le Carré 1999: 25)

Although Leamas's decision at the end of the novel – to go back over the Wall to his death rather than continuing to validate Control's 'dirty game' and amoral view of Cold War conflict – tends to morally invalidate Control's position, I would agree with Eric Homberger's assessment that, in spite of this, 'the central theme [of *The Spy Who Came in from the Cold*] is a conflict in ways of living, and ultimately of social systems, which are rooted in respect for individualism, and those that are not' (Homberger 1986: 50). Tony Barley, also writing on Le Carré, suggests that the 'secret world is a world apart but it is not united', encoding conflict between 'blatant Cold Warriors and humane liberals' (Barley 1986: 11), indicating the *practice* of the Cold War is a site of contestation; so is its ideology. Control lays bare the disturbing ideological implications of the Cold War: that to defend freedom, one must become the same as those who threaten freedom. The 'violator' is once again the guarantor of the power of the 'protector'.

It is in the scenes that follow the death of Otto in *The Innocent*, when Marnham and Maria embark upon the dismemberment of the body that will also sunder their relationship, that the duality of the protector/violator masculine subject is brought to light. Having accidentally killed Otto, the pair convince themselves that the body must be disposed of rather than brought to the attention of the police, compounding the accidental violence with a deliberate and systematic violation of Otto's body that McEwan narrates in grisly detail. The boundaries between subject and object, between protector and violator, between 'innocent' and guilty', become blurred. Just before he has to rush to the bathroom to vomit, Marnham comes to the realization of Self in Other, Other in Self: Otto's exposed innards, of 'liverish reds, glistening irregular tubing of a boiled egg bluish white, and something purple and black' were also 'in himself' (McEwan 2001: 169). Kiernan Ryan quotes McEwan himself in demonstrating the almost over-coded analogy between Otto's dismembered body and the divided Berlin. McEwan said: 'I wanted to show the brutality man can aspire to by comparing the dismemberment of a corpse to the dismemberment of a city: the bomb-devastated Berlin of the postwar' (Ryan 1994: 58). Otto's body, Berlin and Germany itself fall into metonymic relation, but they not only symbolize the particular violence done to and by middle Europe, but also the violence the Cold War visits upon the subject, splitting and dismembering. This violence and fracturing is not confined to Berlin: it is transnational, the state of the 'Western' male subject.

The figure of the 'war hero' Otto, like Johnnie Vulkan's past in *Funeral in Berlin*, and the irresistible approach of the 'soldier within' in Marnham's fantasies, indicates the ineradicability of the recent (Nazi) past, the return of the repressed. In Berlin espionage fictions, the Nazi past haunts the present, just as the bullet-scarred walls of Maria's apartment are a constant indi-cator of slippage 'through the frontier of time'. In his article 'Narration and Unease in Ian McEwan's Later Fiction', Jago Morrison, while not men-tioning *The Innocent* explicitly, suggests that 'in Berlin ... historicization becomes neutralization, with the symbolic demolition of World War Two painted not in terms of euphoria but of blankness' (Morrison 2001: 266). The consignment of Nazism to the past, Morrison suggests, is represented in McEwan's *Black Dogs* (1992) as a dissolution of meaning, not a liberating or even comforting indicator of change or reconciliation. In *The Innocent*, McEwan's deployment of the rape-fantasy 'soldier within' indicates not the neutralization of Nazism and its 'legacy', but its ineradicability, for it is contained as a potentiality within masculine subjectivity rather than either a 'universal reference point of human depravity' or a 'warning from history'. This is not to say that McEwan dehistoricizes or dislocates the experi-ence of Germans (and Europeans) in the twentieth century, only the extent to which his use of the genre of espionage fiction indicates how it is the constructions of masculinity and subjectivity themselves that must be explored and exposed – no matter how gruesome the result.

There was a 'lost' subtitle of *The Innocent*, that according to Jonathan Coe's contemporary review, had been 'abandoned somewhere between proof and finished copy' (Coe 1990: 22), but which was reinstated for the 2001 Vintage paperback reissue. This subtitle, 'The Special Relationship', relies for its significance upon its popular use to denote the Cold War relations between Britain and the United States. The 'relationship' between Marnham and Bob Glass, whose ebullient and energetic American mascu-linity is defined by, and opposed to, Marnham's Englishness, is a fraught one. Although Glass gives a speech at Marnham and Maria's engage-ment party (I will return to this shortly), on leaving Templehof airport, the glimpse of Maria and Glass together compounds Marnham's paranoia about Glass's true intentions. In an inversion of his own 'Level 4' activities of spying on American colleagues, Marnham feels 'betrayed' that Maria and Glass have been conducting an affair behind his back. Glass becomes a version of the double agent, just as Marnham had done. In an impor-tant corrective to Marnham's self-defeating and self-imprisoning logic of betrayal, Maria's 1987 letter signifies that what Marnham most feared only comes to pass because of his own failings: that Glass's hand on Maria's shoulder at Templhof was, indeed, 'innocent'.

Though hokey, Glass's speech at the engagement party is central to a reading of *The Innocent*'s ending, and is worth giving in full. Glass says:

> 'We all know the kinds of freedom we want and like, and we all know what threatens them. We all know that the place, the only place, to start making a Europe free and safe from war is right here, with ourselves, in our hearts. Leonard and Maria belong to countries that ten years ago were at war. By engaging to be married they are bringing their own peace, in their own way, to their nations. Their marriage, and all others like it, binds countries tighter together than any

treaty can. Marriages across borders increase understanding between nations
and make it slightly harder each time for them to go to war ever again.'
(McEwan 2001: 124)

This 'special relationship' is even more overcoded than the dismemberment
of Otto, and invites a sentimental reading of Marnham and Maria's
proposed wedding. (The film adaptation's 'happy ending', rather than a
'betrayal' of the novel, then becomes a completion of Glass's logic.) Such
sentimentality, it seems, is evacuated by the murder of Otto and the scenes
that follow. That the consummation of the 'special relationship' never
happens, or is delayed until the arrival of Maria (now Glass's widow)'s
letter in 1987, indicates McEwan's understanding that the fissures within
the Cold War subject could not be healed while the Cold War existed,
while the Wall (symbol of the split city) still stood. This 'healing' is at the
centre of McEwan's project in this novel. Jonathan Coe, in his 1990 review,
suggested that 'the conventional trajectory from innocence to experience is
not one that the novel seems interested in following' (Coe 1990: 22), citing
Marnham's numbness as he leaves Templehof. I believe this to be true. *The
Innocent* self-consciously avoids or negates this trajectory, but neither is
the novel a cautionary tale of the dangers of such innocence (such as in
Greene's *The Quiet American* of 1954). Perhaps one could less charitably
characterize the novel in terms of a longing for, or a nostalgia for, an
'innocent' pre-World War 2 and pre-Cold War subjectivity (perhaps Kim's
underlying unitary subject), the very thing it seems to dissect in the figure
of the 'soldier-subject'.

However, the serendipity of the novel's publication – the last sentence,
which imagines Marnham and Maria looking 'at the Wall together, before it
was all torn down' (McEwan 2001: 226), was written before the events
of November 1989, and in fact McEwan was awaiting publisher's proofs of
the novel when the Wall fell – attests to McEwan's political sophistication,
rather than naivety. If *The Innocent* wants to return to a state of innocence, it is not in the past, but the future: not before the Wall went up,
but after it has come down. Although in interviews in the early-1990s
McEwan expresses pessimistic opinions about Europe's future, the ending
of *The Innocent* is hopeful, pregnant with possibility. In a necessarily open
and ambiguous fashion, *The Innocent* does offer the possibility of a healed
Berlin, a healed Germany, and a healed masculine subjectivity.

CHAPTER THREE

Operatives

Paranola

Where the British espionage fictions of the Cold War stressed the role of
the double agent, the protagonist of a narrative of penetration of national
security from without, in postwar American fictions, the key note is betrayal from within. Richard Hofstadter, in his crucial essay 'The Paranoid
Style in American Politics' (originally delivered in November 1963), which
we will look at in detail, notes that '[t]heir predecessors discovered foreign
conspiracies; the modern radical right finds that conspiracy also embraces
betrayal at home' (Hofstadter 1966: 24). The espionage and thriller fictions
we will consider in this chapter take conspiracy to be a central fact in postwar
American history: conspiracies of the left, and conspiracies of the right.

Hofstadter understands the 'paranoid style' to be a transnational, rather
than a peculiarly American, phenomenon. However, it is particularly useful
in considering American espionage fictions because of what Peter Knight
has called 'the emergence of what might be termed a culture *of* conspiracy'
(Knight 2001: 28) in the postwar United States, from the National Security
Act of 1947 to the Watergate scandal of the second Nixon administration. Hofstadter considers that the 'paranoid style' — which has the qualities
of 'heated exaggeration, suspiciousness, and conspiratorial fantasy' (Hofstadter 1966: 3) — comes in a series of waves, which he traces back as far as
anti-Catholic and anti-Masonic conspiracy tracts in the late-eighteenth and
early-nineteenth centuries. The paranoid style is ever-present in modern
culture as a kind of 'minority disposition', but more popular movements
which adopt this style 'are mobilized into action chiefly by social conflicts
that involve schemes of values and that bring fundamental fears and hatreds,
rather than negotiable interests, into political action'. This becomes particularly urgent when 'the representatives of a particular political interest ...
cannot make themselves felt in the political process' (Hofstadter 1966: 39).
We will return to the phenomenon of male 'dispossession' in contemporary
culture in Chapter 4. In explaining politically right-wing conspiracies,
Hofstadter borrows the notion of dispossession from the social and political
theorist Daniel Bell. The radical, conspiracy-minded right feel that 'America
has been taken away from them and their kind, though they are determined
to repossess it and to prevent the final destructive act of subversion'
(Hofstadter 1966: 23). In a sense, then, Hofstadter's understanding of the
'paranoid style' and conspiracy-thinking is a mode of political thought and

action resorted to by those who feel that they have no agency within the political field. It becomes a means by which to 'mobilize'.

The 'paranoid style', in fact, rests upon a fantasy of agency. Not only does a 'vast and sinister conspiracy, a gigantic and yet subtle machinery of influence' work beneath the apparent surface of social, political and cultural life, but this conspiracy is '*the motive force* in historical events' (Hofstadter 1966: 29). Although Hofstadter does not go so far, it may not be exaggerating to suggest the presence of conspiracy-thinking acts as a distorted reflection of a kind of compensatory fantasy of the dispossessed: of untrammelled agency and power. History, for the paranoid, is 'distinctly personal: decisive events are not taken as a part of history, but as the consequences of someone's will' (Hofstadter 1966: 32). Underlying the anxiety of conspiracy-thinking is a fantasy of heroic counter-agency: that the conspiracy may itself be stopped by what J. Hoberman characterizes as the 'Secret Agent of History'.

Drawing upon the same sense of paranoia as the thinking of the excluded or dispossessed, but in a rather different register, is Fredric Jameson's 'Totality as Conspiracy' (1992). Jameson suggests that paranoia and a belief in conspiracies is a function of the subject's dislocation in the contemporary 'world system': that there is 'some deeper incapacity of the postmodern subject to process history itself' (Jameson 1992: 16). This can be related to what Jameson calls, in *Postmodernism, or, The Cultural Logic of Late Capitalism* (1991), the failure of 'cognitive mapping' in contemporary social and cultural conditions: that

> the latest mutation in space [which Jameson uses as a concrete metaphor for social conditions as a whole] – postmodern hyperspace – has finally succeeded in transcending the capacities of the individual human body to locate itself, to organize its immediate surroundings perceptually, and cognitively to map its position in a mappable external world. (Jameson 1991: 44)

It is perhaps worthy of note that Jameson's figure of a 'world system' of capital also has shades of conspiracy-thinking. Not only is the paranoid subject produced by social conflict, in Hofstadter's terms, but is actually a version of the 'postmodern subject' that is produced by late (consumer, corporate) capitalism. The paranoid is the obverse of the organization man, produced by similar conditions. Paranoia is, however, a way of making meaning. Peter Knight quotes Jameson to suggest that 'Conspiracy ... is the poor person's cognitive mapping in the postmodern age; it is a degraded figure of the total logic of late capital, a desperate attempt to represent that latter's system' (Knight 2001: 19). Conspiracy thinking or paranoia takes the place of an understanding of the totality of the social conditions of late capitalism, supplanting a false and fantastic totality in place of a 'true' or 'real' political understanding. It is a form of false consciousness, then, which redirects the dispossessed to misunderstand the true nature of their dispossession.

At the core of postwar conspiracy narratives is the assassination of John F. Kennedy. Peter Knight calls this event the 'primal scene of post-modernism', a point where the distrust of the 'master narratives' (as suggested by Jean-François Lyotard in *The Postmodern Condition* (1984)) of progress or Marxism finds, in retrospect, some kind of 'myth of origin' (Knight 2001: 116). Jameson suggests that the assassination of Kennedy is 'paradigmatic' for that of later killings, such as Malcolm X or Martin Luther King, but argues that it becomes so not by its political meaning or social symbolism, but its elevation by the mass media into a repeated public and collective event (Jameson 1992: 47). One would think that Jameson would resist an understanding of President Kennedy's assassination as a 'loss of innocence', but this is what Peter Knight suggests has become the commonplace answer to the contemporary prevalence of conspiracy theories. He writes:

> The other common explanation for the prevalence of conspiracy theories is that the traumatic assassination led to a widespread loss of faith, not just in the goodness of America that Kennedy seems to represent, but in the legitimacy of the authorities who investigated the murder. Everything began to go wrong after that moment, the argument runs. (Knight 2001: 78)

We will return to a cultural nostalgia for the Kennedy era in Chapter 8. Here, Knight emphasizes that this (paranoia-inflected) need for a mythic origin point for a loss of innocence does little to provide a sense of totality or coherence, but feeds 'an anxiety about the irredeemable strangeness of reality in postmodern times' (Knight 2001: 78). The 'strangeness of reality' is perhaps, in Jameson's terms, another failure of 'cognitive mapping'. It is not that the Kennedy assassination causes dislocation, but becomes a convenient origin point for it. It is, in fact, another misapprehension of the world system.

Jameson does concede that the (American) public collective 'broods [upon assassination] like a many-headed private investigator', assassination becoming 'one of the most frequently rehearsed motifs or fantasy-narratives, not to say obsessions, of the current political unconscious' (Jameson 1992: 46). It would be difficult to deny, one would think, that the reason for this is due to historical factors, the importance of the 'bad trip' of what Jameson calls the '60s gone toxic' (Jameson 1992: 42): the litany of assassination victims – JFK, Malcolm X, King, Robert Kennedy. As Knight suggests, there is some basis of paranoia in 'reality'; Hofstadter also notes that other historical manifestations of the 'paranoid style' were responding, in some way, to actuality. In the post-World War 2 period, paranoia could be said to be a reaction to a whole series of developments which imply the workings of a 'secret state': from the National Security Act of 1947, through internal FBI investigations of subversion, through the assassinations of the 1960s, to the Watergate affair. Gore Vidal coined the term the 'National Security State' to characterize these developments. He suggests that a document known as NSC-68, which committed the United States to an escalating militarism to fight the Cold War, was nothing less than a *coup d'état*: he argues that NSC-68 inaugurated 'the strict control of our economy and the gradual erosion of our liberties, all in order to benefit the economic interest of what is never, to put it tactfully, a very large group – defense spending is money but not labor intensive' (Vidal 1994d: 1023). There are shades here of Eisenhower's 'military-industrial complex', C. Wright Mills's 'power elite', and also of the 'paranoid style'. According to Vidal's analysis, paranoia and conspiracy-thinking may be a rational way of understanding the path of recent US history.

In this chapter, we will look at key fictions such as the 'paranoid histories' of James Ellroy, and 1970s conspiracy thrillers such as *The Conversation* (1974) and *The Parallax View* (1974) that are organized around the possibility, or fact of, assassination. We will try to approach the question Jameson posits with regard to representations of the 'assassination plot' in fiction and film: 'what relationship this particular fictional assassination plot is supposed to entertain with the one real-life assassination that has, in our time, had general philosophical significance', that of President John F. Kennedy (Jameson 1992: 47). The answer to this, for John Frankenheimer's *The Manchurian Candidate* (released in 1962), seems to be anticipatory or even prophetic, though its narrative is actually set in the mid-1950s. The narrative of *The Manchurian Candidate* is as follows. While on patrol in Korea, a group of GIs are captured and taken to Manchuria, where they are 'brainwashed' into believing that one of their number, Sergeant Raymond Shaw (played by Laurence Harvey), is a hero. His Captain, later Major Bennet Marco (Frank Sinatra) cites him for bravery, and Shaw ends up winning the Congressional Medal of Honor. However, Shaw has been psychologically manipulated to become an assassin, an agent, placed inside the United States. It is only when Major Marco has nightmares that reveal the process of brainwashing (and when he is believed by his superiors) that the purpose of the brainwashing begins to become clear.

Shaw is the son of Eleanor Shaw Iselin (Angela Lansbury), who is married to (and is the power and brains behind) Senator John Iselin (James Gregory), a McCarthy-type figure who is propelled to the Vice Presidential nomination through a campaign of denouncing (imaginary) Communists inside the Defense Department. Eleanor Iselin is a domineering, manipulative figure, a demonic mother who most resembles a perverse femme fatale from film noir (she even has a blonde coiffure that resembles Kim Novak's in Hitchcock's *Vertigo* (1958)). Shaw 'loathes and despises' his mother and stepfather, yet is unable quite to cut the apron strings; in a drunken, self-pitying and self-loathing confession to Marco, Shaw reveals how he had fallen in love with Jocie Jordan (the daughter of a liberal senator in Iselin's party) one summer, but had been forced to break it off by his mother, who characterizes Senator Jordan as a 'Communist'. 'She won, of course,' says Shaw, 'she always does'. The day after being forced to give up Jocie, Raymond joins the Army.

Undoubtedly, this is a way in which Shaw is attempting to fix a sense of adult masculinity in the face of his mother's campaign of infantilization. (She calls both Raymond and Iselin 'her boys' in an early scene.) What it results in, however, is further trauma. *The Manchurian Candidate* is certainly influenced by the anxieties surrounding the soldier-subject that I analysed in Chapters 2 and 3. Major Marco is a version of the 'damaged soldier' who appears in *The Blue Dahlia* (and who reappears after the Vietnam War as the 'vet'), while Raymond, Congressional Medal of Honor winner, is a 'hero' who finds it difficult to reintegrate into society because of his emotional coldness (a coldness which makes him admirably suited to be processed into an assassin). Raymond Shaw is, in fact, an ideal type of the soldier-subject: he, in contrast to Marco, is unafflicted by bad dreams. As an assassin, he is the perfect type (he is even called a 'mechanism' by his programmer) because he is without interiority, an agent without agency: he has neither conscience nor guilt, because he kills purely as an instrument of someone else's will. What *The Manchurian Candidate* reveals, in the 'killing machine' alter-ego of the war hero, is the violence that accompanies the soldier-subject, a violence that needed to be suppressed for the soldier to be reintegrated into postwar society. (We find similar issues in terms of re-integration of the violent man in the Western, considered in Chapter 7.) The assassin-mechanism Raymond Shaw echoes the figure of the ideal soldier, the MI trooper in Heinlein's *Starship Troopers*: he is an instrument, lacks true agency, is an efficient and reliable killer; yet, while the violence of the MI troopers is legitimized by being turned outward against the threatening Other, *The Manchurian Candidate* expresses the other (fearful) potentiality of this figure, that it may be turned against the civil society that it is meant to protect.

The traumatized masculine subject, Raymond Shaw, is also clearly Oedipalized in this film. In Hitchcock's *North by Northwest* (1959), which we will look at in the next chapter, the irresponsible (mother-dominated) male must forge a Cold War masculinity away from the influence of his mother; this is connected to a heterosexual romance, so that normative Cold War masculinity (and his role in the affairs of the National Security State) is sealed by marriage. Here, though, as we have seen, Eleanor Iselin blocks Raymond's marriage in order to bind him to her more fully. The anti-Communist invective she provides as a rationale for rejecting Jocie Jordan masks, it would seem, an unhealthy maternal jealousy. Further, in one of the film's most unsettling moments, just before Raymond is sent to assassinate the Presidential nominee — leaving the path open for Iselin's nomination — Eleanor kisses her son full on the mouth, a sexual rather than motherly act. Compounding this transgression is the revealed fact that Eleanor Iselin is her son's 'American controller': she is a Communist agent herself, who is using assassination and McCarthy-ite tactics to place the 'Manchurian Candidate' in the White House.

It is only towards the end of the film, when Marco tries to 'deprogram' Raymond, that he achieves a full, adult subjectivity. Traumatically, though, this subjectivity brings with it the full knowledge of his guilt of the murders of two soldier comrades, his boss, his wife and Senator Jordan. The face of Laurence Harvey stares full-face back at the audience at this point, the horror of his awakening written across his features. Harvey, not the most expressive of actors, seems to relax at this point, the stiffness that characterizes his performance – ideal for the priggish Shaw – loosened. When Marco sends Raymond back to his controller to receive his final instructions – and the kiss – he begins to doubt the efficacy of the deprogramming, as Raymond does not contact Marco as per instructions. The Convention takes place in Madison Square Gardens, and Raymond perches in a booth at the back of the auditorium with a sniper's rifle, his sights trained on the Presidential nominee. As Marco searches for him, the film unsettles the audience by making Raymond's status utterly ambiguous: is he still the 'killing machine', or has he recovered agency?

As the Presidential nominee comes to the phrase 'give my life before my liberty' – the trigger for the assassination – Raymond changes target, and shoots first Iselin, then his mother, dead, both through the forehead. The betrayed – the traumatized son and war veteran, Raymond Shaw – ultimately betrays his mother and controller in turn. When Marco reaches Raymond, he is told: 'You couldn't have stopped them, the Army couldn't have stopped them, so I had to', before Raymond turns the gun on himself. The trigger phrase, and Raymond's self-sacrifice (just when he has finally won a sense of self) indicates *The Manchurian Candidate*'s negotiation with the figure of the patriot and 'citizen-soldier' that we analysed in Chapter 1. While the Presidential nominee's rhetoric echoes Jefferson's dictum that 'the Tree of Liberty must be refreshed from time to time with the blood of patriots' (Heinlein 1970: 113), it is the 'patriot' Raymond who lays down his life for his country. In the film's coda, Marco gives a revised Medal of Honor citation almost direct to camera: Raymond had been 'made to commit acts too unspeakable to be cited here .... He freed himself at last and at the end heroically and unhesitatingly gave his life to save his country.' Raymond becomes the ideal of the citizen-soldier. However, the ending masks a troubling ambiguity. Raymond's ascension to heroism validates the very means by which the Manchurian Candidate was meant to achieve the Presidency: assassination. Like later police thrillers such as *Dirty Harry* (1971), which we will look at in Chapter 5, *The Manchurian Candidate* seems to legitimize extra-judicial killing if the cause – a patriotic one – is right.

The conspiracy thriller

In his BFI Classic essay on the film, Greil Marcus suggests that Major Marco's final speech, which carries 'the weight of the idea of one's country, one's community, one's social identity', is 'no less a fantasy, no less an absurdity, than anything else in *The Manchurian Candidate*: the idea that a single person could ruin the commonwealth, or save it' (Marcus 2002: 64–5). This kind of thinking may well be 'absurd', but as we saw above, the 'fantasy' of agency is bound up with the mode of the 'paranoid style' and is a signature discourse of the 1960s and 1970s. A much later paranoid thriller based on assassination – Alan J. Pakula's *The Parallax View* (1974) – seems, in retrospect, a reprise of many of the issues of *The Manchurian Candidate* but from the Watergate era of conspiracy rather than the Kennedy era. The central figure in *The Parallax View* is Joe Frady (Warren Beatty), an investigative reporter who is set up in the narrative as rather troublesome to his editor: he is independent, aggressive, and has a history of alcoholism. Early in the film, on the Space Needle in Seattle, he witnesses the assassination of a liberal senator who had been described by a female reporter as an 'ideal father, ideal husband [and] ideal leader of our country' – a telling conflation. When, some years later, the same female reportor comes to him with a paranoia-inflected story that six of the eighteen witnesses to the assassination have themselves died, and then she herself 'commits suicide', Frady is impelled to investigate.

What Frady uncovers is a secret organization called 'The Parallax Corporation', who recruit assassins by means of psychological testing and profiling. One of the most arresting sequences in the film is when Frady penetrates the organization by means of a fabricated questionnaire, and undergoes 'the test', in which key phrases and images are flashed onto a screen (the screen *we* watch) to cue emotional responses. Repeated words are: love, mother, father, me, home, country, God, enemy, happiness, which are followed by different sequences of images accompanied by powerful music. To begin with, the images connect in uncomplicated ways with American ideological constructs, so 'home' is followed by an image of apple pie, and 'country' by the Stars and Stripes or images of Lincoln or Washington. As the sequences progress, however, it becomes clear that the images are attempting to trigger an underlying pathology, what Fredric Jameson calls a 'political unconscious' of 'home-grown American comic-book fascism' (Jameson 1992: 62). For the viewer, the images suggest a matrix of power, sexual abuse, superhero fantasies (the image used is Marvel Comics' Nordic superhero-God, Thor), racism and racist violence, non-normative or 'perverse' sexuality, and homoeroticism. In a film which is clearly patterned upon the Kennedy assassination, it is curious to note that *The Parallax View* seems to posit an assassin-subject straight out of the Warren Commission: a damaged masculinity results in the 'lone gunman'. Although, by the paranoid 1970s, the assassin works for a corporation, the kind of subjectivity proposed is the same. The assassin here is *not* a normative subject.

According to Jameson, neither is he 'organization man', though he does concede the resemblance:

> What must be stressed is that the institutional construction of the conspirator figures is not to be confused with the essentially satiric portrayal of

'organization men' and the new corporate personality which culturally precedes it and which it is no doubt, in another sense, a kind of structural variant. (Jameson 1992: 59)

Instead, Jameson suggests that the conspirators of the Parallax Corporation, the faceless, identity-less suits that populate conspiracy thrillers of the 1970s, constitute a new form of collectivity. A figure such as Beatty's Joe Frady, whose 'rebellious' subjectivity in fact perfectly suits him to the role he is invited to play by the Parallax Corporation, represents 'the historical disappearance of [the rebel] from a bureaucratic and corporate universe' (Jameson 1992: 56). His kind of unlicensed, uncontrolled violence is not recuperated into the construction of a new social order, as it is in other generic forms (such as the Western). Instead, argues Jameson, *The Parallax View* refuses 'to project even the shadow of some older "positive" hero' (Jameson 1992: 58). Where, I have argued, *The Manchurian Candidate* ultimately reconstitutes the assassin in the form of the heroic and self-sacrificial 'patriot', the end of the later film denies any such gesture.

The closure of *The Parallax View* superficially resembles that of *The Manchurian Candidate* to an extent that I believe it to be a deliberate intertext. Frady follows a Parallax operative (actually the one who shot the liberal senator at the beginning) to a Convention centre, where rehearsals for a political rally are taking place. As Frady traces the labyrinthine corridors of the building, it becomes clear that other Parallax operatives are there and are aware of Frady's intentions. When another senator is assassinated, Frady is present on a gantry and visible to the rehearsing marching band: he is what Lee Harvey Oswald called a 'patsy'. He has been set up all along to take the blame for this assassination, and in fact his 'rebel' masculinity ideally suits him for the role of 'lone gunman'. (The film ends, as it had begun, with a quasi-Warren Commission affirming a 'lone gunman' solution to the assassination, and quashing conspiracy-inflected rumours.) *The Parallax View* denies Frady even the kind of agency afforded Raymond Shaw at the end of the earlier film: Frady is merely an unwitting pawn in a much bigger series of moves.

In *The Parallax View*, not only is agency evacuated, but so, seemingly, is ideology. Where, in *The Manchurian Candidate*, the conspiracy plot is in the service of Communist infiltration (typed, rather unconvincingly even for 1962, as a monolithic Sino-Soviet entity), the Parallax Corporation is as instrumental as the operatives it runs. In the film, it works to put a bomb on an aeroplane of one senator, then uses Frady to assassinate a rival senator (they are shown in dispute on the front page of a newspaper). The only hint of who Parallax might be working for is when an operative interviews Frady, who is offered employment by the 'Manufacturers Intelligence Group'. Presumably, in the world of *The Parallax View*, assassination has become a tool of industrial espionage. In Francis Ford Coppola's *The Conversation* (1974), surveillance operative Harry Caul works for a shady 'Director' of a corporation, who, Caul fears, is planning murder. Conspiracy has devolved merely to a personal murder plot. Where Eleanor Iselin's conspiracy worked for ultimately explicit political ends, the conspirators of later films seem to exist of and for themselves; there is no other end in view, necessarily, than to keep their secret operations secret. That is, essentially, why Frady is killed at the end of *The Parallax View*.

Pakula's film is also notable for its cinematography. As in his earlier *Klute* (1971) and later *All the President's Men* (1976), which was based on the newspaper investigation into the Watergate cover-up, Pakula uses the 'International Style' architectural modernism favoured by corporate American in the 1960s and 1970s to express a pathology not dissimilar to that uncovered in the 'test': the labyrinthine corridors, shiny marble atria, and identical offices (staffed by identical operatives) signify authoritarian impulses. Fredric Jameson, as intimated in a quotation above, has consistently used architecture or space as a figure for changed relations in a postmodern world system. These 'hyperspaces' are concrete, but act as metaphors for the kind of dislocation experienced by the contemporary subject. In *Postmodernism* (1991), it is the Bonaventure Hotel in Los Angeles which is the signature building of the new 'hyperspace'. The Bonaventure, argues Jameson,

> is a total space, a complete world, a kind of miniature city: to this new total space, meanwhile, corresponds a new collective practice, a new mode in which individuals move and congregate. (Jameson 1992: 40)

While Pakula's corporate modernist towers are really of an earlier era, I still think it is legitimate to argue that in the paranoid conspiracy thrillers of the 1970s, they are used to suggest a new form of social space, a disorientating and alienating one which conforms much more to Jameson's characterization of a 'postmodern hyperspace' than the utopian impulses Jameson detects at work in the architecture of the high modernist Le Corbusier. This is most pertinently revealed in the ubiquity of surveillance in these new spaces, a ubiquity that extends to the conspiracy thriller form as a whole.

Mike Davis, in *City of Quartz* (1990), pinpoints the increasing use of surveillance and security systems, particularly in Los Angeles, to control and dominate social and urban spaces. He writes:

> The American city, as many critics have recognized, is being systematically turned inside out – or, rather, outside in. The valorized spaces of the new megastructures and super-malls are concentrated in the center, street frontage is denuded, public activity is sorted into strictly functional compartments, and circulation is internalized in corridors under the gaze of private police. (Davis 1998: 226)

Davis even notes the LAPD's plans to place a geostationary surveillance satellite in orbit above Los Angeles to combat auto theft. The ubiquity of CCTV networks in the cities of North America and Europe denote a regime of maximal visibility, one that precludes deviant behaviour. This corresponds to Michel Foucault's well-known figure of the panopticon. This is a field of vision, immanent with power, which is based on Jeremy Bentham's model of a specular prison. In this model, prison cells are arranged in a circular pattern about a central guard watchtower. Entrances and exits to this tower are shielded, so the prisoners do not know whether the tower has guards in it or not. They must assume, therefore, that it is always occupied, that the disciplinary gaze is always upon them. This gaze both constitutes the subject as a subject (in her/his cell) and supervises them, ensuring the prisoner internalizes the controlling gaze. Foucault suggests that this model was, from the beginning, 'a diagram of the mechanism of power reduced to its ideal form' (Foucault 1991: 205).

Foucault's panopticon is a metaphor for the internalization of a controlling gaze of power, one that ultimately renders surveillance unnecessary. Like the panopticon, like the Army in Heinlein's *Starship Troopers*, the corporate architecture of the conspiracy thriller is a kind of disciplinary institution, designed to control its inhabitants. The spaces of Pakula's conspiracy thrillers certainly tend towards the panoptic, but the subjectivities produced by them tend to be more fractured than the ideal prisoner-subject invoked by the panopticon. This can be particularly seen in the divided subjectivity of the 'call girl' Bree Daniels in Pakula's own *Klute*, and in Harry Caul, 'king of the buggers', in Francis Ford Coppola's *The Conversation*.

Klute is dominated by sound recording, as is *The Conversation*. In both, a recorded conversation is replayed again and again, and is central to the narrative. In *Klute*, this is a recording of the voice of Bree Daniels (Jane Fonda), a call girl who is undergoing therapy and nurtures ambitions to become an actress. (We see that her acting skills in faking an orgasm with a client or 'john' – where she looks at her watch mid-coitus – are much better than her acting skills in reading for theatrical parts.) In fact, Bree 'acts' continually: she projects a mask or persona, of the cynical, manipulating femme fatale, in order to remain in control of the life she is trying to live. However, paranoia is beginning to encroach: she feels that she is being watched or followed. As in other conspiracy thrillers, of course, paranoia is revealed to be a rational processing of actuality. Bree is being watched by Peter Cable (Charles Cioffi), who has murdered a prostitute and a friend of his who had interrupted him in violence, then sent John Klute (Donald Sutherland) to investigate the disappearance of his murdered friend. Cable is a version of the 'bent insider' that recurs in police thrillers such as *Bullitt* (1968) and *Magnum Force* (1973) that we will look at in Chapter 5, but is also surrounded by the signs of personal betrayal that accrue around the double agent of British espionage fiction (see Chapter 2). As the narrative progresses, Cable transforms into a masculinity-distressed 'psycho', the kind of troubled subject that we will find in the next chapter. *Klute*, then, stands at a curious and revealing generic junction.

John Klute, the detective, is also a watcher: he bugs Bree's apartment to find information, but is drawn into a romantic relationship with her, despite initially spurning her sexual advances (attempts at manipulation or a frankly admitted economic exchange: sex for tapes). However, in contrast to Cable's violent and misogynist sexuality, Klute is quiet and restrained (if somewhat paternalistic), offering Bree an alternative to her divided subjectivity, in marriage. (Perhaps we can see in *Klute* a distaff version of *North by Northwest*'s psychological trajectory here.) He is not himself affected by the matrix of conspiracy and surveillance, partly because he comes from outside the city, but also because he represents a kind of moral uprightness (and innocence) at odds with the men of Bree's world. Christine Gledhill suggests that Klute and Cable actually function in the film as 'symbolic extensions of the heroine's divided self' (Gledhill 1980: 112). This division itself actuates a potentiality for sexual betrayal: the coding of espionage fiction is here relocated onto the sexual activity (and agency) of the female protagonist which, as Gledhill suggests, indicates its connections to film noir.

However, I think it is incorrect to view Klute and Cable as stable, unitary identities that reflect Bree's duality. This is revealed in the many shots in *Klute* that show mirrored reflections, not only of Bree, but also of Klute. In one crucial shot, the signature atrium space of Pakula's films creates two Klutes, as Sutherland is reflected in a polished marble wall surface. That Klute, like Bree, presents a persona of control, while repressing a turbulent emotional life, is revealed when Bree's former 'old man' or pimp, Frank Ligourin (Roy Scheider), tries to take her back to 'the Life': Klute violently attacks him (and by extension, her perceived betrayal). Not only is Bree 'rescued' or 'cured' by her heterosexual romance with Klute (much more effective than therapy), Klute himself becomes much more able to express emotion, and in fact moves from 'innocent' provincial detective to an operator who is able to entrap Cable, his erstwhile controller. Klute's own 'divided self' is pointed towards a more unitary stability by his romance with Bree.

The repressed or overly self-controlled masculine subject is also central to a surveillance and conspiracy narrative in *The Conversation*. Harry Caul (Gene Hackman) inhabits, at the beginning of the film, an entirely instrumental subjectivity. He is a surveillance operative, working freelance for faceless clients. He records other people's lives, but confesses 'I don't care what they're talking about, I just want a nice fat recording'. This separation from emotion is, it is revealed, and effect of past trauma: a previous bugging job had led to the murders of three people. To see himself as an instrument, then, an analogue of the recording machines he uses so skilfully, enables him to avoid the strictures of conscience: to become like Raymond Shaw. His own apartment, however, reveals his personal paranoia. The door has four locks, and the décor is deliberately impersonal. 'I don't have anything personal,' he tells an overly intrusive neighbour. Harry Caul (whose name signifies the mask or persona he presents) is, however, unhappy; not unlovable like the priggish Shaw, but loveless, too introverted and repressed to be able to conduct a relationship.

In the film, his one long-standing female companion withdraws from his life, and a brief sexual liaison results in betrayal when crucial tapes are stolen. Ironically, the man who is surrounded by communication technologies finds real human contact almost impossible.

Caul is, then, emblematic of the personal corrosion undergone by the masculine subject who is entwined with surveillance and the clandestine life. John Cawelti and Bruce Rosenberg have suggested the malign psychological effects that the world of the operative has in espionage fiction:

> Participants in the clandestine world live in a state of psychological tension which resembles, in some of its characteristics, the pathology of schizophrenia. This tension results from their dual views of the world. First, there is the 'reality' constituted by the secrets shared with other members of the clandestine group. ... Yet, since the preservation of the clandestine group requires that these secrets remain hidden from other persons, a clandestine participant must also live as a member of the ordinary world, pretending to share its view of reality. ... This slipping in and out of the ordinary world is characteristic of schizophrenic illness. (Cawelti and Rosenberg 1987: 17)

Indeed, in *The Conversation* Harry Caul becomes increasingly prey to a kind of psychic disintegration. He suffers nightmares then, when trying to prevent another murder precipitated by his surveillance information (he has in fact misunderstood it, in a typical paranoid moment), he succumbs to the visions of blood and murder that threatens to blur the distinction between what is 'real' and what is paranoia-induced hallucination. At the end of the film, Caul discovers that he has himself been bugged, and the apartment that symbolized his emptied, controlled subjectivity is reduced to ruins by his search for the device. Caul, the king of the buggers, himself becomes a shattered victim of surveillance.

'I'm the only one who knows what this means'

In *American Tabloid* (1995) and its sequel *The Cold Six Thousand* (2001), the crime writer James Ellroy turned to a conspiracy-informed fictional 'history' of the post-World War 2 United States, written in a percussive and fragmented style that drew on the increasingly concentrated writing of his neo-noir LA Quartet (which we will look at in Chapter 6) and the sensationalism of scandal magazines and *National Enquirer*-style tabloids. In an epigraph to *American Tabloid*, Ellroy wrote:

> America was never innocent. ... You can't ascribe our fall from grace to any single event or set of circumstances. You can't lose what you lacked at conception.
>   Mass-market nostalgia gets you hopped up for a past that never existed. ...
> It's time to demythologise an era and build a new myth from the gutter to the

stars. It's time to embrace bad men and the price they paid to secretly define their time. (Ellroy 1995: n.p.)

These two books, then, take upon themselves the status of 'myth' rather than fiction or history, although the books are themselves populated with figures from the 'real' 1950s and 1960s, such as Howard Hughes, J. Edgar Hoover, Teamster boss Jimmy Hoffa, various Mafia bosses and the Kennedy brothers. As self-conscious myth, both books deploy larger-than-life character types whose interwoven narratives involve them in clandestine activity against Castro's Cuba, in the Civil Rights movement, in Vietnam, and in the assassinations of both John and Robert Kennedy. In fact, each book leads up to a moment of assassination: *American Tabloid* ends in November 1963 with the assassination of John Kennedy, and *The Cold Six Thousand* in June 1968, with the death of his brother, Robert. As Ellroy's invocation of 'bad man' might suggest, these narratives also seem to work to place the agent or operative back at the heart of conspiracy-inflected 'history', while at the same time reconstituting a kind of heroic masculinity that is at once attractive and morally compromised.

Both books are organized around homosocial male relationships, with a triumvirate of men at the centre of each book. In *American Tabloid*, these are Pete Bondurant, a French-Canadian initially working for Howard Hughes, whose main responsibilities are providing dope and scandal-gossip for his boss (and coincidentally, extortion monies for himself); Kemper Boyd, an FBI agent who 'retires' (at J. Edgar Hoover's request) to become part of CIA operations against Cuba, and a close associate of the Kennedy family; and Ward J. Littell, another FBI agent, in this case with left-liberal convictions, who is removed from the service and becomes a Mafia lawyer. The crucial relationship between Boyd and Littell is typed as brotherhood, to ensure symbolic continuities with the macrocosmic 'historical' narrative of John and Robert Kennedy. There is also a strong element of surrogacy involved, for both Bondurant and Boyd suffered the loss of their brother in early years; most particularly, each was responsible for his own brother's death. Bondurant's doctor brother François was in a Los Angeles house, involved in an illegal abortion racket, when Bondurant set it alight and shot dead all those who ran out as part of a 'contract hit'; Boyd accidentally killed his brother in a hunting accident. For Boyd, the unstable 'weak sister' Littell becomes a surrogate 'little brother' who he seeks to protect and advance. Further to this psychological complex, Boyd is attracted to John Kennedy and particularly the glamour and lifestyle (rather than political ambitions) he represents. He is, in a sense, 'star struck'. Littell, by contrast, is attracted to the Jesuit probity of Bobby, and the younger Kennedy's campaign against the Mafia once he becomes his brother's Attorney General.

Homosocial bonds express the different character types of Boyd and Littell, but are fundamentally unstable. When Boyd discovers that Jack Kennedy has said that 'Kemper's one great regret is that he's not a Kennedy [and that] [h]e's living out some kind of unsavoury fantasy', Boyd's emulating love turns into hatred (Ellroy 1995:512). In fact, Boyd's disintegration had begun sometime earlier. In analogous terms to those described by Cawelti and Rosenberg above, Boyd's multiple involvement in clandestine operations leads to a corrosion of the self. Earlier in the novel, he had been careful to keep different elements of his life (FBI agency, CIA agency, involvement in narcotics, wooing an estranged and illegitimate sister of Jack Kennedy) 'compartmentalized'. As the book nears its conclusion, however, these compartments start to disintegrate, and Boyd begins to behave in ever more pathological ways. In fact, he begins to exert the kind of violent masculine agency that had previously been the uncomplicated province of Pete Bondurant.

If Kemper Boyd is a troubled version of the suave James Bond at the beginning of the narrative, by the time of his death, he is displaying the fractured and compromised subjectivity of the double (or in his case, 'quadruple') agent. Bondurant, by contrast, is almost a version of Donovan Grant in *From Russia with Love*: his physical hugeness is constantly emphasized, and the exercise of his own will or desire is usually exerted through physical violence, or the threat of violence. In the course of both novels, Bondurant kills dozens, if not hundreds, of people, and in *American Tabloid* seems largely untroubled by conscience. He is also untroubled by ideology; though a devotee of the 'Cause' (to oust Castro), he is only an anti-Communist in the sense that Communism is 'bad for business'. His primary motivation is money, and latterly, survival. In *The Cold Six Thousand*, however, an ageing and increasingly infirm Pete Bondurant, corroded by his growing sense of guilt for his crimes, begins to go the same way as Boyd. Inhabiting a more unified subjectivity, however, he survives to be reunited with his wife Barbara. This moral trajectory softens Bondurant and renders him more heroic, legitimizing the murders that he has committed. He becomes, in the second novel, another 'victim' of Dallas, but the enormity of this event helps mask the dozens of others he has killed. He is 'fried/fragged/*frappéed* ... frazzled and free' in the alliterative rhythms of Ellroy's prose (Ellroy 2001:670), and the text encourages the reader to be glad that he has survived.

Although Ellroy seemed to disavow a 'loss of innocence' in the epigraph to *American Tabloid*, the centrality of 'Dallas' in both texts seems to suggest that, as Peter Knight argued, the assassination of John Kennedy was indeed some kind of 'origin point' for the American malaise. The first novel works through the vectors that led up to 1963; the second works through the violent consequences. 'Dallas' is then a vortical point around which all the events of the two books circulate. Curiously, the assassination itself is proposed by the character who is otherwise the 'liberal' moral centre of both books, Ward Littell, who, even though fatally compromised (and whose homosocial and political attraction to Bobby also turns into hatred), channels illegally expropriated funds to Communist and Civil Rights activists throughout, partly to assuage his own conscience. It is the 'liberal' Littell who approaches Mafia boss Carlos Marcello with a plan:

We've all been thinking of it. You can't get a roomful of the boys together without somebody bringing it up. ... I'm saying that it's so big and audacious that we'll most likely never be suspected. I'm saying that even if we are, the powers that be will realize that it can never be conclusively proven. I'm saying that a consensus of denial will build off of it. I'm saying people will want to remember the man as something he wasn't. (Ellroy 1995:538)

Of course, this speech reads as retrospective conspiracy-history put into the mouth of a protagonist before the fact, which it is. However, it is worth noting the way in which Ellroy couches the genesis of the plan to assassinate President Kennedy: it involves another displacement of agency. 'We've all been thinking it,' says Littell. The assassination is somehow already out there in the zeitgeist, a 'Let's Kill Jack metaphysic' waiting to be made manifest (Ellroy 1995:568). 'Dallas' is not originated: it becomes the origin point in itself.

In *The Cold Six Thousand*, the homosocial organization switches from brotherhood to fatherhood, with attendant surrogacy. Kemper Boyd (killed by Littell at the end of *American Tabloid*, almost as a gesture of mercy) is replaced in the homosocial triangle by Wayne Tedrow Junior, a Las Vegas cop sent to Dallas by his racist Mormon father on the day of John Kennedy's assassination, to perform his first 'contract hit'. Rather than form bonds with Littell, however, Wayne gravitates towards Bondurant, who had witnessed Junior's botched attempt to complete the hit. Bondurant becomes a surrogate father, mentoring Tedrow's introduction into the world of the clandestine ('the Life'). Tedrow Junior is even called '*le fils de Pete*' at one point (Ellroy 2001:577). In a typical Oedipalized trajectory for the clandestine operative, Tedrow Jr beds his stepmother Janice then achieves full violent, masculine subjectivity at the end of the novel (replacing both Pete and Littell) by helping, and watching, Janice kill Tedrow Senior. (Junior's sexuality in the novel is primarily voyeuristic, therefore not adapted to the heterosexual Cold War normative.) *The Cold Six Thousand* approaches more nearly the kind of 'erotic triangle' suggested by Eve Kosofsky Sedgwick in *Between Men* (1985), where the role of the woman is to mediate (and disguise the primary relationship) between the two male rivals for her love. In fact, there are two interlocking triangles in this novel: Barbara Bondurant is the third point in a triangle that has Pete and Junior at its base; Janice Tedrow is the mediator between Ward Littell and Junior. Although *The Cold Six Thousand* repeats *American Tabloid*'s rewriting of history as conspiracy, its interpersonal economy is surprisingly patterned upon the narrative structures Sedgwick identifies in the nineteenth-century novel. Unlike *Klute*, though, a romance narrative offers no kind of escape or resolution for the protagonists.

The social vision of *The Cold Six Thousand* is apocalyptic, as conspiracy-inflected narratives often are. The key word throughout the novel is 'HATE': racial hatred, class hatred, or personal hatred is the dominant motivational force behind most of the characters, and, by extension, the turbulent and violent social and political scene of the mid-1960s. The predominance of hatred expresses the corrosion evident in Ellroy's America since 'Dallas'; the belief within the story, in the minds of conspirators and others, that the actions of bad men (that is to say, assassination) can restore the United States to some kind of order are revealed as a symptom of that corrosion. Assassination begets assassination, but there is no way back to order, no way back to the innocence of the unitary subject in Ellroy's fiction. His intent may have been to build a unifying myth, 'from the gutter to the stars': but by the end of *The Cold Six Thousand*, despite his attempts to reconstitute some kind of 'heroic' masculinity, the male subject still lies in fragments on the floor.

CHAPTER FOUR

The Psycho in the Grey Flannel Suit

Masculinity has been periodically in crisis over the last hundred years or so. The end of the nineteenth century, the 1950s and the 1990s have all witnessed a cultural discourse that represents hegemonic masculinity as somehow in decline, a symptom of a social and cultural body in crisis. For this chapter, the connections between the 50s and 90s are most pertinent, particularly in terms of genre. I will argue that the 1990s saw a revisiting of the masculinity issues of the 1950s, to do with consumerism, the 'organization man', and 'emasculation'; and also a self-reflexive redeployment of crucial generic motifs. These revolve around two figures: the 'psycho' and the 'man in the grey flannel suit', the subjects of a pair of films Alfred Hitchcock made in 1959 and 1960: *North by Northwest* (1959) and *Psycho* (1960). Robert Corber, in his *In the Name of National Security* (1993), suggests that the two films form an inverted dyad in terms of representations of masculinity; in relation to the films *The Game* (1997), *American Psycho* (1999), *American Beauty* (1999), *Fight Club* (1999) and *Falling Down* (1991), I will argue that the two figures of troubled masculinity come together in a late-twentieth-century matrix of popular representations of the (white) male beset by problems of agency within the fields of home and work.

North by Northwest and *The Game*

Steven Cohan, in his article 'The Spy in the Gray Flannel Suit' (which was largely incorporated into *Masked Men*), suggested that *North by Northwest* had not been, up to that time, 'analyzed in depth as a significant mediation of the culture's own preoccupation with a masculinity crisis' (Cohan 1995: 46). Robert Corber argues that in the figure of Roger Thornhill (Cary Grant), *North by Northwest*'s narrative — where Thornhill is drawn into a Cold War espionage plot that is resolved by saving, then marrying the heroine — is in fact an ideologically loaded narrative. Thornhill is revealed, at the start of the film, to be somewhat beholden to his mother, considering he is a forty-something advertising executive with two ex-wives. Corber suggests that the character of Thornhill represents a masculinity undone by a failure of motherhood, in which, in the terms of Philip Wylie (who coined the phrase 'momism'), 'domineering and over-protective mothers disrupted the Oedipal structure of the middle-class nuclear family by smothering their sons with "unnatural" affection' (Corber 1993: 197). This 'demonology of motherhood' was also, contends Corber, blamed for the 'infiltration' of communism into American life. (We can clearly see these discourses at work in *The Manchurian Candidate* (1962), discussed in the previous chapter.) Corber argues:

> This discourse of momism located the sources of communism and homo-sexuality in incompetent mothering and in doing so ensured that women's child-rearing practices contributed to the reproduction of the national security state. (Corber 1993: 213)

Masculinity, then, is clearly connected with the ideological imperatives of the American nation-state. To fail in producing hegemonic masculinity is to open the floodgates to communism. As we saw in the work of Klaus Theweleit in Chapter 1, the feminine, or feminization, has a long connection with the communist 'flood' (particularly in fascist discourse). An armoured masculinity must be therefore produced to withstand it. The hegemonic masculinity of the Cold War United States, the domestic breadwinner, is then a 'strong' masculinity produced to withstand feminiza-tion and communism, and the nation-state works hard to maintain it. In *North by Northwest*, argues Corber, 'the American government is able to suture Thornhill's identity by creating a fantasy scenario that organizes his sexuality in such a way that it conforms to the nation's security interests' (Corber 1993: 213). The narrative of *North by Northwest* not only produces an adult, domestic masculinity in Thornhill's marriage to Eve Kendall (Eva Marie-Saint), but also an ideologically sanctioned Cold War subject, willing to participate in the espionage manoeuvres against the Soviet 'enemy'.

Cohan attempts to compromise Corber's model, while acknowledging its critical acuity. Cohan suggests that Thornhill's 'masquerade' as George Kaplan, the fabricated spy-persona, in fact destabilizes representations of gender through an alignment with what he calls the 'performative ethic [of] the new professional-executive class [and] that new class's own anxieties about self-presentation' (Cohan 1995: 46). Masculinity, in Cohan's argument, becomes not a stable ideologically constructed identity, but a shifting 'gender performance'. He begins with the scene in which Thornhill (as Kaplan) is shot by Eve Kendall to prove her loyalty to the enemy spy (and her former lover), Vandamm (James Mason). The scene is in fact a fabrication, a staged scene, which ties in to the ongoing motif of theatricality and performance in the film. (When first picked up by Vandamm's men – erroneously – Thornhill protests his innocence. 'Your performance makes this whole room a theatre,' purrs Mason.) Cohan reads this, initially, as the turning point in the film. It is where 'George Kaplan' is killed, 'the fictional identity that has in effect been serving as an instructive masculine persona for Roger'; and where Roger Thornhill finally assumes a 'heroic masculinity' that will enable him to rescue Eve and resolve the narrative in both espionage and romantic terms (Cohan 1995: 44).

In stressing the motif of 'falling', however, Cohan indicates the incomplete suturing of the Cold War subject in *North by Northwest*, preferring a reading which reaffirms the 'vulnerability' and instability of the masculine subject through the constant relation of that subject to masquerade and performativity. (We will return to the notion of 'falling' later in the chapter.) This is symbolized in Cary Grant's 'Gray Flannel Suit', the uniform of the 1950s 'organization man'. The 'Man in the Gray Flannel Suit' was, according to Cohan, 'responsible for legitimating the hegemony of the professional-managerial class' (Cohan 1997: 38), but also, because it 'had to do with the way advertising, increasingly directed toward male shoppers as well as female ones, [it] revised what had been presumed to be an absolute gender divide: masculine production versus feminine consumption' (Cohan 1995: 52). The need for the American economy to expand its range of consumers, argues Cohan in *Masked Men* (1997), increasingly created the need to construct the masculine subject as a consumer (which results in the 'playboy' persona of late-1950s sex comedies starring Rock Hudson and Doris Day, and is also, one might add, connected to the fantasy figure of James Bond). Problematically, this also feminized the male, signifying to a further necessity of buttressing a 'strong' Cold War masculine subject. Hegemonic masculinity, then, helped produce as well as ideologically fix anxieties surrounding the crisis in masculinity in the 1950s.

A similar crisis pertained around the turn of the millennium, and the late-1990s films I shall analyse in this chapter certainly respond to, and represent, the lineaments of this cultural phenomenon. John Beynon, in *Masculinities and Culture* (2002), suggests that 'the summer of 2000 could justifiably be described as the "masculinity-in-crisis-summer"', that crisis signifying a redefinition of masculinity that was caused by changes in employment patterns, the loss of the 'breadwinner' hegemon and the high profile of feminized 'New Man' models, and particularly the loss of masculine 'rights' (Beynon 2002: 79, 77). While Beynon does not accept the idea of a 'masculinity in crisis', a key indicator of the current interest in masculinities was 'the commercialization of male appearance and the widespread acceptance of more androgynous identities' (Beynon 2002: 77), a return to the issues of the 1950s, where the consumerist male was a feminized male. Yvonne Tasker (1993), Tim Edwards (1996) and Kenneth MacKinnon (1997 and 1999) have all argued that there is a greater visibility of the masculine body in contemporary culture. Tasker insists on the visibility of 'built' bodies and the centrality of the bodybuilder action star in the 1980s. She suggests:

> The visibility of the built male body, in both film and advertising images, represents part of the wider shift in the male image, and in the range of masculine identities, that are on offer in western popular culture. ... Images of the built male body form only a part of the new visibility that surrounds male bodies and masculine identities within both popular culture and academic inquiry. (Tasker 1993: 73)

Tim Edwards's focus is upon fashion, and the increasing use of the male body to market consumer commodities, a process which itself fetishizes and reifies the male body. In 'Pump Up the Postmodern', Edwards traces the changing imperatives of 1990s British culture. He suggests that 'images of masculinity are an increasingly pervasive aspect of consumer-oriented society', but that

> despite this apparent plethora of images of masculinity, the content of these representations remains quite extraordinarily fixed. The men concerned are always young, usually white, particularly muscular, critically strong-jawed, clean shaven (often all over), healthy, sporty, successful, virile, and ultimately sexy. (Edwards 1996: 2)

Edwards's argument is similar to that of Michel Foucault in his *History of Sexuality* (1990). Foucault argues that the increasing medicalization and control of sexuality in the nineteenth century came about not through suppression, but through maximal visibility. The increasing contemporary visibility of male bodies signals an appropriation of divergent and non-normative sexualities and subjectivities, a closing of dissent and resistance. Rather than the visible male body being any sign of the overturning of patriarchal imperatives of female objectification, Beynon cites it as a cause of yet further anxiety. We shall return to this issue below.

Beynon's stress on the changing nature of male employment and the decline of the 'breadwinner' hegemon is clearly crucial to the late-1990s 'crisis'. 'The man in the grey flannel suit' returns symbolically in the 'worker drones' of *Fight Club* and *American Beauty*; but first, I would like to turn to David Fincher's *The Game*. David Fincher's films have repeatedly considered the problematic of contemporary masculinity. In Fincher's third film, *The Game*, Michael Douglas plays the protagonist Nicholas Van Orton, a wealthy business executive who lives inside the cocoons of his gated mansion and BMW. The film begins with inserted footage that signifies the 'home movie': soundless, grainy and over-exposed, this footage – of an archetypal American successful family, replete with images of the father in grey flannel – that is soon stitched onto Van Orton's memories of childhood. The seeming normativeness is itself revealed to be a façade, a performance: Van Orton witnesses his father committing suicide, falling from the family mansion's roof (another reference to the vulnerability of the 1950s 'breadwinner').

Van Orton is first seen in a privileged domestic environment that is at once homely and empty; he lives alone and the TV spools behind him, broadcasting market reports. Van Orton has allowed the breadwinner imperative to dominate his life to such an extent that he has lost his wife, is childless, and seems entirely enclosed by his working function. In fact, as the disclosure of his father's suicide reveals, Van Orton's current self-control or emotional withdrawal is a symptom of childhood trauma. When his brother Conrad (Sean Penn) introduces him into the 'Game' of the title, a vigorous pastime for the male elite, he pitches it as something of a palliative: after completing his own 'game' in London, he has never felt better. When Van Orton alludes to his brother's troubled past, Conrad reveals that he is 'off' medication or any other form of psychological crutch. Clearly, the trauma of childhood was shared by the younger sibling; clearly, the older Van Orton is in need of the same therapy that has produced his brother's contentment.

The narrative is patterned on a mixture of *North by Northwest* and the paranoid conspiracy thrillers of the 1970s: a respectable if stolid businessman is drawn into a matrix of femmes fatales, obscure forces, and people attempting to kill him. In an early scene where Van Orton visits CRS, the corporation that stages the 'Game', he is subjected to the kind of psychological testing that forms the entrance exam for assassins in *The Parallax View* (1974) that was considered in the last chapter. Indeed, Van Orton is even subjected to a kind of images-plus-trigger words sequence that forms a crucial part of the earlier film. After his fortune and status are reduced (and Douglas sports a scar on his nose to signify his rediscovered 'heroic' masculinity), the narrative ends with Van Orton, believing that he had mistakenly killed his own brother, committing 'suicide' by throwing himself off the roof where the shooting takes place. This is in itself a fake, as he plunges through a glass ceiling onto a stunt air cushion, surrounded by tables where guests at his birthday party await him. Finally, the 'Game' is revealed: Conrad is alive, and all events have been part of the game. Van Orton recapitulates his father's death in order to be reborn; his act of falling, like that of Roger Thornhill in *North by Northwest*, recuperates a 'healed' masculinity.

As the film closes, he is reconciled with his ex-wife (heavily pregnant, signifying the necessity for 'proper' mothering) and asks the key female protagonist in his 'Game' for a date (played by Deborah Kara Unger, who as 'Christine' or 'Claire' seems to forget herself what is real and what imaginary, what is her 'true' identity and what is performed). He is returned, then, to a form of normative heterosexual masculinity that defuses the problematic isolation of the 'new' 'man in the grey flannel suit', but *The Game*'s critique of a 'breadwinner' hegemon – in the shape of the trauma-tized, introverted Van Orton – lacks a critique of the economic system that produces it. Early in the film, Van Orton behaves not unlike the corporate sharks of Oliver Stone's *Wall Street* (1986), which finds its emblem in the figure of Gordon Gecko, corporate raider – also played by Michael Douglas. Stone's film connects this form of aggressive individualism to the fracturing of post-industrial communities in America in the Reagan era. However, like the other films that will be considered in this chapter, *The Game* tends to deflect this critique into a narrative structure of the troubled male and his trajectory of personal redemption.

The Game is a pastiche, what Fredric Jameson calls a 'blank parody', complicit with rather than critical of the ideological implications of the generic form it recapitulates (Jameson 1991: 17). *The Game* repeats the narrative scheme of *North by Northwest*, but in its attempts to reconnect the affectless contemporary white male with a simulation of 'life' rather than its actuality, indicates a change from the ideological imperatives of the Cold War that drove the narrative resolution of Hitchcock's films. This is even revealed in the title of the film. As we saw in Chapter 2, espionage fictions traditionally use the metaphor of spying as a 'game', derived from Rudyard Kipling's *Kim* where British espionage is called 'the Great Game'. In *North by Northwest*, this discourse emerges when Roger Thornhill is told by the spymaster The Professor (Leo G. Carroll) that Eve Kendall must fly off with Vandamm to maintain her cover, after she has 'shot' George Kaplan: 'I don't like the games you play, Professor,' says Thornhill. (The Professor's reply — 'War is hell, Mr Thornhill, even a Cold one' — indicates that Thornhill has still not internalized the 'adult' imperatives of this particular spy game.) What *The Game* does reveal, however, is that beneath the masquerade of everyday existence lies the potentiality for violence, spectacle and excitement, in the form of a rediscovered 'heroic' masculinity that is disavowed by the 'man in the grey flannel suit'.

The mask and masquerade: *Psycho* and *American Psycho*

Cohan, in 'The Spy in the Gray Flannel Suit', insists on the notion of masquerade to investigate the masculine subject. In the collection *The Masculine Masquerade*, which also contains Cohan's article, Harry Brod investigates the use of masquerade as a rethinking of male subjectivity, particularly the centrality of *performance* in relation to subjectivity. Drawing on Paul Hoch's *White Hero, Black Beast* (1979), Brod argues:

> what is being masked and repressed to present the face of masculinity is an earlier more 'feminine' anal eroticism, a repression also linked to the suppression of homosexuality. The masculine mask is worn in order to achieve a normative performance-oriented phallic heterosexual male sexuality .... There is, however, a crucial difference between the conceptualizations of gender as performance and gender as masquerade, for masquerade invokes a distinction between the artificial and the real. Behind the facade of the mask lies the *real* face, to be revealed when the masquerade is over. (Brod 1995: 17)

The 'Gray Flannel Suit' is a kind of masquerade or mask; what Cohan argues, however, is that there is no 'authentic' or unitary identity presupposed by this metaphor; there is nothing underlying the mask. The masquerade *is* subjectivity, constantly performed. Both *North by Northwest* and *The Game*, however, encourage the illusion that such an unproblematic, 'authentic' unitary subjectivity does underlie the suit, promoting an identification with a masculine subject that is at once 'heroic' and reinserted into the domestic sphere. This, as we saw in Chapter 1, was an urgent cultural and social problem in the period immediately following World

War 2; it recurs in the United States after Korea and Vietnam, and is also found in Britain in the form of the 'soldier-spy' considered in Chapter 2. Generically, the problem of violence and masculinity can also be found in the figure of the 'psycho' in the horror film (particularly in the 'slasher' variant), to which we will now turn. Here, the motif of the mask becomes even more dominant.

In Alfred Hitchcock's *Psycho* (1960), the male 'psycho' of the title, Norman Bates (Anthony Perkins), is, like Roger Thornhill in *North by Northwest*, dominated by the figure of his mother. Bates has also been insufficiently Oedipalized, but for him, there is no possibility of a resolution in heterosexual romance. Indeed, what Corber calls his 'dangerously disturbed behaviour' is explained within *Psycho* itself as the product of 'his troubled relationship with his mother' (Corber 1993: 184). Another instance of momism leads to 'a split in Norman's personality', where the internalized jealousy of his mother causes him to kill the object of his desire, Marion Crane (Janet Leigh). However, Corber calls attention to the inadequacy of the psychological explanation proffered in the film. *Psycho* reveals, instead,

> [t]he limited ability of the state and its representatives to organize and regulate the social field. Norman and his mother are not the only characters in the film who refuse to abide by the 'laws' that regulated Oedipal desire in the 1950s. Marion, too, resists the authority of the state and its representatives to legislate psychosexual norms. (Corber 1993: 190)

While the generic connection between the espionage thriller and the construction of an ideologically sanctioned masculine subject is an explicit one, here Corber directly inserts the horror genre into this field of analysis. *Psycho*, he argues, 'stresses the points of resistance' to the construction of the breadwinner; 'the discourses of national security engender counter-fantasies' (Corber 1993: 216). The hegemon is disrupted at the point of his construction.

Norman's split subjectivity, in which he masquerades as his own mother to unleash the terrifying force of his repressed sexuality (as violence), is also bound up with voyeurism. Before he kills Marion Crane, he watches her in the adjacent cabin to his office through a peep-hole hidden behind a painting. The editing encourages the spectator's identification with Norman's voyeuristic gaze: we see through his eyes. Unsurprisingly considering that the film was made under the guidelines (albeit loosening ones) of the Production Code Administration, the film cuts away from Janet Leigh as she undresses, and cuts back to her as she dons a robe prior to showering. This withholding of the pleasure of voyeurism gains a belated release in the famous shower scene that follows soon afterwards, in which Leigh's body is shown, but fragmented into different parts by the editing and then attacked with an over-large kitchen knife. We will see in the next two chapters that the lone 'rogue cop' is also bound up with voyeurism and violence, suggesting that the figure of the 'psycho' and the 'rogue cop' have troubling affinities.

The 'split subject' of the slasher/horror film is not identical to that of the spy text; rather than the overt ideological imperatives of the Cold War pulling the male subject in several directions and fracturing it, here it is desire that is the cause of fragmentation. As we saw in Chapters 1 and 2 with regard to the homecoming soldier, 'strong' hegemonic masculinity is guaranteed by the very violence that it attempts to suppress in the necessity for the reinsertion of the male into the domestic sphere. We will see in the next chapter that in 'rogue cop' thrillers, it is the law itself that is guaranteed by extra-judicial violence. Limit is guaranteed by, yet destabilized by, an excess that lies within the construction of the boundary itself. In *Psycho* and the slasher film, the male gaze (constitutive of male desire and of the female object of that desire) is usually connoted by voyeurism, and the excessive violence of male desire made manifest in the punishment of sexual activity and the erotic object.

This destabilization is manifested in what Carol J. Clover, in *Men, Women and Chainsaws: Gender in the Modern Horror Film* (1992), calls 'gender distress'. Clover suggests that sexual repression lies at the heart of the 'psycho' male subject:

> The notion of a killer propelled by psychosexual fury, more particularly a male in gender distress, has proved a durable one, and the progeny of Norman Bates stalk the genre up to the present day. (Clover 1992: 27)

This 'psychosexual fury' is determined by sexual repression. Clover suggests that 'violence and sex are not concomitants but alternatives' in the slasher film (Clover 1992: 29). Why has this figure proved so durable? The excess of desire that turns to violence surely reveals further cultural anxieties about masculinity, and it is certainly no coincidence that the crucial period for the 'slasher' subgenre was directly after the end of the Vietnam War. The split subjectivity of the 'psycho' is one where the legitimating violence of the hegemonic male finds excessive manifestation rather than resolution.

The split subjectivity of the 'psycho' is at once revealed and disguised by the 'mask' he wears, whether that is Mrs Bates's clothing in *Psycho*, the William Shatner mask worn by the 'psycho' Michael Myers in John Carpenter's *Halloween* (1978) (or many another killer in the 'slasher' subgenre). The mask of the serial killer Patrick Bateman, in the screen version of Bret Easton Ellis's *American Psycho* (1991), is the overcoded uniform of normativeness that derives from texts such as *North by Northwest*: his Armani suit. Mary Harron's film of *American Psycho* (1999) is faithful to Bret Easton Ellis's dissection of American society in the 1980s. In the novel, Patrick Bateman (the eponymous psycho) and his circle of Wall Street colleagues enjoy a life of conspicuous consumption, but the hedonistic spin on the 'grey flannel suit' is revealed to be empty, just as Nicholas Van

Orton's was in *The Game*. Where Van Orton's traumatized male subject is healed through his immersion in a paranoia-inflected fake 'reality' that is more stimulating than his 'real' life, Bateman's alienation from the world of business and consumption leads directly to psychosis. There is no redemption in heterosexual romance for Bateman; he and his identikit colleagues denote the desirable female body by the term 'hardbody', reiterating the objectification motivated by their desiring gazes. For Bateman, sexual desire is displaced by violence, as it is with other 'slasher' killers, as Carol Clover notes above. The 'hardbody' becomes the object of (and reflection of) a violent, pathological male desire.

In *American Psycho*, normative heterosexuality is displaced by narcissism and repressed homoeroticism. The privileged young men in *American Psycho* who form a homosocial group are obsessed with their own physical condition, attending the gym and building their bodies. Like the female 'hardbodies' they objectify, they also render their own bodies as objects. Bateman (Christian Bale) fetishizes his own body, and the opening scenes of the film represent Bateman's autoerotic enjoyment of his own hardbody in the shower. *American Psycho*'s first sequence after the titles represents Bateman's 'morning routine', one dominated by the use of callisthenics and male cosmetics. It also features Bateman's narratorial voice as a non-diegetic track, offering a litany of facial scrubs and exercise routines. It begins with a tracking shot down a corridor in Bateman's apartment in the American Gardens building in New York. The visual space is dominated by white walls, blond wood and light; the second shot stages Bateman's empty bed. Bateman's body, bisected by Calvin Klein shorts, is first glimpsed in the third shot, exiting a corridor. The film cuts on motion to Bateman shot from behind, still clad in shorts, urinating into the toilet bowl. In both, Christian Bale's body is located as a small component in the screen space, emphasizing his bodily isolation. The next shot cuts to Bateman looking at himself in a framed poster for *Les Misérables* which hangs above the toilet stall. This visual motif of mirrors is a recurrent one in the film, signifying Bateman's narcissism, but also his duality: 'normal' and 'psycho' selves.

However, this appearance/reality dyad is undermined by the next sequence of shots. Bateman removes a blue gel facemask from the refrigerator and wears it while working out. This mask is the shape and size of Batman's, another popular masked character which returned in the 1980s. The concept of the mask is then introduced as a dominant visual signifier with regard to Bateman, one which is complicated by the final shot of the sequence. Bateman, in close-up, stares into the mirror while applying 'an herbal facial mask'. The camera, however, elides the 'real' Bateman and concentrates upon the image in the mirror: he becomes his own reflection or mask. There is no 'real' Patrick Bateman: as the voiceover suggests, 'I am simply not there', as he peels the transparent gel, like a snakeskin, from his face. The middle of the sequence features Bateman in the shower stall. These shots are from behind or below: in all three contemporary films discussed in this chapter, the entirely naked male body may only be shown from the back or above the waist. The penis is entirely negated, removed from the visual field: the body of Christian Bale is staged to suggest nakedness, but the camera resolutely places the penis outside the image. The same visual rhetoric can be found in the other films in this chapter.

Bateman's high-style apartment, like that of Harry Caul in *The Conversation*, expresses his personality: consumerist, aspirational, yet devoid of the marks of comfort or homeliness. Like Nicholas Van Orton's mansion in *The Game*, it is literally and figuratively empty. As we saw in Chapter 3, the paranoid conspiracy thriller of the 1970s, particularly in the hands of director Alan J. Pakula, uses modernist architecture as an index of authoritarian impulses behind contemporaneous American political and social developments. Here, Bateman's apartment, like the identikit IKEA-furnished one of the Narrator in *Fight Club* (see below), expresses anxieties about individuation and conformity that the film diagnoses as being at the heart of Bateman's psychosis. The apartment could be seen as a microcosmic version of Jameson's 'postmodern hyperspace' (for which see Chapter 3 and below): it expresses the dislocation of the contemporary world system that induces the symptoms of schizophrenia (in Jameson's formulation) or here, psychopathology.

In a scene which exposes the circulation of looks that constitutes male desire in *American Psycho*, yet which compromises the institution of the male gaze, Bateman fucks (for this sex act primarily involves power) one prostitute from behind on the bed, while another watches him through the viewfinder of a video camera. Bateman, however, is neither intent on the woman he is fucking, nor the look of the camera, nor that of the woman behind it: instead, his desiring look is fixed on his own image in the mirror, and he attempts a series of heroic poses, watching himself. The spectatorial look elides the space between Bateman, his body and his look into the mirror: the mirror is the camera lens, not of the diegetic camera, but the one shooting the film *American Psycho*. Bateman, in effect, cavorts and performs for us, and his look is reflected in our own.

Where, in this scene, Bateman is clearly aroused by the fantasy of heroic masculinity, in the next sequence another of the homosocial group, Luis Carruthers, misreads Bateman's homicidal grip around his neck as a homosexual embrace, resulting in Bateman's paranoid and homophobic reaction. Bateman – sporting a pair of highly fetishistic black leather gloves – reacts badly to this uncovering of uncoded male desire for a male body, a desire that casts ironic shadows on Bateman's own narcissism and his homicidal acts. Bateman's own hardbody is clearly available as a homoerotic site of desire, and its display in *American Psycho* denotes the male body both as spectacle and as anxious subject. Bateman's own obsessions with the 'hardbody' are reflected in the twin loci of his cultural discourses, pornography and slasher/horror films. In both, the body is exposed, made visible, individuated through spectacle, its hardness penetrated and wounded.

A later sex scene is abruptly terminated in the spectacle of murder. The film cuts to the fleeing prostitute, running from Bateman down an empty corridor. Bateman enters, naked except for a 'box-fresh' pair of white sneakers, and clutching a buzzing chainsaw. This rewriting of *The Texas Chainsaw Massacre* (1974) (which spools on video behind the body of Bateman as he works out) exposes the visual rhetoric of the hardbody of the 1980s (the period setting of the film), and also the ideological and cultural frameworks in which contemporary films are produced and consumed. There is a paradoxical acceptability of the chainsaw as a monstrous phallic symbol, one which, in the framing of the shots, always masks Bateman's own tumescence. Violent male subjectivity is less shocking than the sight of what Tyler Durden, in *Fight Club*, will call 'a nice, big cock'.

Fight Club

In David Fincher's *Fight Club* (1999), the locus of masculine affectlessness is sited not in an economic elite that can afford the serious frivolity of the 'Game', but in the single, consumerist existence of the office 'drone'. *Fight Club*'s Narrator is no high-living Patrick Bateman: he is an office worker who processes information that will determine whether or not certain types of automobiles are recalled if they have faults. Like Lester Burnham in *American Beauty*, his working life is a repetitive and alienating round of seemingly pointless activity. Also like Lester Burnham, his revolt against the life of the 'drone' signifies the kind of white-male disenfranchisement that John Beynon saw as an effect of the 'crisis' in late-1990s masculinity caused by changing working patterns and the failure of the 'breadwinner' type. Neither the Narrator nor Burnham is the primary income-provider for a nuclear family: the Narrator is a singleton, while Burnham's economic activity is secondary to the 'emasculating' success-ethic of his driven (if neurotic) wife. In their rebellions against this disenfranchisement, both protagonists attempt to reconstitute a 'heroic masculinity' – the Narrator through his projection of Tyler Durden, Lester Burnham through body-building – that tries to resolve the contradictions between the masculine fantasies offered by contemporary culture and the 'reality' of social and economic marginalization.

Violence is central to David Fincher's *Fight Club*, and its representations of masculinity. This emphasis has, in fact, led to the controversy surrounding the film, and its denunciation. Henry Giroux castigates the film as infused with 'fascist' discourse and imagery; he suggests that '*Fight Club* comes dangerously close to giving violence a dangerous and fascist edge' and judges the film to be 'morally bankrupt and politically reactionary' (Giroux 2001: 273, 274). He is particularly suspicious of its role as a form of 'public pedagogy', suggesting that it offers proto-fascist solutions to its critique of contemporary capital. Warren Smith highlights the 'designer nihilism' that the film 'peddles' (Smith 2001: 164). Paolo Palladino and

Teresa Young (2003) are more temperate in their judgement, but criticize
Fight Club's 'facile' narrative resolution and complicity with a reconfiguration of time and space that corresponds with a global order posited after
9/11, that places a 'civilized' Self in contradistinction to a non-civilized Other.

Certainly, *Fight Club* ostensibly negotiates the 1990s 'crisis in masculinity' by way of a reassertion of 'strong' masculinity through violence.
Krister Friday (2003) suggests that *Fight Club*'s construction of masculinity
ties into what she suggests are narratives of 'male victimization and its
related symptomology as a redress for a perceived political and social
emasculation' that predominate in 'post-sixties, white male fiction' (Friday
2003: par. 7). As in David Savran's work, Friday organizes a reading of the
text through *Fight Club*'s 'central symptom, masochism', which affords
Tyler Durden and the other men a 'new masculine identity' (Friday 2003:
par. 16). Friday stresses the film's 'historical self-consciousness' and suggests
that it is the absence of a sense of 'periodization' or history itself that is
diagnosed as the root of the failure of masculine subjectivity (Friday 2003:
par. 21). In this sense, the Narrator/Tyler Durden, the split subject of *Fight
Club*, become another effect of what Fredric Jameson calls 'postmodern
hyperspace', the social and cultural dislocation and alienation of the
contemporary subject that we saw in Chapter 3, which leaves them floating
free of history and unable to 'map' their situation politically.

In *Fight Club*, this dislocation is explicitly a result of the detrimental
effects of consumerism on the young, economically successful male. As in
American Psycho, the disconnected male conspicuously consumes (and
displays) pristine arrangements of home furnishings; for him, IKEA
catalogues are the new pornography. These singletons find it difficult to
find resolution in romance, but as Palladino and Young note, the film does
actually rely on this trope to afford the masculine subject a form of 'healing'
or 'redemption' by the end of the film, just as in Fincher's previous film, *The
Game*. The very end of *Fight Club*, however, which sees the Narrator
(Edward Norton) and Marla Singer (Helena Bonham Carter) holding hands
as the towers of capital are blown down by Durden's operatives, is ironized
by the flash-cut of a large penis, signifying that this romantic-apocalyptic
ending is still another phallic fantasy of masculine recuperation and power.

The status of the 'reconstructed' males is ironized throughout the film, in
fact. A third of the way through *Fight Club*, after Tyler Durden (Brad Pitt)
has begun to set up the 'franchises' of the Fight Clubs, he makes a speech to
the male crowd collected in the basement which outlines the gap between
representations of heroic masculinity and mundane reality. 'Man, I see in
fight club the strongest and smartest men who ever lived,' he says, stirring
feelings of disenfranchisement.

> I see all this potential. And I see it squandered. Goddammit, an entire generation
> pumping gas. Waiting tables. Slaves with white collars. Advertising has us
> chasing cars and clothes. Working jobs we hate to buy shit we don't need.
> We're the middle children of history, man. No purpose or place. We have no

Great War. No Great Depression. Our great war is a spiritual war. Our great depression is our lives. We've all been raised on television to believe that one day we'd be millionaires and movie gods and rock stars. But we won't. And we're slowly learning that fact. And we're very, very pissed off.

Note how the 'soldier' subject haunts this speech, the 'greatest generation' (the fathers of this generation of men) given much easier access to 'heroic' masculinity through their historical moment. The speech prises apart the fantasy-masculinities of 'movie gods and rock stars' and the mundane reality of the 'drone', but replaces this fantasy with another (more 'authentic') fantasy of the heroic male of an earlier time. The male violence, an expression of discontent and a desire to reconstitute the 'strong' masculine subject, ironically echoes the very violence of the wartime soldier that had to be suppressed to reinsert him back into the very domesticity that *Fight Club* (and particularly *American Beauty*) seems to critique. Ironically, as the speech progresses, it becomes apparent that the rhetoric belies the reality of the Fight Clubs: that those that are drones in the workplace become drones in the new masculinity.

Tyler Durden himself is a fantasy of agency: not only does he 'look how you want to look, fuck how you want to fuck', but he is able to organize alienated young men into some kind of movement of resistance to contemporary capital. He is the type of aggressive individualist, the 'rebel', that Fredric Jameson saw to be in opposition to the faceless bureaucratic collectivity of the 1970s paranoid conspiracy thriller. By the end of the 1990s, this faceless collectivity has returned to its consumerist, conformist guise of the 1950s. Durden has, in fact, a clear relation to the figure of the 1950s 'hipster' that we will encounter in the next chapter. This figure, in the words of David Savran, offers 'a "life-giving answer" to a pathological society ... and [is,] as a pathologized figure himself, a psychopath' (Savran 1998: 49). The 'hipster' is a rebellious version of the outsider male, a 'psychic outlaw' who, Savran contends, is 'the fragmented, decentered, ephemeral subject of late capitalism' (Savran 1998: 49). Durden, who is revealed to be an idealized masculine projection of the Narrator, clearly corresponds to Savran's description of the hipster, indicating another continuity between 1950s and 1990s. The split subjectivity of the Narrator/Durden makes manifest a fantasy investment in individualist non-conformity that is the inverse image of the 'organization man' or 'drone' that seems to dominate representations of masculinity in both decades.

Most writing on *Fight Club* tends, as I have indicated above, to address the text on the level of narrative, or in Giroux's case as a form of 'public pedagogy'. The analysis I shall offer here of the spectatorial structures of the film are analogous to the suggestion made by Julian Murphet in his *Literature and Race in Los Angeles* (2001). In it, Murphet suggests that the crime writer James Ellroy's engagement with African-American culture in his 'LA Quartet' goes beyond the racist language used by the 1950s cops and the racial emphases of the narratives. Ellroy's prose, suggests Murphet, incorporates bebop rhythms and slang to effect a linguistic 'white jazz', an engagement with black-American experience at the level of discourse. Murphet's own analysis then moves from the representational to what he calls the 'semic'. Similarly, in relation to *Fight Club*, I now want to turn from the narrative or representational to the visual or scopic to elucidate the film's negotiations of masculinity and violence.

The visibility of the male body in *Fight Club* is central to an understanding of its scopic economy. *Fight Club*'s representation of the male body begins not with the body of Brad Pitt, nor with that of Ed Norton, but with the prosthetically enhanced spectacle of the excessive body of Robert Paulson (Meat Loaf), Bob with 'bitch tits' (which are on display throughout Meat Loaf's screen time). Bob inhabits and represents the excessive body, the masculine body rendered monstrous through a process of feminization and maternalization. The narrator of the film meets Bob at a support group for testicular cancer, 'Remaining Men Together'. In discussions with friends and colleagues about this film, it became apparent that there were several different readings of that particular phrase. Are those men who gather together the remainder of the masculine gender? Is it in togetherness that they can remain men, retain masculinity? What differentiates this support group is that they constitute (in the rhetoric of Palahniuk's novel) castrated men, the absence of testes determining their societal and psychological fragility.

These bodies are hidden, shameful, betraying, finding their emblem in Bob's 'unnatural' breasts. An indication of the sophistication of the film is that Bob reveals his history to be that of the bodybuilder. His built male body was created by steroids, and proved to be temporary and prey to the feminization anxieties present in both the armoured musculature of the 80s action heroes and the 'psycho' masculinity explored above. Significantly, while the injunction in the Fight Club arena is 'no shirts, no shoes', Bob's bitch tits remain covered for the entirety of the film, though are hardly invisible. Where the novel of Chuck Palahniuk emphasizes castration as an emblem of the 'denatured' contemporary male, Fincher's film ironizes this sense through the split consciousness of Tyler Durden and the Narrator. Here, the split indicates that the violence guaranteeing the 'strong' male hegemon is not recuperable to a contemporary, consumer-oriented 'breadwinner'.

Opposing the excessive body of Bob is the sculptured hardbody of Brad Pitt as Tyler Durden. Pitt's body, suggests Pamela Church Gibson, 'is fetishized, offered up, commodified ... he is the fantasy wish-fulfilment of the narrator' and, one presumes, the point of identification and desire for the audience (Church Gibson 2004: 185). The Narrator, in a central scene, suggests that when newcomers came to Fight Club, they were a 'wad of cookie dough'; after a few months, they were 'carved out of wood'. The rhetoric of objectification in this representation of the masculine hardbody is explicit and easily decoded; however, the film goes on to make several visual puns which compromise and ironize this rhetoric. Tyler and Narrator get on a bus, in which are advertisements for Gucci (though the Narrator also mentions Calvin Klein and Tommy Hilfiger). 'Is that what a man looks like?' asks the Narrator, rhetorically and derisively. The sequence then cuts to Pitt fighting a physically imposing man who has just brushed past them on the bus, and as he rises, the camera frames and stages Pitt's body in exactly the same way that the anonymous torso of the male in the Gucci advertisement had been staged. The visual pun emphasizes that what the Fight Club and *Fight Club* offers as representations of masculinity are not revolutionary, nor do they resolve the anxieties in contemporary masculinity, but can only offer restagings of the same commodification, and the traces of homoerotic desire through bodily marks of violence.

This is most clearly articulated in a late scene in the film, where the Narrator, in a rage of sexual jealousy, violently and repeatedly beats the face of the blond young man who he fears has supplanted him in Tyler's affections. The sequence is an almost explicit staging of Steve Neale's male spectatorial paradigm. In 'Masculinity as Spectacle', Neale argues that when the male body is staged (in the place of the feminine) as the object of the male look, the gaze marks or wounds the body: 'the male body cannot be marked explicitly as the erotic object of another male look: that look must be motivated in some other way, its erotic component repressed' (Neale 1993: 14). The wounded male body is then cancelled or disavowed as a site of desire, while an arena of violence at the same time allows the body to be staged for spectatorial pleasure. In the scene from the film, Edward Norton's Narrator straddles his victim Angel Face (Jared Leto) during a fight, moving his torso as during sex, while smashing the object of male beauty. As he rises, his apologia is: 'I felt like destroying something beautiful'. While the blond young man is therefore acknowledged as an object of beauty, and a fitting recipient of the male desiring look, this is negated and destroyed by an act of sexual violence. In Britain, the BBFC demanded and obtained cuts to this sequence, in which the spectacle of male violence to a male body is again displaced, this time to cutaways to the face of Ed Norton, spattered with the other's bodily fluid: blood. Once again, sex is displaced by violence.

The 'hardbody' or built body, and the feminized body and Bob, are both excessive bodies: the former signifies an excessive and parodic version of masculine normative subjectivity, and the latter the male body rendered monstrous by feminization and maternalization. Ironically, Brad Pitt's body in *Fight Club* is also marked with the signs of the feminine. In a key scene, Tyler Durden kisses the hand of the Narrator, then pours lye on the saliva to create a chemical burn. The shape of this burn suggests both the shape of the mouth and female genitalia; this scene encodes a revealing conflation of masochistic violence, the male wounded body and feminization. The hard bodies of Pitt and Norton are not invulnerable: here, they are even invaginated. This imagery links the hardbody even more closely to the monstrous (feminized) masculine body of Bob.

The bodies of the men of *Fight Club* are then multiply gendered. The split subjectivity of the Narrator/Durden can be seen as a form of 'gender distress' and is connected to homoeroticism and narcissism as well as violence, as it is in *American Psycho*. This distress is a symptom of the pathology induced by contemporary consumer capitalism, which splits the masculine subject, the fissures in the 'man in the grey flannel suit' revealing the 'psycho' within. We return here to Harry Brod's understanding of masquerade: that this presupposes that the 'authentic', unitary self underlying the mask can be made manifest. The problem may be that this unitary self is, in fact, not a 'healed' subjectivity, but a psychotic one.

American Beauty

Directed by Sam Mendes, *American Beauty* (1999) is centrally concerned with both critical masculinity and with homoeroticism, but, I will argue, ultimately offers a spectatorial pleasure which does not ultimately invalidate the male body as a site of desire. *American Beauty* narrates the disintegration of the Burnham household, and is focalized by the narrator Lester Burnham, a forty-something male drifting through parenthood and marriage. Lester is another 'victim' of white male dispossession and 'emasculation' that is common to the 'crisis' texts of the late-1990s. The spectre of castration is raised in a fight between himself and his wife Carolyn (Annette Bening), witnessed by their daughter. Lester says: 'your mother seems to prefer I go through life like a fucking prisoner while she keeps my dick in a mason jar under the sink', just prior to hurling a plate of asparagus against the wall in a violent show of masculine assertion.

Lester is also the locus of representations of the male body. His first act of rebellion is to descend to the basement, root out his previously unused weights, and then strip naked. It is night, so the darkness outside transforms the window into a mirror: Lester watches himself while pumping iron. He is unaware that his young next-door-neighbour, Ricky Fitts, is watching him, through the lens of a palmcorder. The point-of-view assumes that of Ricky's camera as he zooms in to the beatific smile on Lester's face. Where, in *American Psycho*, the intercutting of two shots from a camera viewfinder represents alienated and homicidal male desire, the visual texture of *American Beauty* itself is disrupted by grainy, degraded video footage. *American Beauty* corresponds to a realignment of the scopic or visual economy in contemporary society, one which now corresponds not to the principles of voyeurism, and so constitutes a gendered gaze, but to the principles of ubiquitous surveillance.

In *American Beauty*, the use of camera technology differs from both *Fight Club* and *American Psycho*. Distinguishing *American Beauty* both from the classical Hollywood spectatorial economy, and the reconsiderations of the representations of masculinity in *Fight Club* and *American Psycho*, is the character of Ricky Fitts (Wes Bentley). Ricky is, from the beginning, seen with video-camera technology surrounding him; he seems to be the archetypal male voyeur, the spectatorial bearer of the 'look'. The film begins, however, with his video footage of Lester's daughter Janey (Thora Birch), declaring a patricidal desire. The audience is encouraged to speculate upon the potentiality for violence behind what appears to be the mask of Ricky's serenity. Later in the film, when this scene is explored in full, the audience discovers that while Janey is being filmed, she is clothed, and remains so; and during the course of the scene, she takes the camera and points it at the naked Ricky. This staging of the reversal of the gaze is emphasized by Ricky's words. Janey asks: 'Don't you feel naked?', to which Ricky replies, perfectly comfortable with Janey's look and the gaze upon him: 'I am naked'.

Televisual technologies disrupt the unitary gaze in the *mise-en-scène* of this sequence. It begins with video footage, the camera pointed at Janey, operated by Ricky. However, when Janey takes the camera and points it at the male, this is staged from the side, Janey facing Ricky who is offscreen left. Behind her, displayed on a monitor, is a feed from the video camera. There are four distinct gazes in this shot: the audience gazing at the screen; Janey, through the camera, at Ricky; Ricky, at Janey; and Ricky's face, displaced, looking straight back at the audience from the television screen. This disruption of the process of looking recurs throughout the film, the feeds from Ricky's camera displayed within the frame, displacing and othering the gaze. It is circulated through the camera technology itself. Ricky's image is itself staged three times within the same frame in this sequence; in a shot looking over Janey's shoulder, we see the 'real' Ricky on the left of frame, the televisual representation on the right, and in miniature, his image on the viewfinder of the camera that Janey holds. The male body is then not fragmented or sundered by violence, but is staged multiply, whole in each repeated image.

The naked body of the actor Wes Bentley is no hardbody. It is not the sculpted muscularity of Brad Pitt, nor the excessive built body of the 1980s action hero; and nor is it the monstrous feminized body of Bob Paulson (Meat Loaf). Ricky's body is neither hidden, nor does it approach the maximal visibility of the type desired by Lester, one which deflects and displaces the homoerotic look. *American Beauty*'s visual paradigm, located in the body, practice, and point-of-view of Ricky, is neither voyeuristic nor spectacular, but panoptic. Ricky Fitts is a product of a society in which the camera gaze of surveillance is everywhere. The character and representation of Ricky Fitts seems to be a different kind of spectatorial pleasure on offer for the male subject, a beauty found in the male body, but a male body not maximally visible, muscularly armoured and anxious. The look is not displaced, as in Richard Dyer's analyses of male pin-ups, nor disavowed into narrative cancellations of the male body as pure spectacle (physical activity, sports, violence). Unlike the narcissism and sexual repression of *American Psycho*, *American Beauty* incorporates the possibility of homo-eroticism, and the male desiring look for the male body, into the narrative and thematic structure. When he decides to become fit, Lester seeks out his male neighbours for advice. He joins them as they jog: they are a gay male couple. When they ask him what his goals are, Lester replies, with admirable candour: 'I want to look good naked'. Implicitly, there is an acceptance of the desiring gaze playing upon the male body. The male here does not look, but is the object of the look.

This opening up of the possibility for homoerotic desire is not without an awareness of cultural anxieties surrounding it. There are parallel scenes in *American Beauty* and *Fight Club* in which the disaffected protagonist blackmails his immediate superior into funding his desires to leave the drudgery of work. In *Fight Club*, this is achieved by the Narrator (Ed Norton) beating himself up in his superior's office; in *American Beauty*, this scene revolves around Lester's threats to reveal the misuse of company funds for sexual ends, and to accuse his male superior of sexually propositioning him. There is also a series of visual puns which suggests a sexual relationship between Lester and Ricky, which actually concerns the shared consumption of cannabis, but is one which is misread by diegetic spectators. This begins when Ricky first approaches Lester when serving at a function: his first line, 'Do you party?', is highly ambiguous, and Lester has to ask Ricky for clarification. Once outside, the hotel manager says: 'Look, I'm not paying you to ... do whatever it is you're doing out here'. They are, in fact, getting high. Most importantly for the narrative, Ricky's father, Colonel Fitts, a closeted homosexual whose sexual repression results in physical violence towards his son, sees what appears to be Ricky giving Lester a 'blow job', when in fact the wall between windows masks Ricky's true activity: making Lester a joint. This misrecognition of homoerotic desire ultimately leads to Lester's death, but not through the homophobic reaction that the Colonel had displayed earlier. The Colonel's misrecognition leads him to approach, and to kiss, Lester; when this is rebuffed, the Colonel returns to kill his neighbour. Desire betrays the male body, and is purged, once again, by violence.

Where in Michael Powell's *Peeping Tom* (1960), the camera-wielding voyeur and murderer, Mark Lewis (Carl Boehme), is portrayed as being produced by the trauma of perpetual surveillance as a child, Ricky Fitts is a product of a society in which the camera gaze of surveillance is everywhere, as Mike Davis analysed in his seminal 1990 text, *City of Quartz*. Ricky's look in *American Beauty* is not one of voyeurism, but one of surveillance; he does not generate the gaze, but channels the panoptic gaze that surrounds and interpellates himself and all the characters. The spectator of the late 1990s and early 2000s is positioned differently in a range of delivery modes. The space of consumption in live feeds available on the Internet from any of the 'reality' shows proliferating in television cultures constructs new subject positions, and new pleasures. This change, and its incorporation into the spectatorial economies of Hollywood cinema, suggests a re-evaluation of both 'masculine' and 'feminine', 'male' and 'female' subjectivities as they are brought into being by the experience of watching film.

Falling Down

The homicidal voyeur has become central to both an understanding of the processes of spectatorship and as the limit-case of male subjectivity. The self-conscious staging of male voyeurism, and voyeurism's explicit identification with the camera lens, and its ultimately homicidal look, are ones which place the horror/slasher movie at the centre of considerations of the male gaze, and also (white) male subjectivity. Richard Dyer, in his BFI Modern Classic text on David Fincher's *Seven*, notes that the 'serial killer has become a widespread figure in films, novels, television series, true crime coverage and even painting, poetry, opera and rock music', and that 'they have increasingly been seen to be expressive specifically of masculinity in contemporary society' (Dyer 1999: 37). More particularly, Dyer suggests that serial killer masculinity is coded as white masculinity. Where, he suggests, in contemporary culture '[w]hite masculinity occupies the space of ordinariness', films such as *Seven* render this 'notional invisibility' visible (Dyer 1999: 45). They also stage ethnic or racial difference. Dyer continues: 'If [Morgan] Freeman/Somerset's blackness alerts us to the whiteness of serial killing, [Brad] Pitt/Mills's whiteness perhaps suggests the serial killingness of whiteness' (Dyer 1999: 40). Dyer's racial or ethnic reading of masculinity is, I think, vital in not falling into the trap of universalizing the sense of crisis in masculinity of the 1950s or the 1990s. The films I look at in this chapter represent *white* masculinity; nowhere is this more evident than in Joel Schumacher's *Falling Down* (1991).

Jude Davies and Carol Smith interpret the characterization of the central figure of *Falling Down* as an 'ordinary man' (in the pre-release promotion of the film) as a means by which to 'maintain the culturally central focus of white masculinity' (Davies and Smith 1997: 31). This cultural narrative, predominant by the end of the 1990s, is foreshadowed by Schumacher's 1991 film. Like *The Game*, *Falling Down* stars Michael Douglas, this time as a worker in the Californian defence industries who has, as the film begins, just been laid off. This film, then, is historically sited at the very end of the Cold War; little wonder, perhaps, at the nostalgia for Cold War masculinity we will find in Chapter 8 if its end precipitates the kind of economic marginalization that precipitates the 'crisis' of the end of the decade. For most of *Falling Down*, which traces the path across a 'balkanised LA' (Davies and Smith 1997: 34), the central protagonist is known as 'D-FENS', named after the number plate of his car that he abandons in a jam in the first five minutes. D-FENS (whose real name is revealed later as 'Bill') seems to occupy an instrumental subjectivity, determined by his occupation, just as Harry Caul had been in *The Conversation*. When this is withdrawn, however, the basis of stable identity fragments, and D-FENS sets off on an increasingly violent odyssey across the city.

Clearly, D-FENS is another version of the anxiety-ridden 'breadwinner'; we soon find out, however, that he is estranged from his ex-wife, who fears him and shuns contact (partly to protect their young daughter). The motivation for this estrangement, which is of itself another index of D-FENS's marginalization and alienation as a masculine 'breadwinner', is not revealed until much later in the film, when D-FENS breaks into his former home to watch video footage of himself with his wife and child. As in *The Game*, home movies reveal trauma: as a father he is overbearing and causes his child to cry. The most telling image is a freeze-frame of his ex-wife Beth, clutching her daughter, gazing fearfully into the eye of the camera. D-FENS's later violence is not only an expression of his economic marginalization: he already inhabits a masculinity disposed to uncontrolled violence.

The figure of the 'breadwinner' is doubled in Detective Prendergast (Robert Duvall), who is at first trapped in the same traffic jam as D-FENS and ultimately tracks him across the city to Venice Beach, where Beth still lives. Prendergast's own white masculinity is troubled and compromised: his wife is portrayed as a neurotic shrew, and they had lost a young child to cot death (in somewhat ambiguous circumstances). Prendergast is on his last day as a robbery detective, but is alienated from wiseacre colleagues who rib him. This comes to a head at Prendergast's leaving party, where he punches a fellow detective who had made a cutting remark about his wife. This restoration of a 'heroic' or 'strong' masculinity is repeated in Prendergast's own relationship with his wife; just before the climax of the film, he tells her to 'shut up' over the phone and to have dinner on the table when he gets home. (The end of the film suggests that he has in fact reneged on his promise to retire.) Where D-FENS's violent masculinity is problematic (and is resolved at the end of the film by his self-willed death), Prendergast stands as a legitimated white male whose recuperation of a heroic, violent masculinity is, in most senses, a healthy and positive one.

Davies and Smith's reading of *Falling Down* works against accusations that the film is a racist or 'fascist' text. Although they concede that D-FENS's later behaviour 'is more violent, less justified, and more directly readable as vigilantism' (Davies and Smith 1997: 34), directed against the multi-ethnic patchwork of contemporary Los Angeles, they suggest that this is compromised by two scenes. First, D-FENS passes a similarly dressed African-American male who is protesting his own loss of employment, indicating that 'it is economics rather than ethnicity which most determines power'; secondly, D-FENS refuses the overtures of Nick, the neo-Nazi store owner (Frederick Forrest), creating a 'problematic differentiation of D-FENS from a recognisably fascist version of white masculinity' (Davies and Smith 1997: 35). This differentiation is 'problematic', argue Davies and Smith, because of the film's fundamental incoherence, which at the same time offers the 'persecutions' availing D-FENS as a kind of narrative rationale for his behaviour, while making sure that 'D-FENS is disallowed from benefiting from such discourses' (Davies and Smith 1997: 35). Though they note the generic importance of 'vigilante pictures' on *Falling Down*, I believe a clear intertext here is Don Siegel's 1971 police thriller *Dirty Harry*, which has itself been accused of validating an extra-judicial 'vigilantism'.

Both films are narratively organized around the doubled protagonists of the 'psycho' (Scorpio and D-FENS) and the cop who tracks them (Harry Callahan and Prendergast). Both end in a form of hostage situation; both end on a pier. However, where *Dirty Harry*'s Callahan resorts to extra-legal violence and torture to stop Scorpio (tending to identify the cop with the 'psycho' criminal he tracks), in *Falling Down* it is D-FENS himself who resorts to excessive violence, and Prendergast is so decoupled from this kind of violence that he even forgets his gun before trying to apprehend D-FENS. Where, in 1971, as I shall argue in the next chapter, the connection between the law and legitimating violence is a troubling one, here the distinction between the vigilante and the cop is much more apparent. Rather than the crucial distinction being between the white masculinities of D-FENS and the neo-Nazi Nick, I would argue that the narrative is actually organized to maintain the distinction between D-FENS and Prendergast. Richard Dyer concurs, suggesting that 'the very unobtrusiveness of Prendergast/Duvall allows him to occupy more comfortably the ordinariness that is the white man's prerogative' (Dyer 1997: 221). At the end of *Dirty Harry*, Callahan provokes Scorpio into raising his gun so he can shoot him dead; in *Falling Down*, D-FENS raises a toy pistol and is shot by Prendergast. D-FENS is the agent of his own death. Where Harry Callahan walks away from the body of Scorpio, who floats in a reedy pool, Prendergast looks down at the body of D-FENS floating in the Pacific, and it is at this moment, we must presume, that he decides that he is 'still a detective'. The gesture of refusal in *Dirty Harry* is inverted here; Callahan throws away his badge, but Prendergast embraces a restored masculinity that is contained within the structures of the law. If D-FENS is the figure of white masculine resentment and marginalization in *Falling Down*, the film suggests that he cannot be reinserted into the domestic sphere. His violence has taken him 'too far'. It is Prendergast, who reorganizes his own masculinity and domestic relations in the course of the narrative, who reasserts the centrality of the 'breadwinner'.

Richard Dyer, in his reading of *Falling Down*, asserts the Western, rather than the police thriller, as intertext. At the end of the film, Dyer writes, D-FENS 'pursues [his family] on to the pier, off land, as far as you can go, the end-point of white Westward expansion, and here he is finally killed by Prendergast . . . . His death is the only possible logical outcome . . . because there is – literally, figuratively, historically – nowhere else to go' (Dyer 1997: 218). Dyer sees the affinity of whiteness with death as a terminal anxiety in a film like *Falling Down*: that white subjectivity is approaching a kind of 'dead end'. As the end-point of expansion, the expression of the closed frontier, California becomes vital in the ideological narrative of masculinity and the American nation-state. Over the next four chapters, we will investigate police thrillers set in San Francisco and Los Angeles, and then the importance of the frontier to the Western and space fictions.

CHAPTER FIVE

Rogue Cops I: San Francisco

Out of the West

At the beginning of *Coogan's Bluff* (1968), the first of five screen collaborations between director Don Siegel and star Clint Eastwood, a Jeep drives
towards the camera, out of the desert. The landscape is iconically of the
American West; the Jeep, in place of the horse, places the film in the mid-
to late-twentieth century. (Contemporaneous Westerns such as Richard
Brooks's *The Professionals* (1966) and Sam Peckinpah's *The Wild Bunch* (1969)
both use the automobile as a sign of encroaching modernity and the end of
the West. We will consider both in Chapter 7.) The driver of the Jeep is
Deputy Sheriff Coogan (Eastwood), who is tracking a criminal, and has been
doing so, it later transpires, for three days. His quarry is, curiously, a Native
American man perched up among some rocks, who wears a loincloth but
aims a modern high-powered sniper-rifle at the approaching Jeep. From the
very beginning, then, *Coogan's Bluff* begins to collapse generic markers:
as we will see later in this chapter, the most celebrated Siegel/Eastwood
collaboration, *Dirty Harry* (1971), also begins with a lone sniper looking
down at a victim from the heights a San Francisco skyscraper rather than a
rocky knoll. Having tracked the 'Chief' Running Bear (Rudi Diaz), Coogan
disarms his prey and then tells him to 'get his pants on'. He then drives
them both to town, and presumably, ultimately returns the Chief to his
'true' place, the Reservation (which is stamped on the sole of Running
Bear's discarded boot like a mark of ownership).

The narrative of *Coogan's Bluff* is, essentially, that of a culture clash,
between the values of the West (embodied in the tall, tough Eastwood) and
the values of the East, embodied in New York City's police force and
counterculture scene. Siegel emphasizes the contrast by cutting from a
scene where Eastwood is in a tin bath, being soaped by his lover and
harangued by his boss – bathing scenes in Westerns usually portend a shift
from wilderness to town – to a Stetson-hatted, bolo-tie and cowboy-boot
wearing Westerner arriving by Chinook helicopter to the roof of the then
Pan-American building in New York, where he disembarks at a helipad.
Much is made of Eastwood's Western status – he is consistently called
'cowboy' and 'Texan', even by the hard-bitten police Lieutenant played by
Lee J. Cobb – and this is emphasized when he meets the probation officer
Julie (Susan Clark) after being given short shrift by Cobb. Julie is being
sexually harassed by one of her clients, though is in control of the situation,

when Coogan steps in, cuffing the parolee across the face and forcing him to flee. Julie reacts with dismay at Coogan's actions, and then with a mixture of derision at Coogan's machismo and attraction to it. (The 1970s television series *McCloud*, a virtual 'spin-off' from *Coogan's Bluff*, in which Dennis Weaver also played a Western sheriff in New York, downplayed the machismo, and softened Coogan's Western harshness to a quasi-Southern gentility.)

Coogan's errors throughout the film occur because he does not understand, and is unwilling to learn, the 'rules' of New York City, be they in the matter of extraditing the criminal Ringerman (Don Stroud) he seeks to return to Arizona, the sexual politics of the urban late-1960s, or those of the counterculture 'underground' that he tries to penetrate in order to track down his prey. While the film certainly makes comic play of the clash of cultures, and points out Coogan's failings when he steps outside of procedure – the prisoner escapes and Coogan is himself beaten about the head – the film ultimately valorizes the values of the West against those of the East. Coogan is tough, persistent, resourceful, and capable of resolving the narrative through violent means. He is also an outsider in New York, lending Coogan a kind of attractiveness that his otherwise harsh persona might dispel.

Unusually for the Eastwood 'cop' persona at this time, Coogan is also sexually attractive, even to the extent of being something of a predator in sexual as well as police matters. He has sexual relationships with three women in the film, the most peculiar being with Ringerman's girlfriend Linny Raven (Tisha Sterling), who plays a hippified 'kook' version of the film noir 'B-girl'. However, throughout the film, there are intriguing suggestions of a knowing 'queering' of the Eastwood machismo. When he first enters the New York police station house, what appear to be a group of 'busted' gay men pass appreciative remarks about Coogan as he passes: 'Get her' and 'Look at those heels'. This seems to be particularly focused upon the Western clothing (perhaps we should say 'costume') that Eastwood wears. As in another film from 1969, John Schlesinger's *Midnight Cowboy*, which also features a Westerner coming to New York in the shape of the callow Joe Buck (Jon Voight), the masculine associations of cowboy garb in the contemporary city are somewhat ambiguous. When Joe proposes to make money from being a gigolo, his erstwhile friend 'Ratso' Rizzo (Dustin Hoffman) tells him that his look is 'fag stuff. Strictly for fags'. In parallel scenes, while Joe's Western demeanour sits well at the 'happening' he visits in *Midnight Cowboy*, Coogan stands out in (and head and shoulders above) the crowd of hippy dancers of the 'Pigeon Toed Orange Peel' club, where he picks up Linny. After she sleeps with him then betrays him to one of Ringerman's friends, Coogan fights his way out a pool hall, beaten and bloodied. Back at his hotel room, he opens the door to Julie, who has discovered his 'infidelity'. What is curious about this scene is that Eastwood is framed from the waist up, with his shirt off – a highly unusual 'beefcake' pose, and one that repeats shots from the beginning of the film.

While the succession of heterosexual encounters (overly) demonstrates Coogan's 'straightness', then, recurrent visual display of Eastwood's body marks him as a site of desire in a way that is highly unusual. (In *Magnum Force*, the 1973 sequel to *Dirty Harry*, Eastwood has a succession of heterosexual encounters but is never seen unclothed. In 1977's self-directed *The Gauntlet*, as washed-up cop Ben Shockley, he also is shown partially unclothed, but bruised and bloodied.) In most of Eastwood's films that rely upon his tough 'cop' persona, sexuality is largely downplayed or bracketed off entirely. This reinforces the coding of the Eastwood character as 'straight' in a multiplicity of ways: morally upright, conservative, heterosexual. The curious and low-key 'queering' of Coogan anticipates the ambiguities that surround the character of Harry Callahan, who Eastwood plays in *Dirty Harry* and four sequels.

Dirty Harry is set in San Francisco. The narrative of the film is as follows. The film begins with a lone sniper sitting atop the Bank of America building, who spies on, then fatally shoots, a young woman swimming in a rooftop pool below. Detective Harry Callahan (Eastwood) is assigned to the case, and with a new partner (college graduate Chico Gonzalez, played by Reni Santoni) seeks to track down the killer, the self-proclaimed 'Scorpio', who threatens more murders if he is not paid a ransom. After Scorpio abducts a 14-year-old girl, Callahan tracks down, shoots and then tortures Scorpio to obtain her whereabouts. Although the girl is dead, Scorpio goes free. The final resolution comes when Scorpio hijacks a school bus, and Callahan chases him to the outskirts of the city, where Scorpio is shot and killed. The final shot of the film is of Callahan throwing his police badge into a river.

Dirty Harry was derived from a script called 'Dead Right', in which a disillusioned older New York cop had decided to take the law into his own hands. It had been slated for production with Frank Sinatra in the title role (renamed *Dirty Harry*), but when Sinatra 'cut his hand' prior to production, the script was offered to Eastwood. Pre-production images of Sinatra's Harry (much like Sinatra's persona in the 1968 film *The Detective*) exhibit a world-weariness at odds with Eastwood's performance. Paul Newman also turned the script down, unsurprisingly: as a delegate at the 1968 Democratic Party convention in Chicago, the scene of police riots against anti-war and counterculture demonstrations, Newman would hardly have wanted to star in a film which validated extra-legal police violence. Newman was also the star of such films as *Hud* (1963), *Cool Hand Luke* (1967) and *Butch Cassidy and the Sundance Kid* (1969), where he played largely sympathetic and anti-authoritarian characters. Eastwood accepted the script, but insisted that Don Siegel be chosen to direct, and the script was remodelled. These changes included a relocation, suggested by Siegel, from East Coast New York to San Francisco, close to Eastwood's hometown and epicentre of the counterculture (Siegel 1993: 358).

The same tension between 'straight' and 'hip' (or 'hippy') that we found in *Coogan's Bluff* is also apparent in San Francisco police procedurals, and for

Dirty Harry, one must presume that the city was deliberately chosen to bring these distinctions into relief. San Francisco had always been a left-leaning or liberal city. In the words of Rebecca Solnit, the nineteenth-century city 'was celebrated as a cosmopolitan version of the Wild West town, with malleable social mores, eccentrics and adventurers a big part of the social mix' (Solnit 2000: 32), exhibiting mythic 'Western' values of egalitarianism, vigour and informality. In the twentieth century, San Francisco became a centre of trade unionism in the United States; was the site of African-American immigration during World War 2; and during the 1950s, was the birthplace of the Beats. It was also the most ethnically diverse city in the US by the end of the 1970s (Solnit 2000: 33). Solnit, who writes in protest against the redevelopment of central San Francisco in the 1990s, identifies the city as a place of change. She suggests that 'since the 1950s San Francisco had been mutating from a blue-collar port city of manual labor and material goods to a white-collar center of finance, administration, tourism' (Solnit 2000: 33). The process of change Solnit identifies was a slow evacuation of the eccentric, left-leaning and tolerant tendencies of the city, towards a homogenized urban centre that looked and felt like any other US city.

In the 1960s, San Francisco became the focus of 'hippy' feeling and was celebrated in Scott Mackenzie's famous song: 'be sure to wear some flowers in your hair'. In J. Hoberman's phrase, San Francisco was the 'wacky, ultra-permissive city of hippies, liberals, homosexuals, and Black Panthers' (Hoberman 2003: 326). (It was also, Hoberman notes, 'the site of the most extensive vigilante movement in American history – the San Francisco "vigilante committee" of 1856, organized by leading merchants to eradicate crime and political corruption' (Hoberman 2003: 326).) Visiting San Francisco in 1967, Joan Didion reported from the city in somewhat despairing terms:

> The center was not holding. It was a country of bankruptcy notices and public-auction announcements and commonplace reports of casual killings and misplaced children and abandoned homes and vandals who misspelled even the four-letter words they scrawled. ... It was not a country in open revolution. It was not a country under enemy siege. It was the United States of America in the cold late spring of 1967 .... All that seemed clear was that at some point we had aborted ourselves and butchered the job, and because nothing else seemed so relevant I decided to go to San Francisco. San Francisco was where the social haemorrhaging was showing up. (Didion 2001: 72)

Didion's San Francisco is peopled by drop-outs and dope-smokers, trippers who give LSD to their children, and countercultural figures such as the Diggers who seem to inhabit paranoid worlds fuelled by 'media poison'. Its presentiments of decline and alienation seem to look ahead to the 'end of the Sixties' of which *Dirty Harry*, and films like it, now seem to be a part.

Taking this in relation to Solnit's understanding of the social and spatial change in the city's fabric between 1960 and 1980, perhaps we can see the end of the 1960s and beginning of the 1970s as a crucial point in the city's history, where the waning of the counterculture inaugurated the end-game of San Francisco's movement from 'liberal' city to 'normative' city. A Redevelopment Agency brochure Solnit reproduces in her book, from 1971 (the year *Dirty Harry* was made) pictures rows of clean, modernist 'dwelling units', with wide pedestrian areas on which children play while parents sit on park benches. The text runs:

> As most San Franciscans know, the Western Addition [a central area of the city] is blessed with some of the city's best weather. It is also within walking distance of the Civic Center and just a quick bus ride from Downtown. And now its renewal ... is more than 50 per cent complete. Just look around ... (Solnit 2000: 47)

Solnit argues that 'urban renewal' means the replacement of low-income housing with office towers, of ethnic communities with civic centres. The brochures and manifestos of the 'urban renewal' movement 'seem at least implicitly a counter-argument to the Civil Rights Movement; they argue a different set of causes than racism, exclusion and poverty for the condition of non-white inner-city inhabitants' (Solnit 2000: 47). To 'renew' the city, then, is to depoliticize it, to create social justice through reordered space. *Dirty Harry* seems to key into a debate that was already occurring in the city about social order and social justice.

Three years before *Dirty Harry*, there had been another San Francisco-set police thriller: Peter Yates's *Bullitt* (1968), starring Steve McQueen in the title role. McQueen's Frank Bullitt is a very different kind of cop, and inhabits a very different kind of masculinity, to Eastwood's Harry Callahan. In the film, Bullitt is asked to protect a key witness against 'the Organization' by Walt Chalmers (Robert Vaughn), a grandstanding politician who wants to use a Senate hearing to propel himself to greater power (and glory). The upright and taciturn Bullitt is unimpressed by Chalmers's blandishments, although a curious throwaway line indicates that there is perhaps a more public persona to the withdrawn Bullitt than there seems to be: 'You make good copy. They love you in the papers, Frank,' says Chalmers. When the informant is shot, Bullitt suspects an 'inside job', and the rest of the film plays out the tactical manoeuvres between Bullitt and Chalmers. While Bullitt has no truck with corruption, graft or influence at higher levels (he explicitly disobeys instructions from superiors he distrusts), he is willing to deal with the 'street', gaining key information in exchange for a promise to try to help reduce the sentence of a prisoner. He is able to straddle 'straight' and 'street' worlds, is at home with, and in, both: policeman as countercultural hipster.

McQueen's star persona informs the character of Frank Bullitt. While immensely tough and capable, McQueen's controlled expression and marked lack of dialogue indicate world-weariness or alienation, while his turtle-neck sweaters, suede boots and muscle car signify his 'hip' credentials. His girlfriend is played by Jacqueline Bisset; early in the film, they go to a jazzy, hip restaurant whose patrons Harry Callahan would want to 'throw a net over'. By the end of the film, however, Bullitt seems to withdraw into something like despair. The last shots are of McQueen staring into his bathroom mirror with anguish written on his face, and then a cut to his gun, the symbol of the personal and ethical corrosion he has to embrace to do his job. As we will see in the rest of this chapter, Harry Callahan's gun has a very different set of connotations.

Frank Bullitt's 'hipster' persona does not seem coincidental in relationship to the film's San Francisco location. In the 1950s, the city was the birthplace of the Beats. David Savran, in *Taking It Like A Man* (1998), suggests that the figure of the Beat is crucial in renegotiations of masculinity in the 50s. He suggests that

> [t]he Beat ... is masculinized by virtue of his resuscitation of the entrepreneurial and maverick self, yet simultaneously feminized both by his sexual dissidence and by the practice of writing itself, that is, by his association with the cultural and artistic sphere. (Savran 1998: 67)

Savran associates the Beat, but differentiates him from, the figure of the 'hipster' that Norman Mailer identified in essays contained in *Advertisements for Myself* (1961). His famous essay 'The White Negro', originally published in 1957, considered the hipster to be at once an 'existentialist' and a 'philosophical psychopath', 'a frontiersman in the Wild West of American night life' (Mailer 1968: 275, 272): note the importance of the rhetoric of the West as the space of freedom here. The hipster or 'white negro' is attracted to what Mailer sees as the crucial elements of an African-American counterculture: marijuana, jazz, a life lived in danger, paranoia, and 'the infinite variations of joy, lust, languor, growl, cramp, pinch, scream and despair of his orgasm' (Mailer 1968: 273). In adopting the hip language and lifestyle of the black community, however, the hipster does not straddle both 'straight' and 'hip' worlds (or white hegemonic and African-American) but is threatened by a possible fragmentation. In Savran's reading, 'the hipster is at once a victim of the repressive and conformist society of which he is a part and a potentially violent, if directionless, opponent of that society' (Savran 1998: 49).

There is, then, a duality or 'double positionality' to the figure of the Hipster that Savran suggests 'would be widely recognized as the postmodernist subject, the fragmented, decentred, ephemeral self of late capitalism' (Savran 1998: 49). In *Bullitt*, the fragmentation of the 'hipster cop', caused by the necessity of participation in two worlds, is represented by a series of shots through glass. (We will find the same images with regard to the 'cop' subjectivity in the next chapter, in Curtis Hanson's *LA Confidential*.) Initially, this is a visual trope for Bullitt's isolation: he is framed in long or medium shots through the window of the nurse's station in the Intensive Care ward or behind the glass of a car windscreen. Towards the end of the film, when Bullitt tracks the Mobster, Ross, through San Francisco airport, Chalmers approaches him for a final time. Bullitt stands facing a large window facing the darkened runway apron, his reflection showing clearly in the glass. In this interview he rejects Chalmers' overtures for a final time, but the reflection here indicates his psychological fragmentation. As noted above, the final shots of the film show Bullitt looking at himself in the mirror, another sign of doubleness. The instability of the subjectivity of the 'hipster cop' foreshadows the necessity, in terms of a reconstructed white masculine hegemonic masculinity, in *Dirty Harry* of the central character, 'maverick' or 'rogue' cop though he may be, to embody 'straight' rather than 'hip' values. Underlying *Dirty Harry* is a project to reconstitute the white-masculine subject in a less anxious form, located at the epicentre of these anxieties, San Francisco.

The release of *Dirty Harry* can be seen as part of a wider conservative retrenchment in American society after the turbulence (and 'liberal dominance') of the 1960s. In 1968, the year of *Bullitt*'s release, the Presidential election had seen the return of Richard Milhous Nixon, the former Vice President who had lost narrowly to John F. Kennedy in 1960. Nixon was from California, and made much of his 'outsider' status. An anti-Communist 'hawk' in the 1950s, and defeated by JFK in 1960, Nixon had come back to win a close contest with incumbent Democrat Vice President Hubert Humphrey in 1968. He had campaigned in the name of the 'forgotten Americans' (a middle America worried by Civil Rights, the anti-war movement, and liberalization in general), but had won the closest election victory in Presidential history largely through the intervention of Governor George Wallace of Alabama, and though seen as a return of America to conservatism, Nixon's first Presidency really had no popular mandate. Later, in 1970, Nixon called upon the 'silent majority' to support him, particularly on Vietnam. This rhetorical device, which had been deployed to mobilize an anti-counterculture reaction from middle-class middle America, indicates an attempt to invert the discourses of marginalization and empowerment which had fuelled the Civil Rights movement, anti-Vietnam war protests, and the rise of feminism. The 'silent majority', in Nixon's terms, was disenfranchised by the 'liberal' east-coast establishment *and* the counterculture.

Eastwood was, according to Hunter S. Thompson, a Nixon favourite. Dennis Bingham writes: 'Hunter Thompson claimed that Richard Nixon lifted a policy against showing R-rated films in the White House theatre so that he could see *Dirty Harry*, declaring, "Eastwood can do no wrong. Let's see the picture"' (Bingham 1994: 180). Peter Lev, in *American Films of the 1970s*, suggests that the word 'dirty' is itself culturally contingent: 'A relevant use of "dirty" circa 1970 would be "illegal, unethical, and violent", as in "dirty" espionage or a "dirty" war' (Lev 1986: 31). *Dirty Harry*, a film which ostensibly sanctions extra-legal violence to overcome an opponent, seems a particularly appropriate text for Nixon to watch.

Not only were the offices of Daniel Ellsberg, a former defence analyst who leaked *The Pentagon Papers*, broken into around this time, but Nixon, from 1970, was conducting an illegal and highly secret war in Cambodia. 'Dirty' Harry Callahan validates the activities of 'Tricky' Dick Nixon, the 'dirty' war of both covered by silence. Silence here, of course, is code for secrecy. Both Eastwood and Nixon, by implication, can 'do no wrong'.

The confession

Dirty Harry begins with a dissolve from a police badge to an extreme close-up of a rifle fitted with a silencer. With this gun, Scorpio kills (or perhaps assassinates) a young woman in a swimming pool below. This visual match implies, though, that behind the badge is a gun. Guaranteeing a system of law, confession and truth there is an ever-present threat of violence. *Dirty Harry* makes manifest these contradictions and exposes the structures of confession which underpin the narrative of detective and police fictions. The confession indicates the operation of power, and takes place at the point of a gun.

Those that confess may, or may not, be redeemed. Richard Nixon, of course, underwent his own rite of expiation three years after *Dirty Harry*, but he never needed to confess. Notoriously, he was given a Presidential pardon, a perpetual right to silence, without ever being accused, in a court of law, of criminal acts. Nixon's own history is continually marked by silence and confession. An advocate of the HUAC hearings, he also became the subject himself of an investigation which he tried to silence through legal and extra-legal means during the Watergate scandal. Nixon, like Harry and other (more mythical) Westerners, was forced to throw away his badge and walk into the wasteland. It is one of the ironies of post-World War 2 history, however, that Nixon, son of the West and fan of Eastwood, was himself redeemed by 'revisionist' right-wing historiography, and by the time of his death had become not the Great Transgressor, but the Great Statesman.

In a key scene from the film, Harry, having already confronted Scorpio and been beaten by him, tracks the killer to his base, the now-disused Kezar stadium, once the home of the San Francisco 49ers. As his partner illuminates the field, Scorpio dashes across, Harry pursuing, gun framed massively ahead of him. After Harry calls 'Stop', and Scorpio obeys, Harry shoots. Paul Smith, in *Clint Eastwood: A Cultural Production*, argues:

> The context into which the film intervened is important here, of course. American culture in the early 1970s was riven with the strife caused by the Vietnam War; the police's lack of credibility and dubious reputation in those years was a result of thousands of incidents of police brutality against antiwar demonstrators. At the same time, citizens' rights in relation to the police had been strengthened by, amongst other things, the Supreme Court's Miranda

decision in 196[6] and the Escobedo ruling: these rulings had produced shrieks of outrage from the right wing, whose complaints about the 'ultraliberal' Warren court have continued ever since. (Smith 1993: 91)

In the 1966 *Miranda vs. Arizona* judgment of the Supreme Court, Chief Justice Earl Warren wrote: 'The cases before us raise questions which go to the roots of our concepts of American criminal jurisprudence: the restraints society must observe consistent with the Federal Constitution in prosecuting individuals for crime'. The balance between state or society and its need (or desire) to prosecute criminals, and the rights of criminals as citizens of America, is one which has been debated ever since the *Miranda* decision. It was, in fact, challenged and upheld in the year 2000. The *Miranda* decision insisted that citizens, when being taken into police custody, must be advised of their rights. These are:

1. The right to remain silent.
2. Anything [you say] will be taken down and may be used [against you] in a court of law.
3. The right to an attorney.
4. If the citizen cannot afford an attorney, one will be appointed by the court.

Miranda upholds the right of the American citizen to silence, the right not to confess. The Fifth Amendment specifically protects the citizen from being a 'witness against himself', from being forced to testify and incriminate oneself. Therefore, the Miranda decision presumes that if a person is not informed of their rights before questioning, any testimony or confession given must, by definition, have been extracted by force.

The torture scene in *Dirty Harry*, although it emphasizes the pain and horror of the situation (and indicates that Harry has transgressed through use of atonal background music), encourages us to identify with Harry. We have been involved not with Scorpio, but in the chase to find the abducted girl; we want Scorpio to give the whereabouts of the girl so she can be found and complete the narrative trajectory of the rescue. For this, we need Scorpio to submit to Harry's demands, to submit to Harry. In short, as spectators, we need Scorpio to confess. The scene makes manifest the hidden violence of confession, but encourages us, the film's viewers, to validate the act of compulsion by a further act of witness. Although this confession takes place between the two men, on a deserted field (Harry tells di Giorgio to 'get some air'), we are a necessary part of the spectacle of confession: the audience. Though seemingly private (only the two men are present), the confession takes place in public, in fact in a designated arena. Scorpio's insistence upon his rights, ironically, encourages us, the witnesses, to validate Harry's attitude: that they are of no importance.

However, we do not see Scorpio give Harry the location. The consummation of the confession is withheld, the moment of subjection lost in the (moral) fog that envelops the scene as the camera lifts high above the stadium in a helicopter. *Dirty Harry* is a film that is aware of its own processes and it is noteworthy that at this critical moment the camera moves away. Perhaps the operation of power is here too crude, too clear, for a Hollywood film to maintain its focus. Conversely, though, it does not allow the spectator a full participation in the moment in which the criminal fully constructs himself as a subject: the moment of confession. Although I concede that *Dirty Harry* does indeed operate as a power-fantasy both for the adult male (women are almost entirely absent from the film except as victims), and for conservative middle America of the early 1970s, I would argue that the film exceeds and disrupts its textual operation in such moments as the torture scene.

This disruption happens again in a following scene, where Harry is interviewed by the District Attorney and told that all the evidence cannot be used because it was gained illegally. In this scene, our sympathies again lie with Harry. The DA mentions *Miranda* as one of the rights violated by Harry's 'police work'. The viewer is, I think, meant to share Harry's outrage at the protection of the criminal afforded by the law, suggesting that the system of law and justice is incapable of dealing with such a person as Scorpio, and thereby validating the use of extra-legal force to stop him. What destabilizes this identification is Harry's ignorance: has he heard of *Miranda*? As a representative of the law, he seems to be in complete ignorance of its operation. How is it possible that he is surprised by the DA's position? Harry's attitude here is excessive (and disingenuous: he remarked 'You know she's dead, don't you?' when told of Anne Mary Deacon's abduction). Not only is the law invalidated, but so is Harry's position. He has no ground other than his too-intimate knowledge of Scorpio ('He likes it') from which to critique the operations of the law. This scene is, strangely, where Harry unwittingly confesses his ignorance of all that constitutes his position as a police officer.

Additionally, the DA in this scene is crudely coded 'liberal', defending the rights of Scorpio and bringing in the opinion of a Berkeley professor. Liberal here also signifies 'effeminate', 'unmanly', one who 'emasculates' Harry or takes away his ability to protect society from the violence embodied by Scorpio. (Chalmers had also angrily directed Frank Bullitt's boss to figuratively 'castrate him' in the earlier film.) However, in one of the film's most effective strategies, Harry is also the outsider, the maverick, positioned against the dominant order. The film's ambiguity allows for a less reactionary interpretation of Harry and the narrative, one in which he is the outsider figure of the Western, whose final act (throwing away the badge) is an understanding of his own transgressions. The character of Dirty Harry, like 'Popeye' Doyle in the contemporaneous *The French Connection* (1971), it should be noted, signifies 'rebellion' while reinforcing the need for brutal police action. As Dennis Bingham says of the *Dirty Harry* films, 'these films ... are clever mixtures of the traditional and countercultural – or at least anti-authoritarian – codes, manipulated to make a reactionary point that is hard to resist' (Bingham 1994: 181). Captain America, the hero of *Easy Rider*, becomes Dirty Harry; the counterculture hero becomes the maverick cop.

The body of the victim, Mary Ann Deacon, is recovered through the confession that Harry extracts through torture. This testimony, though incriminating, is inadmissible; the rifle that Harry recovers is also rendered inadmissible as evidence through Harry's illegal methods, and Scorpio returns to the street. (Here, *Dirty Harry* recapitulates the failure of extra-legal police work found in *Coogan's Bluff*.) Sadakat Kadri, in *The Trial: A History from Socrates to O. J. Simpson* (2005), suggests that the confession has been the evidentiary 'gold standard' in Western societies since the days of the Inquisition. He writes: 'the confession was promoted from a subordinate form of evidence to the *regina probationum* – 'the queen of proofs' – and self-condemnation would soon come to be revered as an almost immaculate guarantor of truth' (Kadri 2005: 50). Historically, Kadri notes, the confession was usually extracted by torture. Violence and the law are, in the confession, inextricably interwoven. '[T]he effect was simple,' states Kadri: 'arrest virtually guaranteed torture, which virtually guaranteed conviction' (Kadri 2005: 66). When Pauline Kael wrote that *Dirty Harry* exhibited a 'fascist medievalism' (Kael 1997: 174), she was perhaps more strictly correct than she knew.

Michel Foucault, in *Discipline and Punish* (1975), suggested that '[t]hrough the confession, the accused himself took part in the ritual of producing penal truth' (Foucault 1991: 38). The violence of the extraction of the confession is masked by the necessity for a repetition 'before the judges, as a "spontaneous" confession, if it were to constitute proof' (Foucault 1991: 39). What is important here is that the confessing criminal is asked to participate in a judicial process: he or she is (violently) brought into being as a subject upon whom the full force of the law may be visited. Foucault, in the first volume of *The History of Sexuality* suggests that the history of Western modernity, one bound up with discourses of rationality and control, is one which uses the confession in a particular way. He argues, 'the confession has become one of the West's most highly valued techniques for producing truth' (Foucault 1990: 59). Foucault insists, of course, that the act of confession is bound up with processes of power. He also inverts the commonly held binary that suggests that the truth lies in articulation: that speaking presupposes release from the constraints of power. Rather, Foucault suggests, 'the obligation to confess ... is so deeply ingrained in us, that we no longer perceive it as the effect of a power that constrains us' (Foucault 1990: 60). Our perception of 'speaking the truth', that it repre-sents a moment or an act of freedom, is an illusion. He goes on:

> Confession frees, but power reduces one to silence; truth does not belong to the order of power, but shares an original affinity with freedom: [these have been] traditional themes in philosophy, ... which a 'political history of truth' would have to overturn by showing that truth is not by nature free – nor error

servile – but that its production is thoroughly imbued with relations of power. The confession is an example of this. (Foucault 1990: 60)

Although I should note here that Foucault's analysis of confession is useful, I should add that I am particularly interested in how it operates in relation to law and justice, rather than in its role in religious rite. The compulsion to confess has a long and unpleasant history of physical enforcement, making manifest its implication with power. Foucault again notes:

> One confesses – or one is forced to confess. When it is not spontaneous or dictated by some internal imperative, the confession is wrung from a person by violence or threat; it is driven from its hiding place in the soul, or extracted from the body. Since the Middle Ages, torture has accompanied it like a shadow, and supported it when it could go no further: the dark twins. (Foucault 1990: 59)

Silence, confession and violence are then interrelated in the discourse of power. Silence, while seeming enforced, in fact is the alibi for confession, the necessity to speak the 'truth': against oneself or one's fellow citizens. That confession, rather than silence, furthers the operations of power is assured by the application of violence. Does silence, then, become a means of resistance?

In the torture scene in *Dirty Harry*, Harry brings Scorpio into being as subject to the law by forcing him to confess. When the DA protests that Scorpio had rights that were violated (to which Harry replies 'Well, I'm all broken up about that man's rights') he attempts to assert a different kind of subjectivity for Scorpio, that of the citizen. Harry would deny him those rights; or perhaps more properly, not consider that Scorpio had recourse to 'rights' because his behaviour meant he had not earned them. There are curious echoes here of the discourse of Heinlein's *Starship Troopers* that was considered in Chapter 1. Dubois, the 'History and Moral Philosophy' teacher, argues that 'a human being has *no natural rights of any nature*' and goes on to dismiss the 'inalienable rights' of 'life, liberty and the pursuit of happiness' enshrined in the American Constitution (Heinlein 1970: 104). Dubois instead elevates the necessity of the role of the citizen-soldier: 'Liberty is never unalienable: it must be redeemed regularly with the blood of patriots or it *always* vanishes' (Heinlein 1970: 104). In its echoes of Jefferson, Heinlein wraps up militarism and heroic sacrifice (which we shall return to in Chapter 8) in the discourse of the founding of the Republic. Harry Callahan, maverick cop and citizen-soldier, is willing to shed his own blood even for a society he no longer believes in.

In so doing, of course, he denies the tradition of rights that is central to the American Constitution. In this, he has not been alone. The Fifth Amendment of the American Constitution protects the right of the American citizen not to speak if that would tend to incriminate them. In the post-World War 2 period, this right has come under increasing attack, but perhaps was most visible at the time of the House Un-American

Activities Committee, the investigations into Communist influence inspired by the paranoid politics of Senator Joseph McCarthy. Many of the witnesses subpoenaed to appear before the committee opted to 'take the Fifth' and refuse to testify against fellow members of the Communist Party, even though some were willing to testify about themselves. Note the word 'testify' here, and its connotations of truth and true witness, re-enforcing Foucault's argument about the role of confession. Arthur Miller, who was called in 1956, after the height of the Committee, wrote *The Crucible* to explicitly compare the role of witness and confession in seventeenth-century witch-trials and 50s America. In his autobiography, *Timebends* (1988), he wrote:

> The main point of the hearings, precisely as in seventeenth-century Salem, was that the accused made public confession, damn his confederates as well as his Devil master, and guarantee his sterling new allegiance by breaking disgusting old vows – whereupon he was let loose to rejoin the society of extremely decent people. In other words, the same spiritual nugget lay enfolded within both procedures – an act of contrition done not in solemn privacy but out in the public air. (Miller 1988: 331)

Miller's insistence on the public nature of this confession is interesting considering he, and other witnesses, refused to take the option of '*in camera*' session, in order that his non-participation in the rite of confession would be (re)marked. In Michel Foucault's sense of confession, this private/public binary does not pertain. The act of confession itself brings into being the confessing subject, establishes positions of authority and subjection, and ensures the operation of power. Confession is a performance, and bringing into being through language, and if necessary, a marking of the body of the confessing subject through violence. Perhaps, however, the act of confession gains more power through enactment upon a public stage, implicating those who spectate in the operation of control and compulsion. By the time Miller testified, the rite of confession itself had become the primary impulse for the continued activities of the committee, and Miller, perhaps not wanting to be thought of as a 'Fifth Amendment Communist', stood rather on his First Amendment rights to free speech. HUAC, by the mid-50s, asked subpoenaed witnesses not to name any new names of those under Communist influence, but only those who appeared on their lists. The 'hearings' (note again the insistence on the acts of speech, witness, testimony and reception in the search for 'truth') no longer sought information, but as Foucault argued, participation.

Clint Eastwood and the Western

Dirty Harry is clearly indebted to the genre of the Western, and Dennis Bingham, in his book *Acting Male*, notes 'its reliance on Western genre conventions' (Bingham 1994: 194). Pauline Kael, in an otherwise damning critique, also noted the generic resemblance: 'our cops-and-robbers pictures are like urban spaghetti Westerns' (Kael 1997: 173). Kael is also hostile to Leone's films. She argues that 'what made these Italian-made Westerns popular was that they stripped the Western from its cultural burden of morality. They discarded its civility along with its hypocrisy' (Kael 1997: 172). We will return to the Western in Chapter 7. Here, though, Kael's insight that 'what the Western hero stood for was left out, and what he embodied (strength and power) was retained' (Kael 1997: 172) is vital to a reading of *Dirty Harry* as an urban Western (taking its cue from the more obvious generic cross-over of the earlier *Coogan's Bluff*).

Like a Western, *Dirty Harry* deploys stand-offs or shoot-outs at key moments during the film, and works towards the final expulsion of the violent criminal through an act of redemptive violence on the part of the lawman. However, as in Ford's *The Man Who Shot Liberty Valance* (1962) and *The Searchers* (1956), this violence means that the hero is himself excluded from the order he protects and brings into being at the end of the film. The reverse of this narrative is that of redemption. In Ford's *My Darling Clementine* (1946), or the Anthony Mann Westerns starring James Stewart, the hero is offered a chance to re-enter society through a purgation of his own history of violence, through a symbolic confrontation with that past.

Is *Dirty Harry* a 'fascist' film? Famously, Pauline Kael characterized *Dirty Harry* as 'a right-wing fantasy about the San Francisco police force as a helpless group, emasculated by the liberals, ... propagand[izing] for para-legal police power and vigilante justice' (Kael 1997: 174). J. Hoberman, writing much later, suggests that 'it may prove more useful to understand Harry as a fascist hero' (Hoberman 2003: 323), though he is careful to historicize his reading of the film. The film manipulates our sympathies to be on the side of Harry, the 'good man' who finds that he must go outside the bounds of law in his fight against Scorpio. Paul Cobley personalizes Harry's actions by arguing that *Dirty Harry* is part of a 'revenge' or 'vigilante' cycle of thrillers that include *Death Wish* (1974) and *Taxi Driver* (1976), though unlike either of these two films (and an important differ-ence), Harry Callahan is a police officer, not an ordinary citizen. *Dirty Harry* seems to offer its central character as a representative of law who must resort to extra-legal force to defeat his psychotic antagonist, thereby exposing as ineffectual any legal means of pursuing criminals and providing a rationale for vigilante-style 'justice'. In essence, the film provides a rationale for police torture when faced with the unmanageable psychosis of the contemporary criminal, but what Harry Callahan represents is an old American figure indeed: the vigilante, or even the militia-man.

Dirty Harry attempts to validate not only extra-judicial police action, and the redemptive violence of the Western vigilante, but a version of (white) masculine subjectivity itself. The centrality of the (straight) white mascu-line subject is suggested by the casting around Eastwood. Scorpio is played by Andy Robinson, the son of Edward G. Robinson, whose hysterical performance was so effective that it hindered his acting career for some years. Scorpio is also clearly gender troubled, an ambiguous figure. He is a loner, a voyeur, expresses his sexuality in violence, and as Paul Smith notes, 'his relation to children in particular is suggestively eroticised' (Smith 1993: 123). Dennis Bingham suggests:

> In *Dirty Harry*, masochism and male hysteria are displaced onto Scorpio (Andy Robinson), the polymorphous villain, who plays 'the bad' *and* 'the ugly' to Harry's slightly ironic 'good'. Scorpio embodies an unrestricted omnisexuality as well as a hysterical reaction to it. (Bingham 1994: 193)

Harry too is a 'man alone', but his status is justified in the back-story by a lost wife. Harry is shown to be a voyeur in several episodes – he has to be 'saved' by Chico from a superannuated vigilante 'mob' at one point after he peeps in a window – and it is not until the sequel to *Dirty Harry*, *Magnum Force*, that the character is represented in any form of sexual relationship. Harry's monolithic silence is in part defined by, brought into being by, the 'excessive' performance of Robinson, just as Eastwood's role as 'Blondie' in *The Good, the Bad and the Ugly* had been defined by the 'Latin' (Method) style of Eli Wallach as 'Tuco'. Harry's 'straight' character is emphasized by the clothes he wears – the tweed jacket, shirt, tie and jumper, slacks – which marks his difference from the counterculture caricatures which otherwise people the film, and from the 'hip' cop Frank Bullitt. Scorpio himself is a rather hysterically distorted representation of the counter-culture, a variant of the 'hipster' who has gone over completely into psychosis, and he prominently displays the 'peace' symbol on his belt buckle in later scenes. It is no coincidence that Scorpio wears this symbol in San Francisco, the city of 'flower power'. Don Siegel, in his autobiography *A Siegel Film* (1993), even suggests that Scorpio 'could have returned from Vietnam bearing a crazed grudge' (Siegel 1993: 370). Although considering Scorpio as an echo of the figure of the Vietnam Veteran is somewhat troubling (suggesting that he too could be a patriot whose blood has been spilled), Siegel's suggestion certainly connects Scorpio to other cultural manifestations of traumatized or damaged masculinity.

Eastwood's identification with the Western furthers a reactionary undercurrent in *Dirty Harry*: to reconstitute masculinity is a less-troubled form, one which is identical with the Western figure of the lone male frontiersman, but it is one which constantly veers towards excess and parody. Dennis Bingham suggests that Eastwood's acting style 'was based on a realization that the foundations of masculine identity had been lost and needed to be massively reconstructed and re-performed' (Bingham 1994: 174). However, Bingham suggests that the only way this could be accomplished was by 'pastiche, in which the discredited myth of the late-nineteenth century frontier lawgiver is replayed with "blank [parody]"' (Bingham 1994: 173). The low-key 'queering' of Eastwood's cowboy persona in *Coogan's Bluff* is a case in point here. Eastwood brings to the role of Dirty Harry the significations which accrued from his performances in Sergio Leone's 'Dollars trilogy' of 'Spaghetti' Westerns: *A Fistful of Dollars* (1963), *For a Few Dollars More* (1964), and *The Good, the Bad and the Ugly* (1966). Leone's films rework the Western to de-emphasize community and law, and replace it with the figure of the bounty hunter: set adrift from history, society and morality. In *High Plains Drifter* (1972), a Leone-inflected Western directed by Eastwood after making *Dirty Harry*, the drifter becomes a force of vengeance, an incarnation of the desire for 'justice' found elsewhere in the Western, but transformed into one that punishes transgressors from beyond the grave. The 'avenging angel' is a performance of violent masculinity also found in Eastwood's *Pale Rider* (1984) and *Unforgiven* (1992), one in which masculine subjectivity is identified with a higher vigilantism. (See Chapter 7 for more on *Unforgiven*.) Eastwood's later Westerns envision a survival of the principle of redemptive violence beyond death, beyond the boundaries of the subject itself. Similarly, in one shot in *Dirty Harry*, Harry is shown standing above a model of San Francisco, like a superhuman force of justice or avenging angel.

Judith Butler's conception of gender as performance has been a suggestive one for film critics, and Steven Cohan, in his article 'The Spy in the Gray Flannel Suit', uses it to analyse Cary Grant's performance in Hitchcock's *North by Northwest*. In this film, Cohan suggests, Grant's costume and performance reflects and critiques the 'performance ethic' of the managerial class of the American 1950s, a masculinity 'tailored' to fit the imperatives of consumerism and conformity. He writes: 'The movie star – whose screen personality is, not accidentally, termed a *persona* – brings to the foreground of popular representation the epistemological problems that Butler describes in her deconstruction of gender identities' (Cohan 1995: 58). The same is true of Eastwood's performances. A certain masculine subjectivity is called up by Eastwood's 'minimal' acting style which compromises the idea of performance itself, makes it seem 'natural'. It is a performance of masculinity that is intended to disguise a critical absence, an authentic and 'natural' masculine self-identity. This is, perhaps, why the character Eastwood played in Sergio Leone's 'Dollars trilogy' – variously 'Joe', 'Manco' and 'Blondie' – have come under the appellation 'the Man with No Name', an explicit suggestion that Eastwood signifies not presence but absence, not identity but performance.

Feeling Lucky

Here we shall turn to two contrasting performances, almost routines, which bookend the narrative of Harry's confrontation with Scorpio. The first takes place as Harry foils a bank robbery on the streets of San Francisco; the second by a mill in a wasteland on the outskirts of the city. In the first sequence, Harry is eating a hotdog in a diner when a shot is heard. Before he is shown exiting the diner, the film cuts to some workmen on scaffolding, explicitly inserting the idea of the spectator into the sequence. The film cuts back to them later in the shoot-out. When Harry shoots at the getaway driver and the car is overturned, Harry walks through the fountain of water from the broken hydrant, the camera tracking behind Eastwood as he walks towards the fallen bank robber. The framing clearly indicates people hiding in their car (afraid of Harry) and crowds on the street as Harry approaches. From the tracking shot, the film cuts to a shot of the pavement, framing the robber's arm, shotgun, and the shadow of Harry's pistol. After a reaction shot of the robber (the actor Albert Popplewell, who played different characters in the first four *Dirty Harry* films), the camera frames the gun, then zooms back and refocuses, framing the gun and Eastwood's face. He then speaks the lines:

> Uh-uh. I know what you're thinking. Did he fire six shots, or only five? Well, in this excitement I clean forgot myself. But as this is a .44 magnum, the most powerful handgun in the world, and would blow your head clean off, you've got to ask yourself one question: do I feel lucky? Well, do you, punk?

This is spoken in a soft, playful fashion, although Eastwood's face is expressionless. It is clearly a performance, one that the character has given before. It simulates confrontation where there is none, as the opponent is already shot, prone, and unarmed. Who is this performance for? It is for the film audience, clearly, a 'routine' to mark the character's difference and authority. Remember, however, that the sequence had carefully inserted the crowd of spectators within this scene, and when Harry is called back to provide the answer to his own question, his response – to point the gun at the robber's head – calls up the possibility of an extra-judicial execution, witnessed by a street full of people. There is a possibility that Harry wants the robber to 'answer', to move and provoke a reaction. There is, however, only silence before Harry picks up the shotgun. There is no need to force confession here, as the robber has been apprehended in the act, has fired at the policeman after due warning, and lies injured on the sidewalk. As Harry turns to go, the sirens of approaching police cars can be heard.

The second sequence is a reprise of the first, and is slightly but significantly different. Here, instead of tracking behind Eastwood, the camera frames him as he walks towards us. No longer on the streets of the city, this performance will be enacted in a symbolic wasteland, without an audience. The background behind Eastwood in the sequence is a bleached-out sky, devoid of the signs of humanity or community. The 'routine' runs as follows:

> Uh-uh. I know what you're thinking. Did he fire six shots, or only five? Well, I kinda lost track myself in all this excitement. But as this is a .44 magnum, the most powerful handgun in the world, and would blow your head clean off, you've got to ask yourself one question: do I feel lucky? Well do ya, *punk?*

Eastwood here is almost whispering. His face works to show anger and emotion, his teeth are clenched together. He can hardly open his mouth to speak. The change in the line from 'in this excitement I clean forgot myself' to 'I kinda lost track myself in all this excitement' emphasizes, ironically, the word 'excitement'. Is this what Harry is feeling? He has, in the course of the narrative, 'kinda lost track' of many things, including his own motivations and the law which he should observe. The last line, with 'punk' almost spat out, is meant to provoke in an entirely different way to the first routine. Here, Harry wants and needs Scorpio to symbolically confess his own nature by reaching for the gun. A literal or verbal confession is not required.

What remains, after Scorpio's death, is silence. Eastwood reaches for the badge that had been used as a symbol of law in the opening montage, and throws it into the creek. Again, police sirens are heard in the background. This gesture is, as I noted above, entirely ambiguous. Those who argue *Dirty Harry* is simply a right-wing fantasy read this gesture as a summing up of the film's case against the system of law: that it no longer provides the protection that society needs. However, the law is largely what has separated Harry from Scorpio, and in divesting himself of it Harry becomes a killer. This, then, becomes Harry's own confession. If we return to the idea that *Dirty Harry* is a Western manqué, the throwing away of the badge also indicates the unredeemed hero, who walks away from society and into the wasteland, excluded from 'order' in the act of creating it.

A more interesting statement would have been to throw away the gun. The .44 magnum is, of course, a phallic symbol, a guarantor of Harry's masculine status and a sign of the patriarchal imperatives at the heart of law. The .44 magnum, though, is no ordinary gun. It is 'the most powerful handgun in the world'. As a guarantor of law, and of Harry's masculinity (and heterosexuality), it is excessive. It is itself implicated in a system of performance, and at key scenes in the film it must be shown. When Scorpio sees the gun for the first time, he says, 'My that's a big one', explicitly homoeroticizing the performance. As with the rite of confession, the audience implied in the *mise-en-scène* of the first 'Do I feel lucky?' speech also signifies the imperative of performance. Harry is displaying the phallus not only to the criminal, but to the crowds, and to us.

The 'liberal' Harry

Although I have aligned my argument with critics such as Kael and Hoberman in considering *Dirty Harry* a film which promotes right-wing politics, it is far from a fascist one, as the foregoing readings of the ambiguities of the film should suggest. Siegel himself (a self-declared liberal) writes in *A Siegel Film* that 'Not once throughout *Dirty Harry* did Clint and I have a political discussion. ... The response of my many friends – members of the "Siegel cult", some of them left wing or Communists, others conservative Republicans or Fascists – has not surprised me' (Siegel 1993: 373). The surprise might be that he would call such an assortment his 'friends'. There is, in *Dirty Harry*, a plurality of ideas and discourses, some which are certainly authoritarian, some of which are more liberal in intent. It is revealing that in *Dirty Harry* and most of its sequels, Harry's partner is not a white male. In *Dirty Harry*, Chico Gonzalez is Hispanic; in *Magnum Force*, his partner is African-American; in the second sequel, *The Enforcer* (1976), his partner is played by Tyne Daly, a woman.

There is clear sensitivity in *Dirty Harry* with regard to race. It was important, declares Siegel, 'to show our audience that Harry was not a bigot' (Siegel 1993: 369). Directly after the first 'Do I feel lucky?' scene, where Harry delivers his speech to the wounded African-American bank robber, Harry is tended by black doctor Steve, who declares that 'we Potrero Hill boys have got to stick together'. (The same scenario plays out very similarly in *Magnum Force*.) Other shots focus on black policemen, and one of Scorpio's victims is a young African-American boy. While one might justifiably analyse this in the same terms that I suggested with Scorpio above – the presence of the ethnic or gender 'other' serves to define the central, hegemonic white masculine subject – there is a clear determination here not to fall into crude 'bigotry'. In *Magnum Force* (1973), Harry's persona is in fact realigned in a more liberal direction, partly through his difference from a group of vigilante motorcycle cops who are organized by Lieutenant Briggs (Hal Holbrook) to 'restore order' to the city by assassinating important figures in organized crime. These cops form a homosocial group and, says Harry's partner, in training 'everyone thought they were queer for each other'. Harry retorts 'If all of you could shoot like them, I wouldn't care if the whole damn department was queer'.

Magnum Force goes to much greater lengths than *Dirty Harry* in establishing Harry's normative heterosexuality; in fact, as noted above, several times in *Dirty Harry* Callahan is revealed to be something of a voyeur. This is to establish him as 'straight' in sexual as well as political terms. In this film, Harry discovers other vigilantes who idolize him, but when they ask him to join them, he replies: 'I'm afraid you've misjudged me.' He ends up defending the system he hates because there is no alternative: that consists of Briggs and the patrolmen. Curiously, he asks Briggs rhetorically: 'What happens when police become their own executioners? Where's it gonna end?' Between *Dirty Harry* and its sequel, he has clearly forgotten the events that created his reputation in the first place. By the end of *Magnum Force*, Harry Callahan is in the position of Frank Bullitt: liberal, upright, and opposed to corruption in high places. However, where *Bullitt* ends in anxious stalemate, with Chalmers driving away from whatever crimes he may have been complicit with, in *Magnum Force* police vigilantism is itself undone by the very 'gun law' it uses. Frank Bullitt's gun is the symbol of his despair; Harry Callahan's is a fetish object that enforces law with violence.

CHAPTER SIX

Rogue Cops II: Los Angeles

Los Angeles assumes a particular place, even perhaps a non-place, in the imaginary of the United States. Where its east-coast *Doppleganger* and inverse image, New York, may be identified by its emblematic buildings and monuments (the Statue of Liberty, the Empire State Building, the Chrysler Building, and until 9/11 the World Trade Center), Los Angeles has no such identifiable icons. Its imagery is derived from Hollywood: the Hollywood(land) sign, the Walk of Fame, perhaps Grauman's Chinese Theatre. New York (and I really mean Manhattan island here) is synonymous with the skyscraper, the steel-frame high-rise which gives Manhattan's blocks their singular iconography. This architecture, dominated by the designs of Mies van der Rohe and others of the International Style, are inextricably linked with modernism and modernity and also, as we saw in Chapter 3, were used by Alan Pakula in his conspiracy thrillers of the 1970s to suggest authoritarian systems of control. Charles Jenks, in his article 'Hetero-Architecture and the L.A. School', suggests that:

> Architectural modernism, in its socially acceptable late and neo forms, becomes the natural expression for modernization .... It's a sad story, repeated in every American city: as building commissions get bigger, more expensive, and closer to the center of action, they become predictably duller, safer, more modernist. (Jenks 1996: 51–2)

Jenks laments the importation of a debased architectural tradition, particularly into the downtown area of Los Angeles, where after the relaxation of zoning laws prohibiting the building of high-rise buildings, over 40 new skyscrapers were built between 1976 and the end of the century. Jenks, an LA-based architect and leader of the self-named 'L.A. School' of architecture (most notably embodied in the work of Frank Gehry), asserts that Los Angeles has its own particular style which has no need of such 'foreign' transplants. LA style is, he argues, heterogeneity. He goes on:

> This heterogeneity, at all levels, is at once excessive in Los Angeles and typical of the world city. London, Rome and Tokyo are also hybrid agglomerations that allow their originating village structure to remain an imprint for later diversity. But none, it seems to me, is so characteristically heteroglot. Even New York City ... seems homogenous by comparison. If the 1940s mayor, Thomas Dewey, called New York not a 'melting pot' but a 'boiling pot', then that makes

Los Angeles, as a form of food, a simmering, spread-out pizza with all the extras. (Jenks 1996: 48)

Jenks uses a wonderfully jazzy metaphor, one which, jokingly, emphasizes the horizontality of LA as opposed to the verticality of New York. Jenks also opposes heterogeneity to homogeneity; implicitly, he also contrasts the 'modernity' of New York's skyscrapers to the 'postmodernity' of the LA School. As in all binaries, this offers a hierarchy of value, and we should be in no doubt as to which is the privileged term. In case we are in any doubt, Jenks also states:

What makes Los Angeles unusual, if not unique, is that it is the primary example of what I have called a heteropolis, a new form of urban agglomeration that thrives on difference. ... It is a place where heterogeneity – of culture and even of flora and fauna – is enjoyed. (Jenks 1996: 47)

Los Angeles becomes, for Jenks, a rather utopian (or perhaps heterotopian) place. The singularity of LA, Jenks asserts, is in its insistent privileging of difference within the fabric of the built environment, a city where difference is 'enjoyed'.

However, look more closely at Jenks's rhetoric and the sutures start to emerge. In his discussion of the importation of the 'dull', 'safe' modernism of New York, there are strong echoes of the anti-immigrant politics of much of Los Angeles's short history. In 1871, for instance, a mob of Anglo vigilantes murdered 20 ethnic Chinese in the 'Chinese Massacre', inaugurating what Edward Soja and Allen Scott call a 'pattern' of the 'social disciplining of [a] "troublesome" minority' (Soja and Scott 1996: 4). Jenks's privileging of the horizontal development of Los Angeles masks its history of expansion, which rests upon real-estate speculation (much of which concerned real estate that was not very real at all), the incorporation of outlying rural spaces into a super-urban sprawl, and the long history of civic corruption which made it possible. Most worryingly, although Jenks celebrates 'difference', the 'heterogeneity' he reads into LA's urban fabric may also be read as ethnic segregation. As Soja and Scott suggest, '[b]y 1970, sociological studies show that Los Angeles now rivalled Chicago as the most racially segregated of all American cities' (Soja and Scott 1996: 10). This segregation was produced by racist employment practices, housing inequalities, and the development of 'white flight' communities (now gated and patrolled) at Los Angeles's margins.

There is, in fact, another 'LA School', but this concentrates on urban geography rather than architecture, and is centred on the Department of Geography at UCLA. In the work of Edward Soja, such as *Postmodern Geographies* (1989), and particularly Mike Davis, in *City of Quartz* (1990), a strongly historicized critique is offered of the development of LA, and implicitly also of the sunny assumptions of Jenks and others who echo the rhetoric of LA's most one-eyed boosters. Soja and Scott suggest that LA has undergone five 'surges' of development, from 1870 to 1990. The first followed the 'Chinese Massacre' and concentrated on luring WASP migrants from small-town mid-America, a short-term boom based on land speculation; the second, from 1900 to 1920, encompassed the installation of industrial development and the immigration of southern and central Europeans, Japanese and Mexicans to supply the workforce. The third, 1920–40, was created by another land boom, the growth of both Hollywood and the aircraft industry, and migration from the Dustbowl states; the fourth, 1940–70, saw the greatest expansion of suburbia, the massive growth of defence-related industries, and the migration of African-Americans from the South to California; and fifth and last, 1970–90, 'mass regional urbanization' (Soja and Scott 1996: 11), the development of high- and low-technology industries, and immigration from the Pacific Rim and from Central and South America.

The irony of the ongoing racism which has marred LA history is that the successive waves of immigration have, in fact, provided the motive force behind California's long (and anomalous) summer afternoon of prosperity. Soja and Scott, like Jenks, consider the diversity of the Los Angeles cityscape, but instead emphasize its economic significance:

> A very different kind of American metropolis was taking shape, one in which the oil derrick, the automobile, the airfield, the movie studio, the beach and mountain community, the immigrant labor camp and factory town, and the all-purpose resort both stretched the urban fabric and pinned it down in an extensive multiplicity or urban places and experiences. (Soja and Scott 1996: 6)

'Multiplicity' rather than 'heterogeneity': Soja and Scott are well aware that the history of Los Angeles is punctuated by urban tensions and ethnic violence, from the 'Chinese Massacre', to the 'Zoot Suit' riots of 1943, the Watts riots of 1965, and the rioting following the Rodney King case in 1992.

In *Literature and Race in Los Angeles* (2001), Julian Murphet analyses how the crime novels that will be analysed in this chapter, by James Ellroy and Walter Mosley,

> circulate around the question of policing and segregation [and reveal] what I have called elsewhere [LA-set noir's] *racial unconscious*, its uncanny tendency to map urban racial unease in terms of black and white, paranoia and violence, consumerism and the void. (Murphet 2001: 39)

Murphet's illuminating analyses demonstrate how crime fictions recapitulate the kind of ethnic spatialization that characterized Los Angeles in actuality, if not in the sunny rhetoric of Charles Jenks or other 'boosters' of the city. The racial division of the city that Murphet diagnoses in the policies of LA Police Chief Parker, who insisted on 'a dualized conception of public space, ... projecting his notion of "good vs. evil" through a racial optic' (Murphet 2001: 46), is repeated in the segregated city of James

Ellroy's 'LA Quartet' of novels, *The Black Dahlia* (1987), *The Big Nowhere* (1988), *LA Confidential* (1990) and *White Jazz* (1992). Murphet suggests Ellroy is committed to a 'spatial mapping [of] whiteness in crisis' in which white supremacy, in the form of LA policing and governance (and the regulation of city space) undergoes an ideological rupture (Murphet 2001: 59). Indeed, Murphet goes on to suggest that in Ellroy's fiction,

> the division of public space between centre and margin is most often explicitly a racial one, 'containing' blacks and Hispanics in segregated urban zones where white power can freely exercise its muscle; on the other [hand], the veritable deconstruction of white subjectivity has clear and determinate links to the impossibility of maintaining this racial division. (Murphet 2001: 59)

We saw exactly the same motifs – white male subjectivity in crisis and the racial mapping of Los Angeles – in Joel Schumacher's *Falling Down* (1991), roughly contemporaneous with Ellroy's quartet of crime novels, in Chapter 4. The anxious or troubled masculinity of the white 'rogue cops' of Ellroy's *LA Confidential*, and Curtis Hanson's 1997 film adaptation, will be the primary focus of this chapter. I would like to begin, however, by looking at Walter Mosley's *Devil in a Blue Dress* (1990), another 'retro-noir' fiction, but this time narrated by an African-American private detective.

At the beginning of *Devil in a Blue Dress*, the first of five novels featuring the same private detective, 'Easy' Rawlins is a veteran of World War 2 who works at the 'Champion' factory, part of the aerospace industry that played a crucial role in Los Angeles's postwar boom. Easy has just been laid off, by his white (Italian-American) boss Benny Giacomo, for refusing to work overtime when he was so exhausted he knew he was bound to make mistakes. The description of Benny Giacomo begins to unsettle the racial categories that segregate the city: 'His salt-and-pepper hair had once been jet black and his skin color was darker than many mulattos I'd known. But Benny was a white man and I was a Negro. He wanted me to work hard for him and he needed me to be grateful that he allowed me to work at all' (Mosley 1996: 58). While Easy is all too aware of the racial codings that inform this employee/employer relationship, this speech introduces a sense of the artificiality of these codings of 'color' that will recur throughout the novel. Easy's awareness of race is an awareness of power in this situation, or rather of his own powerlessness. He refuses to apologize to Benny and therefore does not get his job back, but demands to be treated with respect. This is crucial for Easy's sense of self: 'I wasn't going down on my knees for him or anyone else,' he says when menaced by another white male (Mosley 1996: 51).

Easy is himself part of the African-American immigration into California in the postwar years that Soja and Scott describe as an element in the boom. Easy is from Texas, but 'ran away' from there when his friend Mouse had implicated him in a murder. Easy's conscience is bound up with his sense of masculinity: 'I signed up to fight in the war to prove to myself that I was a man' (Mosley 1996: 42). It is interesting to note here that Easy echoes, nearly word for word, the speech that Juan Rico's father gives to explain joining up in Heinlein's *Starship Troopers*. While I would concur with Julian Murphet's assessment that Mosley's texts function perhaps less as strictly generic texts and more as a 'registering apparatus for the everyday life of LA's black ghettos', mediated through Easy's voice (Murphet 2001: 64), it is revealing that Mosley seems to be as indebted to postwar constructions of a male soldier-subject to construct a normative masculinity as those texts that encode a universalized white masculine hegemon.

Easy's subjectivity is not unitary, however. In times of stress, Easy hears 'the voice'. He first hears it when in Normandy, pinned down by a German sniper. It tells him to kill: and he does. 'The voice has no lust. He never told me to rape or steal. He just tells me how it is if I want to survive. Survive like a man,' Easy confesses (Mosley 1996: 88). The 'voice' within enables Easy to recover a violent masculine subjectivity, which he adopts temporarily to survive. It is a regulated violence, however; it does not exceed social or ethical boundaries, remaining a means by which Easy can retain his self-respect as a black man in a racist America. The 'voice' within, however, does suggest that Easy's subjectivity is at least a double one. Scott McCracken suggests that 'respectability', made concrete in Easy's desire to be a homeowner, is central to Easy's 'double identity': he desires to become part of the black middle class, but 'the precarious position of the black property-owner forces him to keep his status secret' (McCracken 1998: 170). While 'property establishes his right to citizenship', his development into a private detective in *Devil in a Blue Dress* makes him doubly liminal (McCracken 1998: 170).

As in Pakula's *Klute*, masculine double-subjectivity is, in *Devil in a Blue Dress*, mirrored in a split female subject. At the centre of the narrative is Easy's search for a white woman called Daphne, who is revealed to actually be an African-American woman called Ruby. Also as in *Klute*, the detective falls in love with the object of his investigation, but here there is no romantic escape possible. Ruby/Daphne in fact mis-recognizes Easy's masculine subjectivity: 'I'm different than you because I'm two people. I'm her *and* I'm me' (Mosley 1996: 179). She even suggests that their sexual liaison 'wasn't me', allowing her to disavow any emotional connection and take a cab out of Easy's world. By contrast, Mouse, who turns up in *Devil in a Blue Dress* to apply the violent solutions that Easy finds difficult, represents a kind of alter-ego, 'the other side of Easy's bourgeois citizen self' (McCracken 1998: 170). Mouse signifies a kind of black-American experience that is less troubled by the kind of racial categorizations that fracture Easy's own subjectivity, even though his violence is in no way admirable. Mouse's key judgement on Easy runs as follows:

> You learn stuff and you be thinkin' like white men be thinkin'. You be thinkin' that what's right fo' them is right fo' you. She look white and you think like you white. But brother you don't know that you both poor niggers. And a nigger ain't never gonna be happy 'less he accept what he is. (Mosley 1996: 180)

Mouse skewers the double-bind that Easy inhabits with regard to African-American subjectivity: his desire for 'respectability', for the status that property-owning citizenship will confer on him, indicates an internalization of the imperatives of the racially segregated status quo. Easy, because he is black, can never achieve the kind of respect he demands from a racist society.

Southern California, and particularly Los Angeles, is a place of paradox. It is a megalopolis with no identifiable icons in its urban fabric, yet the place which, through Hollywood cinema, massively contributes to the global imaginary. Ethnically and culturally diverse, LA has been riven by rioting and communal violence. It is at once singular and unlike any other US city, yet it is emblematic of the 'world city' and the future development of London, Tokyo or Rome. Finally, and most importantly, it is a place of seemingly inexhaustible economic boom, yet one which has been driven by civic corruption, inequality, and the systematic eradication of any radical political critique within the Californian polity, and also of the very landscapes which sell the 'dream' of the city. The beginning of Curtis Hanson's 1997 adaptation of James Ellroy's *LA Confidential* makes the point admirably. Over archive images of Hollywood stars, the tract homes of postwar suburbanization, and particularly orange groves (citrus was a large part of the early Californian economy), the voiceover narration first 'sells' the imagery, then undercuts its visual rhetoric. The voice is recognizably Danny DeVito, who, it is revealed, is the editor working on copy for the scandal magazine *Hush-Hush*, a magazine that really existed during the 1950s, one that seemingly offered the 'truth' (or 'sleaze') behind the Hollywood image. Although Hudgens's vision is tarnished later in the film, here he speaks true. The irony of the voiceover has its correlatives in LA's history. As Mike Davis has noted:

> One of the nation's most picturesque and emblematic landscapes – the visual magnet that had attracted hundreds of thousands of immigrants to Southern California – was systematically eradicated. ... What generations of tourists and migrants had once admired as a real-life Garden of Eden was now buried under an estimated three billion tons of concrete (250 tons per inhabitant). (Davis 1996: 171)

The image of Los Angeles as 'paradise' is belied by the experience of the millions of Angelinos. Not for them suburban domesticity and the 'land of plenty': rather, urban blight, discrimination, and poverty. The orange groves were bulldozed, and replaced by arid, empty building lots.

The two versions of *LA Confidential*, and the Towne/Polanski retro-noir *Chinatown* (1974), construct crime narratives on an underlying matrix of civic corruption, where narratives of the city's 'development' or expansion are replayed in familial or generational struggle, and where the racial tensions in the city's fabric are insistently turned into anxieties about gender. I intend to intersect five different threads in this chapter: Los Angeles itself and its urban development; the formal and generic motifs of noir fiction and film, and their relationships to Los Angeles, particularly as found in *LA Confidential* and *Chinatown*; hegemonic masculinity as it has been (re)constructed in post-World War 2 America, and its centrality to noir fictions; the importance of this gender politics to the 1990s, as Ellroy's *LA Confidential* was first published in 1990, and Curtis Hanson directed the film version in 1997; and the adaptation of the textual to the visual with regard to *LA Confidential*, and the screen version's regulation of gender and desire. The first question I wish to posit is, therefore: how does the constitution of a (white) hegemonic masculinity in the late-1940s and 1950s, typified by Steven Cohan as the 'domestic mystique', connect with issues of civic governance, particularly in Los Angeles?

Masculinity and governance

The answer, I believe, can be found in the development of popular fictions that deal with crime and criminality, most particularly the film noir and the succeeding 'police procedural'. Both *The Blue Dahlia* and *In a Lonely Place*, that I considered in Chapter 1, are set in California, as are Raymond Chandler's novels and adaptations such as *The Big Sleep* (1946). Mike Davis, in *City of Quartz*, notes that:

> Beginning in 1934, with James M Cain's *The Postman Always Rings Twice*, a succession of through-the-glass-darkly novels – all produced by writers under contract to the studio system – repainted the image of Los Angeles as a deracinated urban hell. (Davis 1998: 37)

The connection of LA to noir, and noir to renegotiations of masculinity, is vital, and suggests my argument in this chapter. LA fictions are particularly well suited to a consideration of the figurations of masculinity in post-World War 2 American culture, partly because these fictions respond so clearly to the massive cultural and societal upheavals which characterize the life of the city in this period. If the city is in a state of perpetual flux and crisis, it is little wonder that masculinity in LA fictions should be too. Will Straw, in an article on the 'lurid city', suggests that 'one of the most significant developments within postwar crime fictions [is] the emergence of the urban policeman as a complex, often tragic figure' (Straw 1997: 119). He continues:

> The policeman will come to stand, in film cycles which continue through to the present, as the locus of fictions which address the relationship between crime, social order and individual morality, and the tensions between professional, bureaucratic and police authority. (Straw 1997: 120)

In the early-1950s, then, the policeman begins to take over from the private detective as a central masculine figure in crime narratives, and there is a decline both in conventional 'mystery' narratives and in the formal coherence of film noir. Josh Cohen, in an article on Ellroy's *The Black Dahlia*, indicates the conscious deployment of this movement from noir to police drama in Ellroy's fictions. He argues:

> As he has explicitly asserted, Ellroy's shift of narrative perspective from the Chandlerian private eye to the waged cop constitutes a critique of the romanticised and historically inaccurate figuration of crime as existential conflict between alienated individual and urban modernity. (Cohen 1997: 169)

In Cohen's estimation, then, Ellroy's men recapitulate the struggle between a heroic, individualistic subjectivity and the organized collective that Fredric Jameson perceived at the heart of the paranoid conspiracy thrillers analysed in Chapter 3. It is no coincidence that Ellroy's crime novels are also saturated with conspiracies. The policeman, in crime fictions of the 1950s and in *LA Confidential*, is identified both as a figure of authority and as the ambivalent, transgressive and doomed male: the fractured masculinity of the 'rogue cop'.

Curtis Hanson's film of *LA Confidential* self-reflexively acknowledges the trajectory from noir to *policier*. Behind Kim Basinger, in the scene which introduces her character, the protitute Lynn Bracken, the 1942 film noir *This Gun for Hire* plays on a portable projector. Like *The Blue Dahlia* analysed in Chapter 1, *This Gun for Hire* stars Alan Ladd as the laconic hero, cast opposite Veronica Lake. Lynn Bracken's client, wearing a private-eye snapbrim, is clearly playing or *performing* (for erotic effect) the role of the noir hero – Ladd to Bracken's Veronica Lake. By the early- to mid-1950s, when the film is set, the iconography of the film noir has become a matter both of cultural memory and of self-conscious role-play: it is no longer available as a 'naturalized' subject position. It has been overtaken, by the 'rogue cop' Bud White who is about to knock on the door, and by the characters on 'Badge of Honor', *LA Confidential*'s homage to the TV show *Dragnet* (which even reprises Jack Webb's famous tag line, 'Just the facts, ma'am'). *Dragnet* later went into TV syndication as 'Badge 714'. As the cynical Sid Hudgens says on the voiceover at the beginning of the film, 'Badge of Honour' (like *Dragnet*) portrays its policemen as heroes, and the LAPD as the 'best police force in the world'. Susan Anderson, in an article called 'A City Called Heaven', exposes the true face of the LAPD, in which she also mentions the 'toughness, efficiency and a kind of L.A. cool' promoted by *Dragnet* itself. 'From the start,' she argues,

> the LAPD was a volatile, corrupt fortress that had sixteen police chiefs in the thirteen years after its founding. In its earliest years, the LAPD was known for two characteristics; graft and corruption and extreme aggression toward the Chinese population, the largest nonwhite group in the city. (Anderson 1996: 352)

By World War 2, the Mexican community in LA had become the focus of its racist policies; in the postwar period, the African-American community has become its 'special target' (Anderson 1996: 353). The connection between governance and racism in LA that I emphasized at the beginning of this chapter finds its most typical, yet provocative and violent, manifestation in the LAPD and its relationships with the city's non-white inhabitants. Ironically, the 1950s and the 'heyday' of Chief Parker (who features in both versions of *LA Confidential*) was the time when the LAPD achieved a 'mythical status' according to Anderson (1996: 353), when the image or *performance* of its virtue (on the likes of *Dragnet*) masked its real operation as the instrument of corruption and repression in the city. It is this 'true' nature that *LA Confidential* reveals.

The title of *LA Confidential* refers to a cycle of 'lurid' and sensational crime films made in the mid-1950s, with titles such as *The Phenix City Story* (1955), *The Houston Story* (1956), *Las Vegas Shakedown* (1955) and *Kansas City Confidential* (1952). Curiously, there was no *Los Angeles Confidential*, suggesting that the ideological work done by *Dragnet* and other representations of LA effectively masked its connections to crime and corruption. This cycle of films was inspired by the Senate hearings on Organized Crime led by Senator Kefauver of Tennessee. Peter Biskind notes that 'On March 12, 1950, the TV cameras started to grind, and senator Estes Kefauver ... began summoning members of the underworld to testify before his Special Committee to Investigate Organized Crime in Interstate Commerce' (Biskind 2001: 196). Biskind comments on the Runyon-esque tone of the questions and answers, but the hearings were a ratings sensation, drawing 30 million viewers.

The hearings themselves fed on the furore created by a series of books written by two journalists, Jack Lait and Lee Mortimer, starting with *New York Confidential* in 1948, which 'offered the "low-down" on vice and corruption in four US cities' (Straw 1997: 113) until a series of lawsuits discredited them in the mid-50s. A parallel phenomenon were the 'scandal' magazines, such as *Confidential* and *Hush-Hush*, the latter of course featured in *LA Confidential*. Lait and Mortimer in fact attacked the Kefauver hearings for 'whitewashing crime', and argued that there existed a '"giant conspiracy" that "control[led] practically all crime in the United States"' (Biskind 2001: 191). The right-wing, paranoid and often racist tone of these books is the very attitude that James Ellroy attempts to portray in his 'LA Quartet' of novels. The vision of LA in these novels does indeed reveal conspiracy and corruption, violence and crime: but the conspiracies in the novels are organized by members of the LAPD themselves, and implicate the entire system of LA governance.

In his essay on Ellroy, Josh Cohen indicates the areas into which this chapter will now move, in analysing *LA Confidential* in terms of masculinity and governance. Cohen suggests that

> [t]he *LA Quartet*, spanning some 23 years in the life of the city, intricately maps its postwar boom, playing out Gothic dramas of criminal excess within the context of the reshaping of its built landscape by the convergent forces of land development and mass cultural spectacle. (Cohen 1997: 168)

Cohen chooses not to follow this line of enquiry and instead figures Los Angeles as a feminized 'object-world' of spectacle in which a 'crisis' of masculine subjectivity takes place. The intersection of familial (and particularly incest) themes with narratives of the expansion of the city provide an illuminating pathway into both Ellroy's *LA Confidential* and a significant intertext for the film adaptation, Robert Towne and Roman Polanski's *Chinatown*. Both trope the development of the city in terms of paternity, foregrounding the figure of the 'bad' or malign father and, as Manohla Dargis notes, 'sons confronting the sins of their fathers' (Dargis 2003: 40).

Chinatown was released in 1974, and its sunny and golden *mise-en-scène* is a clear influence on the look of *LA Confidential*. The narrative is focalized through the private investigator J. J. Gittes, played by Jack Nicholson, who is hired to provide sexually incriminating photographs of the head of Los Angeles's Water and Power department, Hollis Mulwray. It is revealed that Gittes is a pawn in a much larger game, and after Mulwray's murder, Gittes sets out to discover who set him up, and ascertain what conspiracy lies behind the initial events of the narrative. As such, it is in a clear lineage from previous film noir and detective fictions, and is set in the late-1930s (although its exact historical markers are, interestingly, repressed). The detective's quest leads him to knowledge and to a form of self-knowledge, although here it is only an intimation of his own impotence against far larger forces. Gittes discovers that Noah Cross, former business partner of Mulwray and father of Evelyn (Faye Dunaway), Mulwray's wife, is behind both Mulwray's murder and the conspiracy that surrounds it, but what is significant about Cross is that he owns Los Angeles's water supply; that he has been manipulating the supply to further his plans for city expansion into the San Fernando valley; and that he has been conducting a long, incestuous affair with his daughter Evelyn, which has produced a daughter/ grand-daughter. This young woman is the subject of the famous scene between Gittes and Evelyn Mulwray: he slaps her face repeatedly to get at the 'truth' of the young woman's identity, only to get the answers 'My sister', 'My daughter'. Both are true. The young woman is Evelyn's sister *and* daughter, an incestuous and monstrous symbol of the city's self-destructive and monstrous growth. Cross, played with wonderful malignancy by John Huston, is ultimately beyond Gittes's, or the law's, reach. He *is* LA governance, and so therefore cannot be constrained by it. His monstrosity is LA's monstrosity.

The narrative of LA expansion is thereby intersected with a narrative of malignant paternity, and the 'bad father' or evil patriarch attests to anxieties about masculinity and authority as well as civic corruption in LA. In Ellroy's *LA Confidential*, the source of corruption is the Dieterling family, a barely disguised caricature of the Disney empire. The location of murderous violence in one narrative thread is Douglas Borchard, an illegitimate son of the father Ray Dieterling born of a 'disturbed woman named Faye Borchard' (Ellroy 1994: 466), who closely resembles Dieterling's legitimate son Paul. Douglas becomes a child-killer in adulthood, and his father arranges plastic surgery and institutionalization to protect him, but Paul is suspected of the crimes. Dieterling agrees to the 'execution' of his innocent, legitimate son, by a policeman who demands 'absolute justice', sacrificing one son to protect the other, sacrificing the innocent to protect the guilty. This policeman is Preston Exley, the father of Edmund Exley, one of the three main narrative foci of the novel, himself a policeman who attempts to emulate or exceed his father's career. Ed Exley is, ironically enough, a returning war hero in the novel, but Exley's wartime 'soldier-subject' masculinity is compromised by the 'real' story behind his heroism: a mixture of cowardice and opportunism. The son's (Edmund's) threatened exposure of the crimes lead ultimately to the suicide of both fathers.

This summary represents only one of the novel's intricate narrative threads, and one that is entirely dispensed with in the screen adaptation. In another narrative thread, this time central to the film, another monstrous authority figure, the corrupt and racist Lieutenant (later Captain) Dudley Smith (played by James Cromwell), attempts to take over organized crime in LA. Preston Exley is dead in Hanson's screen version: many of his speeches of Ed Exley are uttered by Dudley Smith. In his review of the film for *Sight and Sound*, John Wrathall praises this decision:

> One inspired decision is to eliminate Preston Exley, the cop-turned-property developer who in the novel dominates his son Ed and the city as a whole. This allows Dudley Smith to loom more powerfully as Ed Exley's father figure, *éminence grise* and, ultimately, nemesis. In fact, Smith's opening speech to Exley, in which he tests his willingness to plant evidence, rig crime scenes, beat confessions out of suspects and shoot criminals in the back, belongs to Preston Exley in the book. ... If anything, Helgeland [the screenwriter] and Hanson's devastating ending, in which Exley can only beat Smith by stooping to Smith's cold-blooded, law-bending methods, improves on Ellroy's. (Wrathall 2001: 257)

I quote at length partly because I endorse Wrathall's conclusions, partly to emphasize yet again the connection between malign fatherhood and LA development, but also because it is a rare instance when a screen adaptation is judged to have 'improved' on the source novel. The ending of Ellroy's novel is messy and fails to provide the satisfying narrative resolution found in the film; the death of Jack Vincennes occurs in the last few pages of the novel and is not motivated like (nor is so powerful as) the screen version. However, I will return to the very last sentences of Ellroy's novel at the end of the chapter.

In *Chinatown*, J. J. Gittes, the private eye who focalizes the narrative, is a self-confessed 'snoop', and largely makes his money through preparing evidence for divorce cases. The film actually opens with a shot of photographs of a man and woman having adulterous sex: Gittes has just shown them to the cuckolded husband, 'Curly'. Gittes's status as a private eye is then inextricably bound up with looking and voyeurism, and Nicholson is shown on several occasions with a camera held to his eye.

We encountered several other instances of this in the 1970s conspiracy thrillers in Chapter 3. As the narrative of *Chinatown* makes clear, however, we cannot always trust the evidence of the camera: it requires knowledge-able analysis for its own stories or truths to be revealed. Gittes is profoundly unable to bring this kind of analysis to bear. He tries on several different explanations for the events unfolding around him throughout the film, and in the scene where he slaps Evelyn, the violence is preceded by yet another explication of his version of events. Gittes, as the nose-bandage he sports for half the film suggests, himself represents 'damaged' masculinity.

The title of the film itself, *Chinatown*, refers to some unexplained trauma in Gittes's former life when he was a policeman patrolling LA's Chinatown district. The enigma of the word's significance is reinforced by the end of the film: after Evelyn has been shot, Gittes is dragged away by one of his colleagues who says, 'It's Chinatown', meaning that there is some unforeseen vector or force which renders further action redundant, or that an unknowable and Other space has been reached and retreat is the only option. It is significant for LA fictions that this textual *aporia* is figured in terms of the urban space of LA's oldest ethnic minority. It is also significant that the usual restoration of the legitimate heterosexual couple is undone at the end of the film. Noah Cross regains control over his daughter/grand-daughter after Evelyn's death. The relationship between Evelyn and Gittes is negated: the malign influence of the 'bad father' is restored.

Chinatown is predicated, as is much detective and noir fiction, on the uncovering of secrets. The words 'revelation' or 'uncovering' point to the intensely visual nature of this narrative structure. It is the quest to make the hidden seen, to make the secret manifest, which drives the detective. *LA Confidential* is no different, though the novel's deployment of the Dieterling narrative thread emphasizes this motif more strongly. Its absence in the film adaptation refocuses the crime narrative onto Pierce Patchett's 'stable' of movie-star call-girls, and Dud Smith's takeover of LA orga-nized crime. It also centres the film on the dynamic between the three male protagonists, all policemen, a homosocial triangle that is common to Ellroy's fictions: it is also discernable in *American Tabloid* (1995) and *The Cold Six Thousand* (2001). They are Edmund Exley (Guy Pearce), who begins the film as a sergeant and ends the film a twice-decorated lieutenant; Officer Bud White (Russell Crowe), a 'strongarm' detective who has 'a thing for helping women'; and Sergeant Jack Vincennes (Kevin Spacey), a celebrity-infatuated Narco cop who is the 'technical advisor' on *LA Confidential*'s *Dragnet*-clone, 'Badge of Honor'. This homosocial triangle is mediated by the circulation of looks and looking in the film adaptation of *LA Confidential*.

Each of the three central male protagonists is framed looking in mirrors or glass, staring at and through their own reflections. Ed Exley is shown behind a two-way mirror, 'snooping' on a scene where senior officers are seeking to find scapegoats for a police riot that took place in the Hollywood Station cells, in which Mexican 'suspects' were assaulted. Exley uses the incident to parlay his way to a spot in the Detective Bureau. The shot which shows his reflection is composed so that Exley's self-satisfied countenance is to the left, Chief Parker (the creator of the 'new' LAPD) to the right, and between them a shot of City Hall, until the 1950s the only building to exceed the 150-feet limit in the centre of the city, symbol of power and dominance. Exley is framed as one of Chief Parker's 'coming men', the 'clean-cut hero' as true 'organization man'. The shot also emphasizes Exley's spectacles: Parker, like Dud Smith, warns Ed to 'lose the glasses', emphasizing the performativity required of the LA policeman. A detective has to look like a detective. This mirror motif is repeated at the end of the film, after Exley has shot Dudley Smith in the back. This time, however, he is in the interrogation room and his superiors are outside. The shot assumes the position of the voyeur or watching subject, but here it is the ranking policemen who both watch Exley and are reflected in the glass of the two-way mirror. As in the shot between Exley and Parker, facial images are superimposed, but here Exley has 'substance', and it is the faces of Parker and Loew who are reflected and ghostly. Exley's transition to 'organization man' is signified by his status as the object of another's look, a gaze which authenticates his 'presence' rather than emphasizes his performativity.

Jack Vincennes is the subject of the next mirror-shots. Vincennes is nicknamed 'Hollywood Jack' in the film, whereas in the book he is called 'Trashcan Jack' (which refers to a back-story event when he dumped Charlie Parker into a garbage bin after rousting him for marijuana possession). Jack Vincennes, played with a mixture of suave self-regard and repressed anxiety by Kevin Spacey, is perhaps the most changed character in the film adaptation. In Ellroy's novel, Jack conducts a long and inappropriate relationship (then marriage) with the daughter of the powerfully connected Morrow family. Jack is single in the film, and seems most in love with himself and his own image. The hints of narcissism in Jack's character – the careful tailoring, the well-groomed hair, the stylish manner – destabilize his masculinity to the extent that one suspects that Jack Vincennes is all performance and no substance. In her BFI Modern Classic essay on *LA Confidential*, Manohla Dargis hints at a similar performativity: '[Jack's] personality seems learned from Dean Martin, whose lush-life saunter and slur Spacey lightly borrows' (Dargis 2003: 20). In one shot, Jack looks into a full-length mirror to appraise his trim appearance, but angled side-mirrors split Jack's image, emphasizing duality or potential disintegration. The connection between narcissism and effeminacy also explains the visual composition of the shot that introduces his character. Vincennes is carefully placed, dancing seemingly intimately with a beautiful woman, which seems to assert his heterosexuality (in fact the film is at pains to do so for all three main male characters, a point I shall return to shortly).

However, as the film progresses, Vincennes becomes troubled by his complicity in the exposure and downfall of the young actor Matt Reynolds. In an early scene in the film, Jack 'busts' Reynolds for 'felony possession of

marijuana', and is photographed by the *Hush-Hush* team doing so. Jack gets
kickbacks from his 'celebrity' police work, and later he is offered more
money to tempt the disgraced Reynolds to seduce the closeted homosexual
DA, Ellis Loew. Homosexuality is a source of scandal (and through
blackmail, vulnerability) in the film, though elsewhere in Ellroy's crime
novels it is a disturbing and disruptive potentiality in several seemingly
'straight' male policemen, the most obvious example being LA County
Sheriff Danny Upshaw in *The Big Nowhere*, who eventually commits suicide
when his masculine police persona and his homosexual desire come into
conflict. Vincennes helps persuade Reynolds to bed DA Loew, by telling
the young actor 'think of it as an acting job, showbiz'. This again
emphasizes performativity as central to both gender and sexual desire, and
indicates that Jack knows all about sexual orientation as performance. Jack
goes to a bar and has second thoughts about his complicity in Reynolds's
further disgrace. The gaze into the mirror here represents a form of self-
knowledge, critical rather than narcissistic. Vincennes attempts to save
Reynolds from the fate to which he has consigned him, but when he goes
to the place of assignation, Reynolds has already been murdered.

The third shot is the 'rogue cop', Bud White (Russell Crowe), looking
into his own rear-view mirror, a gaze which is in fact conflated with his
desire for Lynn Bracken (Kim Basinger). Bud, with his 'thing for helping
women', is most clearly situated within a heterosexual frame of reference in
the film, and he is the only one whose narrative trajectory is resolved in a
stable heterosexual relationship by the film's close. As Lynn says to Exley
in the final scene, dialogue lifted directly from the novel, 'Some men get the
world, some men get ex-hookers and a trip to Arizona' (Ellroy 1994: 480).
Bud typifies the 'wartime' masculinity of the late-1940s, the aggressive male
whose soldier-subjectivity is connected to troubling and excessive violence.
It is no surprise, then, that he is the character most rigorously relocated into
the 'domestic mystique' by the end of the film's, and novel's, narrative.
Bud's masculinity, in fact, is least identified with signs of performativity in
LA Confidential.

Jack Vincennes's masculine subjectivity is too destabilized to survive
either narrative: like Danny Upshaw from *The Big Nowhere*, his death
indicates the anxiety-provoking intersection of homosociality and homosexuality. Exley, by contrast, is the 'organization man', whose ambition
marks him as one of the professional 'power elite' of the future. His
heterosexuality is asserted in the film by having sex with Lynn Bracken, but
what Lynn says before sex is of most interest: 'Fucking me and fucking Bud
White aren't the same thing, you know'. Though this can be read as 'having
sex with me isn't the same thing as gaining power over Bud', the
destabilizing homosexual connotations are clear. Manohla Dargis makes
this explicit, citing Exley's 'antagonistic and repressed desire for Bud'
(Dargis 2003: 22–3). This is further emphasized in a previous scene, where
Jack and Exley stand outside Lynn's house and watch Bud and Lynn making
love. The voyeurism constitutive of the male gaze is in evidence here (Kim

Basinger's body is staged for the look of both men and for the audience), but Lynn's comment perhaps makes us retrospectively question who Exley is actually looking at. Is it Lynn (as the narrative would have us believe), or is it Bud? In Exley's case, rather than the problematic of desire marking the male subject for death, as it does for Jack, his role as 'organization man' enables the contradictions between homosociality and homosexuality to be repressed, if not resolved.

This is most apparent in the scene of violent confrontation between Bud and Exley, after Bud has been shown photos of Exley 'fucking' Lynn. This scene is best explored by further recourse to the critical work of Eve Kosofsky Sedgwick, and also Steve Neale's analysis of 'masculinity as spectacle'. In the film of LA Confidential, Jack Vincennes is killed about two-thirds of the way through the narrative, unlike in the novel, where he dies a few pages from the end. This is done, I would suggest, to focus upon the Bud–Lynn–Exley erotic triangle, where desire and the gaze are circulated. Sedgwick suggests that in texts that feature the 'erotic triangle', the relationship between the two men is as important, or is more important, than either relationship between the men and the female erotic object. She writes:

> In any erotic triangle, the bond that links the two rivals is as intense and potent as the bond that links either of the rivals to the beloved: that the bonds of 'rivalry' and 'love', differently as they are experienced, are equally powerful and in many cases equivalent. (Sedgwick 1985: 21)

Further to Sedgwick's argument is that, in a patriarchal and homophobic culture, the repressed element of desire renders representations of possible homosexual relations as homosocial ones, with the 'beloved', or female object, a 'counter' in a sublimated erotic game between the two men. The images of Lynn and Exley, which drive Bud into homicidal rage, compromise Bud's sole possession and knowledge of Lynn as an erotic object, and enforce his equivalence with Exley. This is not necessarily to suggest that Exley desires Bud; however, the insistently sexualized conflict between them does reintroduce the possibility of homosexuality into homosociality, that they are, in Sedgwick's word, a 'continuum' rather than mutually exclusive.

The violence of their final confrontation, if read according to Steve Neale's analysis, also exposes anxiety about male desire. Neale's explored the spectatorial paradigm of Mulvey's 1975 article to open a space for the investigation of screen masculinities. He wrote:

> ... in a heterosexual and patriarchal society, the male body cannot be marked explicitly as the erotic object of another male look: that look must be motivated in some other way, its erotic component repressed. ... We see male bodies stylized and fragmented by close-ups, but our look is not direct, it is heavily mediated by the looks of the characters involved. And those looks are marked not by desire, but rather fear, or hatred, or aggression. (Neale 1993: 14, 18)

The violence between Bud White and Exley corresponds to Neale's paradigm of the male gaze: violence and aggression dominate in a scene which will eventually enforce their mutual need in terms of bringing their investigation (and the narrative) to a successful resolution. One particular image emphasizes the connection between violence, power and sexuality. Bud screws up a photograph of Exley and Lynn and attempts to force it into Exley's mouth. Bud leans over the seated Exley, the framing emphasizing Bud's physical power over his opponent. This, I would argue, is a representation of oral rape, with Bud taking the 'masculine' or dominating position, and Exley (who is seated, his face level with Bud's groin), the subjected, feminized position. Earlier in the film, Jack Vincennes tells Exley that because he had contributed to the downfall of Bud's partner, Bud will 'fuck you for it if it takes him the rest of his life'. Once Bud has done so, here, the bonds of homosociality can be reasserted.

This scene also indicates, perhaps, the limits of Sedgwick's use of the term 'continuum' to characterize the connection between male homosociality and the disruptive possibility of homoerotic desire. 'Continuum' suggests linearity, a spectrum of male behaviour with homosexual desire at one end and violent homophobia (or repression) at the other. The scene of violence between Exley and Bud White, I would suggest, indicates that there is a circular or iterative connection between homosociality and homoerotic desire. The violence of this scene signifies the film's most extreme moment of the repression of homoeroticism, and its repression and transformation into homosocial bonding. However, deploying an analysis of the male gaze here suggests that this moment of homosociality is ruptured by desire, and that the violence is insistently sexualized. The presence of the image of Lynn – the motivator of Bud's homicidal rage – also serves to remind us of the third point in the erotic triangle, Lynn as counter in a sublimated erotic game between the two men. It is at this point of maximal repression of homoeroticism that, ironically, its presence is most manifest.

The final scene of the film emphasizes the connection of Ed and Bud, at the expense of the position of Lynn. After the two men have fought it out with Dud Smith's men at the Victory Motel, their bond forged in mutually supportive violence, the film shifts to Exley receiving his second medal. He walks out of City Hall with Lynn, and finds Bud, wounded and mute, in the back of a car. Bud's enforced silence focuses our attention between the looks passing between the two men. The male gaze is clearly evident here, and the primacy of the Ed–Bud relationship indicated by the visual exclusion of Lynn from their reunion. The two are framed in close-up in two-shot, their faces as close (or closer) than Jack Vincennes and his dance partner at the start of the film. Exley reaches through the window and grasps Bud's hand, and says 'Yes'. This ambiguous and enigmatic word leaves open the status of their relationship, and what kind of 'bond' it signifies. As the car drives away, Bud is in the foreground, waving to Exley: the last shot is a reversed point-of-view of the car as it drives away from City Hall and LA. Again, Lynn is notable by her absence. The novel ends similarly, but emphasizes still more strongly the bond between the two men:

> Ed kissed her cheek. Lynn got in the car, rolled up the windows. Bud pressed his hands to the glass.
>
> Ed touched his side, palms half the man's size. The car moved – Ed ran with it, hands against hands. A turn into traffic, a goodbye toot on the horn. (Ellroy 1994: 480)

Bud is 'the man': what, then, is Ed? The pane of glass becomes highly symbolic of the impossibility of tender, physical (homoerotic) contact between the two men, within the terms of postwar American homosociality. The glass is transparent, hardly there at all, but its presence enforces an unbridgeable distance between men. Like the word 'Chinatown', the pane of glass represents the place where noir fictions may not tread. The continuum of homosociality and homosexuality is ultimately unspeakable for *LA Confidential*, and the gap between the two is represented in the film by the images of Ed, then the car, receding into the distance.

The performativity of masculinity finds its most successful representative in Exley, who is able to alter his relationship to others (and after his murder of some African-American 'suspects', is called another name: 'Shotgun Ed'). Exley's successful masquerade as a detective (and as a morally unblemished policeman) is ranged against other forms of masculinity. Jack Vincennes is conflicted; Bud White symbolizes a kind of anti-masquerade, as he is unable to present himself as anything other than an uncomplicated and somewhat violent man. His masculinity achieves a kind of 'authenticity' denied Exley, a point made over and over again in Ellroy's novel, where Exley's ambition and deception is consistently criticized as deficient masculinity by both Lynn and the rape victim Inez Soto. In the film, however, male masquerade is staged against the figure of Lynn Bracken, who of course 'plays' Veronica Lake for male clients. Female sexuality in *LA Confidential* is bound up with both economics and disguise, but Lynn's masquerade is knowing. When she takes Bud into her own bedroom, it is a revelation of the 'authentic' identity of 'Lynn Bracken', but also a self-conscious *coup-de-théâtre*. She has an awareness of her own role-playing in a way that the masculine protagonists only belatedly reach, if at all. While her sexuality is clearly marked as performative, so, ultimately, is masculine desire; her conscious masquerading serves to foreground the unconscious masquerading of masculinity.

The markers of Lynn's difference can also be found in the social structure of the text: where the importance of the male homosocial groups consistently open the possibility of male homoeroticism, there is no such possibility for Lynn Bracken. The only other female characters of any substance are Susan Lefferts, the prostitute who is killed at the Nite Owl; her elderly mother, Mrs Lefferts; and Inez Soto, the rape victim, whose rather larger role in the novel is compressed to a few scenes in Hanson's film version. This absence of female homosocial bonds or homoerotic desire indicates the monovalent heterosexual femininity of Lynn Bracken, as opposed to the destablized masculinities of Exley, Bud White and Jack Vincennes. Her 'true' identity of Lynn (as opposed to the performance as Veronica Lake), revealed in her small 'hometown' bedroom, is (ironically but not coincidentally) authenticated by her unambiguous heterosexuality. It is also no accident that the least performative, most 'authentic' male, is Bud White, whose masculinity is most rigorously repositioned, within the romance plot with Lynn Bracken.

In Steven Cohan's conception, the hegemony of the 'domestic mystique' in the 1950s, while attempting to impose a hierarchy of hegemonic and subordinate subject positions for postwar American men, actually indicates the constructed, performative and fundamentally unstable categories of gender and desire which are ideologically figured as the normative. *LA Confidential's* versions of masculinity both reinforce the 'domestic mystique' (in the trajectory of Bud White) but also offer rather more conflicted and problematic masculinities in Jack Vincennes and Edmund Exley. The question I would now like to posit, by way of drawing to a conclusion, is: why do novels such as Ellroy's *LA Confidential* (and others in the 'LA Quartet'), and films such as Hanson's *LA Confidential*, find the 1950s such a fruitful period for rethinking hegemonic masculinity in the 1990s?

The answer, perhaps, can be approached by way of Mike Davis's criticisms of what he calls Ellroy's 'delirious parody' of noir (Davis 1998: 45). Davis writes:

> In building such an all-encompassing *noir* mythology ..., Ellroy risks extinguishing the genre's tensions, and inevitably, its power. In his pitch blackness there is no light left to cast shadows and evil becomes a forensic banality. The result feels very much like the actual moral texture of the Reagan-Bush era: a supersaturation of corruption that fails any longer to outrage or even interest. (Davis 1998: 45)

The key phrase here, I think, is the 'moral texture of the Reagan-Bush era'. The all-encompassing conspiracies of *LA Confidential* do suggest a critique of Los Angeles's development, yet, as in *Chinatown*, the revelation of that corruption is followed by an assertion of the limits of 'law', and ultimately, the necessity of forming an accommodation with that corruption. Unlike Noah Cross, Dudley Smith is defeated, but only at the cost of Ed Exley's own complicity with the LAPD's violent and corrupt methods. (Exley's morally conflicted 'victory' repeats the dilemma of Ranse Stoddard (James Stewart) at the end of John Ford's *The Man Who Shot Liberty Valance*, that I shall consider in the next chapter: liberal, democratic sentiments must give way to the priority of violence if the rule of law is to be achieved.) Exley's symbolic patricide also casts the narrative of LA development as generational or Oedipal struggle, but of course Exley will himself take the place of the 'bad father'.

If the contemporary 'crisis in masculinity' is, as Susan Faludi suggests in *Stiffed* (1999), a failure of the fathers of the postwar generation, then it is little wonder that Ellroy and Hanson found the 1950s a particularly significant period for rethinking both noir and postwar masculinities. The 1990s 'crisis in masculinity' is in direct relationship to the renegotiation of male subject positions in the immediate postwar period, for, as the example of Ed Exley suggests, the sons recapitulate the mistakes of the fathers. Ironically for contemporary America, the 'domestic mystique' worked all too well. The problem for the late-1950s was not the insertion of hegemonic masculinity into imperatives of responsibility and domesticity, but the emasculating or feminizing nature of this renegotiation. From the problem of too much (or aggressive/threatening) masculinity, anxieties surfaced about too little assertive masculinity. The same problematic is at work in contemporary American culture and in *LA Confidential*. Bud White's masculinity is too violent; Jack Vincennes too conflicted/effeminized. If the 'domestic mystique', and the elevation of the 'breadwinner' to a masculine ideal, corresponded in the 1950s to the political hegemony of a professional (military/industrial) power elite, what version of hegemonic masculinity would correspond to the ideological imperatives of the 1990s? *LA Confidential's* seeming validation of Ed Exley ('organization man' personified) as the man of the future could indicate a renewed conservative and corporate hegemony. *LA Confidential*, and its renegotiations of both the film noir and postwar masculinities, may be partaking of a wider cultural project to redefine hegemonic masculinity in a manner similar to the early 1950s.

LA Confidential's vision of the continuing centrality of the white male policeman to issues of governance in LA, and to postwar masculinity, has strong and rather disturbing resonances for the 1990s. Although the novel was written and published before the Rodney King beating and the 1992 riots, the film must certainly have been aware of the urgency of gender, power and racial relations to contemporary LA in particular and the United States in general. While racism seems to be part of the everyday discourse for LAPD policemen in both Ellroy's novels and the film of *LA Confidential*, outright critique of this is repressed in the texts in favour of renegotiations of gender and desire. Neither form of *LA Confidential* partakes of Charles Jenks's sunny vision of LA's 'heterogeneity', but it is significant that both are also far more willing to destabilize representations of hegemonic masculinity than they are willing to tackle the long Los Angeles history of discrimination and urban violence. It is paradoxical and somewhat disturbing that the LA noir fictions I have considered here locate their considerations of masculinity and governance through the reimagination of Los Angeles's troubled past, at the same time as they selectively portray that history of expansion and corruption as a series of personal struggles between powerful (white) men.

CHAPTER SEVEN

Old Age Westerns

Western myth and Western ideology

Criticism of the American Western has often concentrated upon its relation to history; or more properly, the ways in which the Western recapitulates the 'myths' of the American West and obscures history. In the 2001 AFI Reader, *Westerns: Films Through History*, the editor Janet Walker suggests that a significant tendency among writing on the Western is to 'receive the western-as-myth as being set apart from history ... [and that] while history is argumentative and discursive, westerns give *narrative form* to ideological beliefs and values' (Walker 2001: 5). Walker criticizes this tendency; the essays collected in the Reader concentrate on revisionist Westerns such as Robert Altman's *Buffalo Bill and the Indians* (1976), where the Western fulfils 'a historiographic function by evincing a self-consciousness about the history writing process at the same time that they share in it' (Walker 2001: 13). Although she suggests that myth and history are in dialogue, that 'there is a historiographic element to mythological discourse [as well as a] mythographic component to history writing' (Walker 2001: 7), Walker's own revisionist project seems to privilege a certain kind of Western. Drawing upon Linda Hutcheon's formulation of the 'historiographic metafiction', Walker argues that this interplay between history and myth is best revealed in self-reflexive Westerns like *Buffalo Bill and the Indians*, which are about the ways in which the West becomes 'the Wild West', a spectacular, and fictional, representation of the true conditions of the frontier.

Walker's argument, however it might want to promote a 'postmoderniz-ing' of the Western, and decentring the opposition between 'myth' and 'history' found in other criticism, in fact preserves those very distinctions, coming down on the side of history. While acknowledging the pervasive-ness of 'myth', Westerns are understood by Walker as recoverable to historiography, because they refer to a 'geographically and historically delimited time and place' (Walker 2001: 13), a rhetorical move that categorizes the Western as a historical fiction and brackets off the hundred-year history of the screen Western (let alone the even older history of the Western novel, traced by Henry Nash Smith back to Fenimore Cooper's Leatherstocking novels, and which encompasses the dime-novel, which fictionalized the West even as it was being settled); a history which says much more about the ideological structures informing the cultural repre-sentation of the United States than it does about how the West 'really' was.

My reading of the Western is political or ideological, because I believe that a fundamental part of the Western's narrative is the encoding of the political development of the United States as a nation-state. This is not a particularly new insight – Andre Bazin argued that 'the western is rooted in the history of the American nation which it exalts directly or indirectly' in 1955 (Bazin 1971: 150) – but it is insufficiently worked through in criticism of the Western. In *The BFI Companion to the Western*, an entry on 'States and territories' suggests that 'only to a small extent ... does the political process of acquiring statehood figure in Westerns' (Buscombe 1993: 225), citing John Ford's *The Man Who Shot Liberty Valance* as one that does depict this process in terms of 'progress, which statehood will bring but which remaining in territorial status will thwart' (Buscombe 1993: 225). In this chapter, I will argue that this seeming absence is in fact an invisibility, brought about by the ubiquity of the ideological narrative of 'progress' towards the nation-state, as a fundamental ideological substrata of the Western and of American culture. The mythic narrative of the Western is underpinned by the ideological imperative of 'progress'. We can see this in the self-consciously epic Western *How The West Was Won* (premiered the same year, 1962, as *The Man Who Shot Liberty Valance* and *Ride the High Country*, both of which I will discuss in this chapter). Filmed and projected with the three-camera/projector process Cinerama, made by three directors (including John Ford) in five segments, and starring a whole galaxy of Hollywood stars, *How The West Was Won*, as its title suggests, fully embodies the myth of progress, though it is one of the very last Hollywood Westerns to do so. A revisiting of the 'settler' epics such as *The Covered Wagon* (1923) and *The Big Trail* (1930), the ideology of progress is explicitly revealed in its estranging final shots: the camera, helicopter-borne, looks down at the clover-leaf-shaped intersections of Californian freeways, then moves to the blue of the Pacific Ocean. At the end of *How The West Was Won*, the frontier is the Pacific shore, and the West has become incorporated into the modern Nation.

The term 'myth', as I have said, is often used in criticism of the Western; its derivation is in part from the classic American school of criticism of American literature, the 'myth and symbol' school, which understood American narratives to be romances, 'mythic' or archetypal struggles. In this conception, Melville, rather than Henry James, is the classic nineteenth-century American writer. 'Myth' is also used in derivation from the work of French Structuralist theorists, such as the anthropologist Claude Levi-Strauss, as in one of the first modern critical texts on the Western, Will Wright's *Sixguns and Society*. Myth, argued Wright,

> is a communication from a society to its members: the social concepts and atti-
> tudes determined by its history and institutions of a society are communicated
> to its members through its myths. (Wright 1975: 16)

Just as 'tribal myths' encode a world-view, and enable the members of a society to operate as a society through the communication of this shared world-view, so, argues Wright, does the Western function as a myth for American society. Setting aside the problem of mapping the cultural processes of a small tribal society onto one of 250 million people, 'myth' here suggests a narrative representation of the society, which encodes certain assumptions and 'concepts' about that society. Wright is using the word approximately to Roland Barthes in *Mythologies*, who analysed key cultural artefacts in the 1950s to reveal the underlying (and underpinning) social, cultural and political structures of postwar France. (The most famous, in 'Myth Today', is his reading of the picture of the black soldier standing in front of the *Tricoleur*.)

Wright's project is also structural: by attempting to map out the narrative functions of the 'classical' Western plot (in the manner of the Russian formalist, Vladimir Propp), Wright is not only trying to formulate a 'universal' narrative of the Western, but to comprehend its social 'meaning'. The problem is, of course, that by conceptualizing in terms of 'myth', the narrative is dehistoricized as it is universalized into narrative functions. It is significant, of course, that Wright does not read the Western in terms of ideology, even though the 'deep structure' of American society and culture is really what he is aiming to reveal. This, I think, is a paradigmatic case for criticism of the Western: with recourse to either 'myth' or 'historiography', the ideological and political implications of the Western can be, and have been, elided, or avoided altogether. In this chapter, I shall use the word 'myth', but not in the sense of an underlying structure of beliefs or assumptions, or the expression of a world-view. For this, I shall use the word 'ideology', in an Althusserian sense. Althusser's definition is: ⊬ 'Ideology represents the imaginary relationship of individuals to their real conditions of existence' (Althusser 1971: 153). Ideology is a false understanding of 'reality' itself, one that effaces its own presence by insisting that the dominant ideology and organization of life is in fact the 'natural' one. I shall use 'myth' in a more limited sense, as an archetypal or symbolic narrative, informed by ideology.

In his revised edition of *Horizons West*, Jim Kitses seems to rather disapprove of 'ideological' criticism of the Western (and gender criticism, as well). What he diagnoses as a 'pervasiveness' of this kind of criticism in recent times troubles him; in texts such as Lee Clark Mitchell's *Westerns: Making the Man in Fiction and Film* (1996), Kitses sees a 'reduction of the genre to its discourse on masculinity' (Kitses 2004: 17). While admitting that these lines of enquiry have been fruitful to understanding the Western (and writing about both ideology and gender in the analyses of key directors), he defends his auteurist approach partly by indicting the reductiveness of others. While, clearly, the Western is not simply 'about' masculinity, my contention here will be that masculinity is a vital construction with regard to the ideological narratives of the Western. My intention here is not to use an 'ideological' criticism as a stick to beat the genre with, but rather, as in the foregoing chapters of this book, to investigate the ways in which masculinity and the nation-state are mutually reinforcing constructions.

The history, myths and ideology of the West were first expressed by the American historian Fredrick J. Turner, in his famous lecture 'The Significance of the Frontier in American History', which he gave in 1893, just three years after the date he himself gave as the 'closing of the Frontier'. The so-called 'Turner thesis' is one of the most important, and widely debated, concepts in American historiography. It is also a recurrent touchstone in criticism of Western films: both Stanley Corkin in *Cowboys as Cold Warriors* (2004) and Philip French in *Westerns* (2005) note its importance early in their books. Essentially, Turner argued that what defined the experience of Americans, and therefore was the foundational principle for the character of American life, was the frontier. (Turner's thesis is implicitly racial, of course, ignoring both slavery and the 'great dying' of the Native American peoples, both more important to a contemporary understanding of the history of the United States of America.)

Turner's thesis buttresses, and is an expression of, 'Manifest Destiny': that it was, and is, the God-given right of the 'American people' to claim the North American continent. The frontier, argued Turner, was the 'meeting point between savagery and civilization' (Turner 1963: 28), the point of evolution (he himself uses this post-Darwinian metaphor) into modernity. It is the experience of the frontier itself, however, which makes the American character:

> that coarseness and strength combined with acuteness and inquisitiveness; that practical, inventive turn of mind, quick to find expedients; that masterful grasp of material things, lacking in the artistic but powerful to effect great ends; that restless, nervous energy; that dominant individualism, working for good and for evil, and withal that buoyancy and exuberance which comes with freedom – these are the traits of the frontier, or traits called out elsewhere because of the existence of the frontier. (Turner 1963: 57)

It is interesting to consider the optimism and vitality of this expression when set against the European tenor of social writing in the 1890s; where European writers worried about 'degeneration' and what seemed to be the 'declining stock' of the Imperial race, the American is manly, virile and active. The frontier, it seems, generates the evolution of the European into the American, in terms very like what would come to be known as the 'melting pot': 'in the crucible of the frontier the immigrants were Americanized, and fused into a mixed race, English in neither nationality or characteristics', wrote Turner; the frontier was 'the line of most rapid and effective Americanization' (Turner 1963: 44, 29).

Turner's mythic narrative of the frontier, however, is not only about the virile American character; it is about American democracy. It is the conditions of frontier life itself, argued Turner, which gave America its quintessentially democratic flavour. '[T]he most important effect of the frontier has been the promotion of democracy in here and in Europe', argued Turner, somewhat tenuously; 'frontier individualism has from the beginning promoted democracy' (Turner 1963: 51). For Turner, American character *is* American democracy, and the typical American character is formed on the frontier. Turner's conception of 'character' I take to mean masculinity, for not only is Turner's writing gendered, but its expression of American-*ness* seems peculiarly male. The very same identification of American-ness with masculinity and Nation can be found in Theodore Roosevelt's phrase of 1899: the cowboy, the Westerner, had the 'stern, manly qualities that are invaluable to a nation' (Buscombe 1993: 181). Turner's conflation of 'character' with 'democracy' is central to the argument of this chapter, as in the Western films I am considering, masculine characteristics are bound up with ideas and ideals of America and American-ness. A kind of martial or violent masculinity is encoded as central to the mythic narrative of the frontier. This is clearly marked in Turner's assertion of the 'importance of the frontier ... as a military training school, keeping alive the power of resistance to oppression, and developing the stalwart and rugged qualities of the frontiersman' (Turner 1963: 38). The centrality of violence to the Western has been a staple of criticism since Richard Slotkin's *Regeneration Through Violence* (1973), which investigated the narratives of redemptive violence that were vital to early American literature, and have remained so, especially in the Western. I shall return to this theme towards the end of this chapter in a consideration of Peckinpah's *The Wild Bunch*.

The implicit importance of the frontier, for Turner, is that is enables the construction of the American nation-state: 'the growth of nationalism and the evolution of American institutions were dependent on the advance of the frontier,' he argued (Turner 1963: 46). The movement of the frontier westward brings the national boundaries ever closer to their present positions, thus giving rhetorical significance to Turner's evolutionary metaphors: the frontier represents 'progress' towards a federated USA. Turner himself characterizes the westward expansion thus:

> The fall line marked the frontier in the seventeenth century; the Alleghanies that of the eighteenth; the Mississippi that of the first quarter of the nineteenth; the Missouri that of the middle of this century (omitting the California movement); and the belt of the Rocky Mountains and the arid tract, the present frontier [in 1893]. Each was won by a series of Indian wars. (Turner 1963: 33)

This last, almost offhand, phrase is one of the few indications that westward expansion and 'settlement' was, in fact, dispossession and exclusion. Turner's list also entirely obscures the historical processes by which land was acquired. These include the Louisiana Purchase of 1803, the Florida Purchase of 1819, the agreement with Britain that the 49th parallel would divide the USA from Canada, and the Gadsden Purchase which defined the border between Mexico and the South-western states of New Mexico and

Arizona (1853). As Rick Worland and Edward Countryman note, '[i]f that
land seemed "free" it was because white Americans did not have to pay the
price of its purchase. That price instead was borne by the Indians and by
conquered south-western Hispanics', whose land was taken away from
them (Worland and Countryman 1998: 185). The Western, like Turner's
frontier thesis, ideologically masks the history of westward expansion/
appropriation through a mythic narrative of progress, and a democratic
ethos forged through the 'pioneer spirit' of the rugged individualist.

The Man Who Shot Liberty Valance

Henry Nash Smith, in his seminal book on the American West, *Virgin Land*
(1950), devotes a chapter to the Turner thesis. Smith suggests that there is a
curious doubleness about Turner's concept of the frontier:

> For him as for his predecessors, the outer limit of agricultural settlement is the
> boundary of civilization, and in his thought ... we must therefore begin by
> distinguishing two Wests, one beyond and one within this all-important line.
> (Smith 1970: 251)

We must not forget, either, that it is the 'line', the boundary, the frontier
itself, that is important to Turner, neither what is before ('savagery') nor
what is behind ('civilization'). What is missing in Turner's conception of the
frontier is the *direction of its movement*: from East to West. As Smith noted,
Turner's argument inadvertently renders the settled land as an undemo-
cratic one, because it is no longer 'free'. Once the frontier passes on, the
settled land becomes enclosed, civilized, subject to community and social
institutions. The conditions of democracy and freedom are produced, in
Turner's thesis, in the moment of contestation, not after land has been
settled. As Smith notes, Turner 'had based his highest value, democracy, on
free land. But the westward advance of civilization had caused free land
to disappear. What then was to become of democracy?' (Smith 1970: 257).
In embodying the democratic moment in a moving boundary, Turner
inadvertently indicates its fragility.

One of the key problems for the mythic narrative of the construction of
the American nation-state is how democracy is produced. Is it the unstable
and shifting frontier that produces democracy, as Turner argued, or the
values of the East, transported West? This is at the heart of John Ford's
The Man Who Shot Liberty Valance. The narrative of the film begins with a
train, symbol of modernity in the Western, for good or ill, arriving at the
station of the small western town of Shinbone, now 'civilized'. Horse-and-
carts trot through quiet streets lined with substantial houses. At the station,
Senator Ranse Stoddard (James Stewart) gets off the train with his wife
Hallie (Vera Miles). They have come home, for the funeral of an old friend,
Tom Doniphon (John Wayne). Accosted by a young cub reporter, then the

editor of the *Shinbone Star* newspaper, Stoddard tells the story of his first
arrival in Shinbone (as an attorney-at-law), how he won Hallie's heart, and
how Liberty Valance — the enforcer of the cattle barons who have ranches
beyond the Picketwire, who menace the citizens of Shinbone — was killed.
The senator is known as 'the Man Who Shot Liberty Valance': in the course
of the film, we find this not to be quite the truth. Ford's film is, though
late in the director's career, still definable in Will Wright's typology of
the Western as 'classical'. The archetypal 'classical Western', according to
Wright, 'is the story of the lone stranger who rides into a troubled town
and cleans it up, winning the respect of the townfolk and the love of the
schoolmarm' (Wright 1975: 32), a definition most applicable to George
Stevens's 1953 *Shane*, but also to Ford's own Wyatt Earp story, *My Darling
Clementine* (1946).

What differentiates *Liberty Valance* from the 'classical' structure is that
the 'lone stranger' is split into two different characters, Stoddard and
Doniphon, played by two actors with widely divergent star personas
(Stewart and Wayne), who embody the values and attributes of East and
West respectively. Laura Mulvey, in 'Afterthoughts on "Visual Pleasure
and Narrative Cinema"', also notes the 'splitting of the Western hero'
(Mulvey 1993: 130); in her reading of Stoddard/Doniphon binary, one
character 'celebrat[es] integration into society through marriage, the other
celebrat[es] resistance to social demands and responsibilities, above all those
of marriage and the family, the sphere represented by women' (Mulvey
1993: 130). Stewart, playing in the main 'flashback' sequences of the film
a character some years younger than Stewart's own age, revives the liberal,
democratic, all-American persona of his Frank Capra movies (such as
It's a Wonderful Life of 1946); John Wayne's Doniphon, individualistic
and physically dominant, recapitulates the heroic (though flawed) figure
found in earlier Ford Westerns.

When he arrives on a stagecoach on the outskirts of Shinbone, Stoddard
is beaten by Valance's gang, and whipped sadistically by Valance (Lee
Marvin), as they rob the coach; taken in at Shinbone's saloon-cum-
steakhouse, Stoddard dons a pinafore and does the washing up in order
to pay his way. He is explicitly feminized, his masculinity softened and
destabilized, as James Stewart's characters were in Anthony Mann's
Westerns of the 1950s (such as *The Naked Spur* (1952) and *Bend of the River*
(1952)) and Hitchcock's *Rear Window* (1954). Stoddard is placed in a
domestic environment (and is counterposed to the 'frontiersman' Doniphon,
who even lives outside the town), and realizes that in Shinbone, law will
make him no money. He turns his hand to schoolteaching, becoming the
feminine figure that often stands in opposition to the lone stranger.

In what I take to be the key scene in *Liberty Valance*, Stoddard conducts a
lesson with a newspaper freshly printed by his friend, the editor Sutton
Peabody (Edmond O'Brien). 'The best textbook in the world,' he proclaims,
'an honest newspaper'. The headline reads: 'Cattlemen Fight Statehood;
Small Homesteaders in Danger'. As the scene progresses it becomes clear

that Stoddard is attempting to educate the people of Shinbone for political reasons: literally, in order to produce a *polis*, a society of voters that elects representatives to the seat of power, Washington. This is made explicit in the slogan on the chalkboard shown behind Stoddard: 'Education is the basis of law and order'. In the rhetoric of the film, statehood equals democracy; to be a Territory is to be at the mercy of the cattle barons and their murderous henchmen like Valance. Stoddard, of course, comes from the East, bringing Eastern values with him (democracy, politics, education); and curiously, with regard to the Turner thesis, the triumph of his values will mean that Shinbone and the West will have to look back East in order to wield political influence. The *mise-en-scène* of the schoolroom signifies the centrality of the nation-state to Stoddard's educational project: on the wall are a crude facsimile of the Stars and Stripes; a copy of Gilbert Stuart's famous (and famously unfinished) portrait of George Washington, the Father of the American nation-state, a painting that was the source of Washington's image on the dollar bill; and a portrait of Abraham Lincoln, hanging behind Pompey's shoulder as he repeats the Declaration of Independence's dictum, 'We hold these truths to be self evident: that all men were created equal'. In fact, Ford's nation-state is racially utopian (excluding Native Americans, that is: Ford's apologetic *Cheyenne Autumn* (1964) was still two years away): Pompey (Woody Strode) is given prominence in the *mise-en-scène*, as are the Mexican faces of Sheriff Link Appleyard's 'family'. Two years before *Liberty Valance*, John Wayne's Davy Crockett (in his self-directed *The Alamo* of 1960) had waxed extremely lyrical about the word 'Republic' in sentimental terms; here, a speech on the Republic (equated with democracy, even the power of the people) is given to the female, immigrant, melting-pot-American voice of the new *polis*.

As Stoddard expounds the rights of the homesteaders, and outlines the necessity for both community and politics, he is interrupted by the entrance of Doniphon, who brings news that two 'sodbusters' have already been murdered by Valance's gang. This seems to bring about Stoddard's defeat: the class is dismissed, and Stoddard himself exclaims that 'when force threatens, talk's no good any more', before riding off (in a cart, not horseback, another sign of his association with modernity), to practise his shooting. However, we have already seen the older Senator Stoddard in the frame-story, before the flashback: his Eastern values will triumph in the end, as they must for the narrative of the American nation-state to reach its known resolution. Here the film adheres to a second part of Wright's 'classical' Western narrative: that the lone stranger, though he 'cleans up' the town through violent means, is incapable of being reincorporated into civil society (the new *polis*) because of his association with violence. In *Liberty Valance*, this narrative resolution becomes the site of knowing self-sacrifice on the part of Doniphon, and also the locus of the film's multiple ironies.

Stoddard understands that talk, in the short term, must give way to force, so arranges to meet Valance on the main street of Shinbone. The shoot-out is a version of the classic narrative resolution of the Western, where the moral order is reasserted through the gun, but here it occurs some three-quarters of the way through the film, not at the end. We see Stoddard face Valance and, though wounded, somehow manage to shoot and kill his opponent, becoming in the popular imagination 'the Man Who Shot Liberty Valance', giving him fame and a popularity that will see him elected as the state's first governor. At the same time, Stoddard had won Hallie from Doniphon, not through an assertion of traditional, violent masculinity, but through teaching her how to read. Jim Kitses, in *Horizons West* (2004), notes that 'the film's spatial logic establishes a relationship between the law, the press and education' (Kitses 2004: 123), a relationship made manifest in the schoolroom. Hallie's rejection of Doniphon is, ideologically, a rejection of the past, of the lawlessness and violence of the frontier and an embracing of the values of the East, of education and civic society. Hallie's choice is an indication of the film's 1962 revision of the Western's gender politics: as an audience, we are invited to validate Hallie's rejection because of the way Doniphon treats both her (and Pompey) as possessions, whereas Stoddard treats both she and Pompey as equals, with courtesy and respect, teaching them both how to read: how to be citizens. The ending of the film, once the Senator's tale is told, indicates that Stoddard's marriage is somewhat cold and distanced, and that Hallie truly loved Doniphon. Why did she reject him? One can only assume that she, too, understood the ideological necessity of embracing the values of modernity rather than those of the past.

Just as Stoddard is to be elected as Shinbone's representative, Doniphon (who had himself refused this responsibility) seeks out Stoddard to tell him the 'truth' of the shoot-out with Valance: that Doniphon had hid in a darkened alleyway, and killed Valance at the same time that Stoddard had fired his 'fatal' shot. Initially repulsed by the lie he had been living, Stoddard is eventually persuaded by Doniphon to carry on for the greater good. As it is usually read, the 'triumph' of liberal, democratic values is rendered ironic by this scene: their victory rests upon a violence which must itself be repudiated. When told this 'truth', the editor of the *Shinbone Star* rejects it with the phrase: 'This is the West, sir. When legend becomes fact, print the legend.' Michael Coyne, in *The Crowded Prairie* (1997), reads the ending of *Liberty Valance* in this way:

> In the end, there is no escape from the manufactured myth – he is a hero to a society which prefers the romantic lie, and with that realisation dies Ranse Stoddard's last illusion of hope and his last shred of innocence. (Coyne 1997: 109)

The 'myth' is that Ranse Stoddard, the lone stranger, the educated man, kills Valance and propels Shinbone and the state towards modernity; the 'truth' is that it requires the values of the old West, in the person of Doniphon, to deliver modernity, while necessarily sacrificing himself.

In this reading, *Liberty Valance* is a sentimental and nostalgic revisiting of the myths of the frontier, and a rather conservative argument for the priority of force over law in dealing with disruption of the community. However, another possible yet more ironic reading offers itself. As a viewer, we only know the 'truth' of Valance's death through Doniphon's own narration: what if he was wrong? What if Stoddard did kill Valance? Doniphon's version is validated by his belief in his own mastery of violence, and his complementary belief (shared by Stoddard) that Stoddard was incapable of killing Valance. As the viewer is presented with the star personae of Wayne and Stewart, we believe this too. We know that Stoddard was prepared to face Valance, to use the Gun, to defend himself and Shinbone's community (in a way that Doniphon seems incapable of doing). What Doniphon's speech does is to convince Stoddard that force must prevail over talk, that the gun must prevail over law: he ensures Stoddard's spiritual and ideological defeat at the same time that he himself, and the values he is associated with (the values of the frontiersman), must be set aside. This inner defeat is signified by Stewart's playing of the older Senator as something of a blowhard, a man set in the persona of pompous politician, and in the seeming distance between Stoddard and his wife Hallie. In this reading of the film, the final triumph of the violent West is in its rhetoric: it convinces democratic society of its priority by arguing that civilization cannot bring itself about, but must be brought forth by violence.

The Man Who Shot Liberty Valance is a transitional Western, between the 'classical' form (which inhabits the ideological landscape of Turner's frontier) and the 'revisionist' Westerns of the 1960s and after. What makes it transitional is that it exposes the Turner thesis to be a fraud, while at the same time adhering to the 'classical' structure of the Western outlined by Will Wright. In *Liberty Valance*, it is not Wyatt Earp, the 'civilized' man of violence and a Westerner, the personification of law and modernity (as Henry Fonda makes him in Ford's *My Darling Clementine*) who is victorious; it is Ranse Stoddard, an Easterner, an attorney-at-law and an educator, but whose victory is presented as a lie, a lie that American society finds it more convenient to believe than the truth. If, as Lee Clark Mitchell suggests, 'Ford ... delights in how such lies [do] not simply misrepresent but actively comprise history' (Mitchell 1996: 23), *The Man Who Shot Liberty Valance* offers all the disruptive and discursive pleasure of Janet Walker's 'metafictional' paradigm, but within the formal parameters of the classical West(ern) it summarizes, commemorates and compromises.

The end of the West(ern): belatedness and the post-classical Western

We will now move on, in rather less detail, to three other Westerns which depict the end of the West: Sam Peckinpah's *Ride the High Country* (1962), for which Randolph Scott temporarily came out of retirement; Don Siegel's *The Shootist* (1976), John Wayne's last film; and *Unforgiven* (1992), so far

Clint Eastwood's last Western. All of these films share, with *Butch Cassidy and the Sundance Kid* (1969) a sense of belatedness, in that their characters have 'outlived their time' (as the town marshall says to Wayne's dying gunfighter, John Bernard Books, in *The Shootist*), and the only thing for them to do is to die, peaceably or otherwise. More precisely, the central protagonists of all these films have outlived the West itself, and are relics of a bygone, heroic time in which their unreconstructed 'frontiersman' masculinity posed no problems, because there was no community or society for their individualism to threaten.

Ride the High Country was released the same year as *Liberty Valance*, 1962, and suffered a nasty fate at the box office, being dumped on the bottom half of a B-grade double bill. It is, however, an excellent film and is now regarded as something of a key Western, starring Joel McCrea and Randolph Scott as two superannuated heroes, living in the early-twentieth century. The film begins with McCrea, playing Steve Judd, a former celebrated US Marshall down on his luck (and down at heel) riding into a small town, whose streets are lined with cheering crowds. He waves, thinking the cheers are for him (later, another character confesses to have 'heard the name' Judd). Peckinpah introduces disturbing elements into the *mise-en-scène*: there is no town marshall or sheriff, but a policeman complete with dark blue serge uniform and helmet; a race is being run between horse and camel; Judd is almost run down by a motor car, as the policeman shouts 'Look out, old timer!' at him. Modernity has overtaken the town, as it has Judd, but the most interesting aspect of the opening sequence is to come. Judd recognizes his old friend Gil Westrum (Randolph Scott) who is costumed as a Buffalo Bill-alike, and whose 'Wild West' shooting gallery trades on a faked Wyatt Earp-style past. Like the 'historiographic metafiction' Westerns praised by Janet Walker, *Ride the High Country* represents the history of the West at a point where it is turned into myth, but there is a serious politics underlying Peckinpah's film. In *Ride the High Country*, the West is transformed into a spectacle, into a commodity that allows the surviving heroes of the past to turn a few dimes and cling on. The West is exploited by the remaining 'frontiersmen' because they have no other choice: in Peckinpah's films, the world of the frontier has been replaced by the world of economics.

We see the same process occurring in Eastwood's *Unforgiven*, in many ways a similar film to *Ride the High Country*. Here, the self-conscious exploitation of the West *as a myth* takes the form of the 'famous' gunfighter English Bob (Richard Harris), who is accompanied on his travels by the dime-novel writer W. W. Beauchamp (Saul Rubinek). When they arrive at Big Whiskey, veteran frontiersman and Sheriff 'Little Bill' Daggett, played by Gene Hackman, sadistically beats up, then imprisons, Bob. In the town jail, Little Bill reads Beauchamp's *The Duke of Death*, a fictionalized account of English Bob's adventures. Cruelly mocking the beaten Bob, Little Bill refers to him as the 'Duck of Death', while explaining to the (soon freed) Beauchamp the 'real' or historical events that lie behind the myth. Here,

Unforgiven's generic and historical knowingness extends to an acknowledgement of the history of the West rendered as myth in the dime-novel, a self-reflexive turn that is part of what John Saunders has called its 'deconstructive project' (Saunders 2001: 118) in relation to the form of the Western. As Henry Nash Smith argued in *Virgin Land*, even as the West was being settled/appropriated, dime-novelists were writing sensational tales of the frontiersmen (and women) for consumption in the cities of the East. This, perhaps, is a more direct representative of the idea of 'historiographic metafiction': history and myth are both in play as intertwined discourses, one inseparable from the other.

Significantly, as Little Bill's debunking of the 'myth' of the Duke of Death goes on, it seems that all he is producing is a counter-myth, with himself at the centre. Perhaps, considering Munny's murderous triumph at the end of the film (unlike the deaths of Judd and Books), the same might be said of *Unforgiven*. William Beard, in *Persistence of Double Vision*, suggests that Beauchamp's sequential interest in English Bob, Little Bill, then at the very end, Will Munny, constitutes an escalating investment in the 'three evolutionary stages' of the 'transcendental mythic hero' (Beard 2000: 82); Beard suggests that Beauchamp's role is to encode a self-reflexive auto-critique of *Unforgiven's* own representation of the triumph of the mythic hero. As I have argued above, *Unforgiven*, like *Ride the High Country*, certainly offers the sophisticated pleasures of generic self-consciousness, but I am not convinced that this auto-critique disables the violent pleasures of Munny's vengeful dispatch of Little Bill and the other men in the saloon.

In *Ride the High Country*, Judd enrols Westrum, and Westrum's young partner (the camel-rider) Heck Longtree (Ronald Starr), into a contract to escort some prospectors' gold back down to the bank in town. Westrum and Longtree plan to hijack the gold, hoping to persuade Judd of the moral 'rightness' of this plan along the way. However, Judd's contract with the bank is more than just a written one; it connects with the Code of Honour which, in many Westerns, differentiates the 'good' man of violence from the bad. This Code that Judd lives by is superannuated, as is he; it bears little relationship to the exploitation and degradation the three men meet with at the miners' camp. The Code that Judd relies upon is an explicitly homosocial one, in Eve Kosofsky Sedgwick's terms: it consists of a set of rituals and relationships between men, and masculinity is defined in relation to these codes, where emotion is displaced into rites of bonding, display or into violence. As Christopher Sharrett has written of *The Wild Bunch*, 'it is clear that the affection men have for each other is consistently translated into violence and bravura acts resulting in destruction' (Sharrett 1999: 87).

As we saw in the structure of the 'classical' Western, the negotiation of the lone stranger into domestic arrangements (replacing homosocial bonds with heterosexual ones) is problematic for narrative resolution of the 'classical' Western, but for Peckinpah and other revisionist directors, this is not an available option for the superannuated frontiersman. In *Ride the High Country*, it is Heck Longtree who meets, and falls in love with, Elsa Knudsen

(Mariette Hartley). This attraction ultimately leads to the final shoot-out in which Judd and Westrum are reconciled, meeting their enemies 'head on', but in which Judd is fatally wounded. Westrum, of course, ultimately adheres to the Code and promises to complete Judd's contract. Heck Longtree's future is with Elsa, in San Francisco, rather than with the outdated homosocial Code of Honour.

The male tripartite relationship of *Ride the High Country* is reflected in Eastwood's *Unforgiven*, where the callow Schofield Kid (Jaimz Woolvett) is similarly set against the 'old-timer' pairing of Will Munny (Eastwood) and Ned (Morgan Freeman). The same narrative structure also pertains: set on one last ride (brought about by an appeal to homosocial bonds), the two old friends embark on a 'contract' with a younger third member, in the course of which one is killed, and ultimately the younger member of the triumvirate rejects the homosocial and violent past. All three later films offer their frontiersmen the opportunity to make a 'last stand', to meet their enemies 'head on'. This symbolizes the necessary exclusion of the Old Men of the West from the new *polis* (and from the new economics of capital), but also their reinscription into myth: they are afforded a nostalgic last 'showdown' in which to demonstrate the frontier masculinity which brought modernity about, but which cannot incorporate them. What modernity can do, of course, is to recode their exclusion as part of the myth of the West, to make the frontiersman a figure of (fraudulent) nostalgia for a (mythic) past when Honour, not law or money, differentiated man from man, group from group.

The exclusion of the frontiersmen is, in *Ride the High Country*, *The Shootist* and *Unforgiven*, narratively complemented by the rejection of the homosocial Code by the young men (who are, in the latter two films, acolytes steeped in the mythic narratives of the frontiersmen they look up to). Where, in *The Man Who Shot Liberty Valance*, the mythic narrative of America is ideologically underpinned by a teleological structure that has the nation-state as its end-point and rationale, *Ride the High Country*, *The Shootist* and *Unforgiven* reread the development of the USA as a rites-of-passage narrative for white-male America. In this narrative, the young must reject the values of the old (just as democratic Americans rejected the values of old Europe) while nostalgically reinscribing the authority of the frontiersman as a validating father figure, gone but not forgotten. As Wendy Chapman Peek has rightly noted in relation to John Ford's Westerns, 'American masculinity ... honors behavior that is ultimately subservient to some manner of father' (Peek 2003: par. 27).

As Thomas Schatz has pointed out, the figure of the young man (or 'initiate' as Schatz calls him) is common in the postwar Western, from *Red River* (1948), through *Shane*, to *Rio Bravo* (1959) and beyond. Schatz (1981) reads this as a conflict between what is inside, and what is outside the bounds of community – the 'initiate' must balance the influences of West and East, frontiersman and (often) a maternal figure. The difference for *The Shootist* and *Unforgiven* is that the initiate or acolyte comes to worship the frontiersman through pre-produced myth, either in newspapers or dime-novels, or oral legends. Experience, for the initiate, removes the blinkers of the mythic narrative and causes him to reject it. Structurally, this is different from a film such as Hawks's *Red River*, where John Wayne plays the older, patriarchal Tom Dunson, who comes into conflict with his foster son Matthew Garth (Montgomery Clift). In *Masked Men*, Steven Cohan (1997) reads this conflict not as a rites of passage by which the younger man is 'hardened' into the ways of the frontiersman, but the reverse: the inflexible, patriarchal Dunson is supplanted by the feminized, 'boyish' Matthew.

Although *Red River* ends with a fistfight between the two men, Cohan argues that the film negotiates the two versions of masculinity rather than offering simple generational conflict or change. 'The closure of *Red River*', writes Cohan, 'appears to reconcile Dunson's and Matthew's opposing masculinities in the name of their resemblance as heroic men', while at the same time 'reify[ing] the myth of the individualistic Western hero' (Cohan 1997: 219, 206). In this, Cohan's reading of the film seems to exemplify what *The BFI Companion to the Western* identifies as the way in which the Western has been portrayed by critics such as Will Wright as 'functioning (like a myth or ritual) to resolve conflicts between key values in American culture' (Buscombe 1993: 181); in Cohan's work, conflicts in American ideology are resolved through the masculine star personae of Wayne and Clift. In *Red River*, Matthew displaces Dunson; in *Ride the High Country*, *The Shootist* and *Unforgiven*, the disillusioned acolyte leaves the range altogether.

Will Wright suggested that the 'professional' Western, a post-1960s development of the 'classical' Western, was, in films such as *The Magnificent Seven* (1960), *The Professionals* (1966) and *The Wild Bunch* (1969), a reflection of the managerial imperatives of the dominant professional classes in the USA at the time. In the 'professional plot', as Wright calls it (Wright 1975: 85), it is the Code of Honour itself that binds the men to each other and provides an ethical framework; the films have no recourse to a wider mythical narrative of the frontier and modernity. The men of the 'professional' Westerns get the job done, and that is all. In *The Professionals*, this Code is revealed when the two central characters (played by Burt Lancaster and Lee Marvin) discuss their mission, to bring back the 'kidnapped' Mexican wife of the railroad magnate Grant. Marvin, in putting off Lancaster's counter-suggestion that they go in search of buried gold instead, says: 'We gave our word to bring the woman back.' Lancaster retorts, 'My word to Grant ain't worth a plug nickel'. Marvin's devastating *coup-de-grace* (which ends the argument) is: 'You gave your word to me.'

The 'professional plot' does not really explain the predominance of the motif of superannuation or belatedness found in many Westerns in the 1960s and after. In some ways, this superannuation is a response to the ageing stars of the Western itself. Both *Ride the High Country*, in the shape of Randolph Scott, and *The Shootist*, with John Wayne, refer to their own star personae, extremely explicitly in *The Shootist*, as we shall see shortly.

There are two other explanations: one is that the ideological underpinnings of the Western ceased to correspond to the cultural and social landscape of the 1960s, with its ideological investment in the nation-state; the other, which I tentatively suggest here, is that the 'old age' Westerns, with their acolyte figures, indicate a greater sensitivity to generational change (or conflict). This seems particularly appropriate to the 1960s, where the younger generation (the Baby Boomers) reject, yet mythicize, the values of their fathers and mothers (the Greatest Generation). It is no coincidence that *The Man Who Shot Liberty Valance* and *Ride the High Country* were released in 1962; this is also the year of *The Manchurian Candidate*, the first James Bond film *Dr. No*, Ian Fleming's (JFK's favourite author) short story 'The Living Daylights' (the only Bond narrative set in Berlin), and the year in which John Le Carré wrote *The Spy Who Came in from the Cold*. The Western's superannuated heroes are overtaken by a new set of ideological contestations, to do with the Cold War, and Cold War masculinity.

The Shootist

Where *Ride the High Country* and especially *Unforgiven* show myth and history as intertwined, Don Siegel's *The Shootist* (1976) tends to efface history entirely, although it seems to correspond to Janet Walker's metafictional imperative. John Wayne's last film, *The Shootist* tells the story of the last week of the famous gunfighter (or 'shootist') John Bernard Books, played by Wayne. Books returns to Carson City, Nevada, in January 1901, in order to confirm the diagnosis of terminal cancer, and thence to die 'with his boots on'. As is well known, Wayne was himself in the last stages of his struggle with lung cancer while making the film, having lost one lung back in the 1960s, and Books's valedictory last stand is, in effect, John Wayne's. The film ensures the collapse of character 'Books' onto Wayne's star persona with its extraordinary montage sequence detailing Books' past. As Siegel explains in his autobiography, *A Siegel Film* (1993), he chose to cannibalize Wayne's own screen history, giving short clips from *Red River* (1948), *Hondo* (1953), *Rio Bravo* (1959) and *El Dorado* (1966) to illustrate Books's earlier, violent career (Siegel 1993: 1–2). *The Shootist* confirms Jim Kitses' dictum that 'the Western is history' (cited in Walker 2001: 1); or perhaps for *The Shootist*, history is the Western. (Kitses also wrote that 'The Wild Bunch* is America' (Kitses 2004: 223), of which more shortly.) Even though Siegel attempts to historically locate the film in time and place (Books reads of the death of Queen Victoria in the Carson City newspaper), in *The Shootist*, American history and the screen history of the Western are collapsed, and embodied in the heroic masculine form of John Wayne.

The montage sequence is not the only element of self-reflexivity in the film. The doctor who confirms the diagnosis of cancer is played by an elderly James Stewart, and two of Books's antagonists in his final showdown are played by actors well known from television Westerns from the

1950s. Richard Boone, 'Paladin' in *Have Gun, Will Travel*, and Hugh O'Brian, Wyatt Earp in *The Life and Legend of Wyatt Earp*, provide fittingly iconic opponents. Curiously, except the opening sequence where Books rides out of the high country towards Carson City, and his later buggy-ride in the country with Mrs Rogers (Lauren Bacall), the landlady who at first rejects him then warms to his courtesy, *The Shootist*'s *mise-en-scène* resembles nothing so much as a TV movie. Filmed partly on location at Carson City (moved from the more suggestive and liminal border town El Paso in the source novel), and on the Universal backlot at Burbank, this town-based Western looks and feels not just modern, but inauthentic, like TV rather than 'history' (or myth). Wayne's big, still-powerful body is hemmed in by the film's predominant domestic and interior set-ups, and even the final shoot-out takes place in a bar rather than on the streets of Carson City; and the screen ratio, while close to the Academy ratio of the classic Westerns of the 1940s and 1950s, cuts off screen space, metonymically repeating the closing of the frontier. Again, 'history' becomes screen history: Siegel rejects the CinemaScope spaces that characterize the Western in the 1960s and after, signifying the shrinking of the frontier, and the space of the individualist frontiersman.

Like Heck Longtree and the Schofield Kid, the young Gillom Rogers (played by Ron Howard as the son of Books's landlady) is repulsed when he experiences this violence not at second hand, in the legendary stories of Books's career, but for real. As in *Unforgiven*, it is the acolyte's discovery that, like his hero, he is willing to shoot to kill (unlike most men) that precipitates his rejection of this path, and those values. In *The Shootist*, Gillom kills the man who has fatally shot Books (with a shot gun, as Munny kills the brothel owner 'Skinny' in *Unforgiven*); he then tosses the gun away. Curiously, the next shot shows Books/Wayne nodding approvingly, a patriarchal and violent frontiersman giving his blessing to the repudiation of violence. Thomas Schatz has suggested that 'Gillum [sic] is caught between the influence of his mother ... and the mythic redeemer-hero, who together represent the west's basic contradictions and conflicts' (Schatz 1981: 54), but Gillom's reaction to killing seems to reject both. He wanders past his mother blankly, not acknowledging her presence, profoundly alienated from both alternatives. There the film ends. Although *The Shootist* gives its heroic protagonist a sentimental last showdown, and offers a closure for the Western and Western hero, it also suggests trouble to come in the new *polis*.

The Wild Bunch

Sam Peckinpah's *The Wild Bunch* (1969) is another end-of-the-West Western, which became notorious for its 'ultraviolent' climax, a revision of the 'head-on' shoot-out, in which the violent individualism of the frontiersman is extinguished in a mixture of battle and massacre. *The Wild*

Bunch has been read as a 'professional' Western by Will Wright (1975), a Vietnam Western by Noel Carroll (1998) and J. Hoberman (2003), and as a response to the conflicted cultural landscape of LBJ's 'Great Society' by Lee Clark Mitchell (1996). Clearly, the Bunch are militarized: in the opening sequence, they ride into the town of Starbuck disguised as US Army personnel in order to rob a bank; the final shoot-out is dominated by a machine gun they later steal from the legitimate US Army. Both Noel Carroll and J. Hoberman read *The Wild Bunch* as a legitimation of US military intervention overseas. Carroll suggests that

> what these ['south-of-the border' Westerns] are about is what Americans want to believe, namely, that American military operations abroad are undertaken in a defence of freedom (Carroll 1998: 60)

which explains why the Bunch are sympathetic to, and are symbolically allied with, Mexican revolutionaries in the second half of the film. Hoberman goes still further in arguing that the film's 'real pleasures' are in 'the thrill of [the] invasion and massacre of foreigners' (Hoberman 2003: 235). I find Carroll's analysis of the underlying premises of *The Wild Bunch* to be persuasive, in that, like *Dirty Harry*, it can enlist liberal or even radical sentiments to the side of violent force. Peckinpah himself suggested that the excessive violence of the film was meant to provoke a reaction in the viewer similar to that of Gillom Rogers in *The Shootist*: revulsion. 'Actually,' said Peckinpah in interview,

> [*The Wild Bunch*] is an antiviolence film, because I use violence as it *is*. It's ugly, brutalizing, and bloody fucking awful. It's not fun and games and cowboys and Indians: it's a terrible, ugly thing. (Farber 1994: 40–1)

Hostile critics are unconvinced by Peckinpah's protestation, and view the ending as an 'orgy' of violence, a celebration rather than a condemnation. The way in which the violence is choreographed and edited in Peckinpah's films (slow-motion intercutting of falling bodies and spurting gunshot wounds) does, I feel, introduce a countervailing aesthetic of violence in his films which tends to adulterate Peckinpah's serious, even political, intentions. What the film makes clear, however, is that the history of the West, the history of America itself, is a violent one, and the narrative of 'progress' one that masks a bloody, violent exclusion and appropriation. In *The Wild Bunch*, the process of exclusion (symbolically, of the superannuated frontiersmen) goes so far that they must escape to Mexico, crossing (and therefore defining) another frontier, this time a national one. In Mexico, the Bunch finally acts out a nihilistic fantasy of 'revolution' against the very American conditions of exclusion that have precipitated their exile. There is no return for them, no redemption: Peckinpah's revisionism extends to the abandonment of the Turner thesis, to the extent that modernity does not equate with progress, but the exploitative domination of the banks and railroads.

However, I would suggest that even these 'end-of-the-West', post-classical Westerns still define their narratives in relationship to the frontier thesis. In *How The West Was Won*, the 'settler trail' leads directly to contemporary California's freeways; in *Liberty Valance*, the frontier thesis is a necessary myth; in the revisionist Western, modernity is represented negatively and accompanied by a sense of loss, and nostalgia for the heroic ethos of the frontiersman. The underlying teleological structure, from Wilderness to Garden, from the West to modernity, is the same. I agree with Lee Clark Mitchell, who argues that:

> Peckinpah was obsessed by the interlinked issues Ford had addressed in *Liberty Valance*, of lost youth, a spiritless present, and nostalgia for a vital past, though he treats them less theatrically, more directly, finally more sentimentally because uninterested in exposing the mythic past as a dream. (Mitchell 1996: 241–2)

In *The Wild Bunch*, this sentimentality is expressed in the final shots, where, laughing, the actors (William Holden as Pike Bishop, the leader of the Bunch; Ernest Borgnine as 'Dutch' Engstrom, his lieutenant; Warren Oates and Ben Johnson as Lyle and Tector Gorch; and Jaime Sanchez as the Mexican Angel) ride off into a filmic Valhalla. The Bunch are incapable of being accommodated by a cynical, corrupt modern United States, so they are rewritten into the myth of the West itself by Peckinpah, and are thereby (ironically) finally incorporated into the 'Dream'.

The Bunch are redundant because their Code, like that of Steve Judd or J. B. Books, has been 'enshrined' in the mythic narrative of progress, and in the Turner thesis comes to embody the very spirit of democracy and law. Their continued existence betrays the myth of the Code, particularly as the Bunch find it very difficult to live by it. As Lee Clark Mitchell notes, Peckinpah 'makes a fetish of the idea of a code of loyalty ... only to reveal that code as honoured more in the breach than in practice' (Mitchell 1996: 245). The Code is expressed by Pike Bishop (Holden) after their attempt to rob Starbuck's bank has gone terribly wrong. It was a trap, organized by the railroads, and led by a former member of the Bunch, Deke Thornton (Robert Ryan) who has been dragooned into leading a rag-tag group of 'gutter trash' bounty hunters to try to capture, or kill, the Bunch. After failing to mount his horse (an indication of old age repeated near the beginning of *Unforgiven*), Bishop rails against the derisively laughing Gorch brothers. 'When you side with a man, you side with him all the way – otherwise you're an animal. You're finished. *We're* finished. *All* of us.' What we have seen is that Pike has just abandoned a young member of the Bunch, Crazy Lee, back in Starbuck; later, in flashback, we find that Bishop 'never got caught' because he jumped out of the window rather than standing by Thornton when the law authorities broke in on them.

Their homosocial Code, which is meant to differentiate the Bunch from other criminals, or the 'gutter trash' of Thornton's group, only pertains at the very end of the film, when Angel is captured by the Mexican warlord

Mapache, and the Bunch go to try to force his release. This act of loyalty is
what precipitates the final massacre, and deaths of all but Thornton and
Freddy Sykes, the 'old retainer' of the Bunch, played by the same Edmond
O'Brien who was Sutton Peabody in *Liberty Valance*. Earlier in the film,
Bishop jokingly compares Mapache to the Bunch, suggesting that they
were all out for what they could grab. Dutch Engstrom is outraged by the
suggestion: 'we don't *hang* nobody,' he declares, then expressing the hope
that 'one day these people will rise up and kick [Mapache] into the gutter'.
'We will,' responds Angel, 'if it takes forever.' The destruction of Mapache's
army, though, is only incidentally revolutionary: the last shoot-out is, as in
The Shootist, a self-consciously (and heroically coded) suicidal escape from
the futility of the remainder of their lives. The ending of *The Wild Bunch*,
with Thornton and Sykes joining the Mexican revolutionaries, some of
whom are from Angel's village, indicates a reversal of the 'rites of passage'
plot found in *Ride the High Country*, *The Shootist* and *Unforgiven*. The last
remaining members of the Bunch – Thornton and Sykes – must learn to be
more like the youngest, and most revolutionary, member of the Bunch,
Angel. The fact that it is for Angel that they finally act on the code of
loyalty, and that Angel's death invokes the carnage, signifies his centrality.
By destroying Mapache's army they complete Angel's revolutionary
trajectory; ironically, it is upon their violence that possibility of social
change rests, recapitulating and revising Tom Doniphon's role in *Liberty
Valance*, but in the open or revolutionary spaces of Mexico rather than the
'democratic' national space of the United States.

To illustrate the compromising of the 'national' narrative in later
Westerns, we will consider an image from *Unforgiven*. After the character
Eastwood plays, Will Munny, the reformed killer and widower, discovers
his friend and partner Ned tortured and displayed in Big Whiskey as a
warning to other lawbreakers, he gulps the whiskey he has sworn off for
ten years, and rides into town to wreak revenge. Here, of course, the
revengeful violence is motivated by homosocial bonds of loyalty and
friendship, just as at the end of *The Wild Bunch*. Unlike Judd, the Bunch, or
J. B. Books, Munny survives the shoot-out, having reverted back to the
killer he had been before his marriage. As has been noted, although
Unforgiven is a self-conscious revision of the mythic narrative of the
frontier, it does not close off the future as other 'post-classical' Westerns
have done. Some critics have read this ending as a failure on Eastwood's
part, a reversion to the quasi-supernatural violent heroics of the Man with
No Name persona. Indeed, as he leaves the saloon full of the corpses of the
men he has killed, Munny makes his escape by threatening to shoot any
man, kill their wife and friends, and burn down their houses, if they try to
stop him, or if they fail to bury Ned 'right'. In fact, Munny plays upon his
own reputation, mythologizing himself as the Killer (the obverse of the
heroic redeemer) in order to secure his escape.

The final shot of the film is overlaid by a title, which suggests that after
the shoot-out at Big Whiskey, Munny gave up farming and successfully ran

a dry-goods store in San Francisco. Unlike the nostalgic, redemptive deaths of Steve Judd, Books or the Bunch, Munny is reconciled to the society of the West. After Munny has killed Little Bill, Eastwood is framed on his horse, in the pouring rain, as he declaims his threat: 'You'd better not cut up or otherwise harm no whores or I'll come back and kill every one of you sons of bitches'. Behind hangs the Stars and Stripes, symbol, as we have seen in *Liberty Valance*, of the Nation and its values. In *Unforgiven*, then, violence and the rule of the violent man are not expelled from American society: they are incorporated into it. Kevin Costner's *Open Range* (2004), the most recent Hollywood Western at the time of writing, makes the same gesture. While it recapitulates many motifs from 'classical' westerns such as *Shane* and *My Darling Clementine*, where the man of violence must ride away, here the violent man is reintegrated into society, and the film ends with a romantic scene in a garden, the imagery of Wilderness finally giving way to imagery of Civilization. This is the inverse of the Turner myth. Rather than the frontier and the West being the crucible of democracy, in *Unforgiven* they are the locus of violence; rather than disavowing 'progress' in favour of a nostalgia for the individual ethos of the frontiersman, the violence of the frontiersman is implicated in 'progress'. *Unforgiven* is perhaps at the end of the long cycle of the 'end-of-the-West' revisionist Western, but it finally returns to the moral complexity, and ideological symbolism, of *The Man Who Shot Liberty Valance*.

CHAPTER EIGHT

The Twilight Frontier

In *Toy Story 2* (1999), the cowboy toy Woody is kidnapped by the unscrupulous Toy Barn owner Al, who wants to sell him to a Japanese toy museum. He is introduced to the 'Round-Up Gang', three other toys who featured in *Woody's Round-Up*, a children's television series of the 1950s: his horse Bullseye, the cowgirl Jessie, and the villain of the piece, the 'old timer' Stinky Pete. While Jessie and Woody must face the troubling certainty that their 'owners' (the children who play with them) will grow up and abandon them, Stinky Pete had never been unwrapped: his trauma is that he stayed on the dime-store shelf while all the other toys were sold. In a key scene, Woody discovers his origins or history when Jessie plays him the last episode of *Woody's Round-Up*. Woody mis-recognizes the 'real' onscreen puppet Woody as himself, and identifies the cancellation of the show with the end of his utility (his 'owner', the human boy Andy, will not play with him any more) and the end of the 1950s (in the rhetoric of the film, the Age of Innocence and the Age of the Western). Stinky Pete's revelation that there was no more *Woody's Round-Up* is delivered in the fateful shorthand: 'Two words: Sput Nik. After that, children only wanted to play with *space toys.*'

Of course, the fear of replacement (by space toys) had haunted Woody in the first *Toy Story* film (1995). Stinky Pete's own superannuation is pointedly compared with Woody's threatened (and impending) 'retirement'; the promised Japanese toy museum becomes a kind of old folks' home, where the toys can be admired at a safe distance. Although Woody buys this argument for a short time − until Buzz himself reminds Woody of his own rhetoric, that 'you are a child's plaything', and toy existence gains meaning *only* in moments of play with the 'owner' − the film reasserts the group or team ethic which had provoked the rescue mission in the first place, incorporating Jessie and Bullseye into a reconstituted 'Round-Up Gang' in Andy's bedroom. (Stinky Pete is excluded from the new consensus.) *Toy Story 2* validates the importance of the team over the individual while providing plenty of space for quasi-heroic escapades. Though it starts as a science fiction film, the end of *Toy Story 2* completes the 'missing' final episode of *Woody's Round-Up* and casts the whole narrative as a kind of captivity Western manqué. Centrally, Woody and Buzz 'wouldn't miss for the world' Andy's growing up, even though it will result in their own abandonment. Woody and Buzz sacrifice themselves for the greater good

(Andy's happiness), consoling each other that at least they will have a friend to rely on in their (or Andy's) old age.

Woody and Buzz seem to represent different times, values and conceptions of masculine heroism, organized around the generic imagery of the two toys: the Cowboy and the Space Ranger. Woody's masculinity is 'soft'; his leadership of the toys is consensual, open to challenge, and reaffirms the importance of group cohesion rather than individual heroism. Initially at least, in *Toy Story* (then replayed through the 'other' Buzz in the sequel), Buzz Lightyear is the individual Hero, the Action Toy, whose single-minded heroic world-view is at first attractive to the other toys, then irritatingly at odds with reality. In the course of the two films, which negotiate their initial antagonism into friendship, Buzz is acculturated into Woody's values, while Woody learns to accept this potential male rival (who produces 'laser envy' in him) into the toy community. Generically, of course, the opposition between the two is also between the Western and science fiction. They are initially seen to be in conflict, their associations with the past/tradition (the Western) and the future/change (science fiction) rendering them incompatible. *Toy Story 2* works to achieve the resolution of this generic conflict through the male 'buddy' system of contemporary action cinema.

For *Toy Story 2*, the launch of Sputnik in October 1957 is also a moment of irreversible and catastrophic cultural change, figured as a moment of transition from the generic dominance of the Western to the dominance of science fiction. The 'history' of Woody's origins is, however, actually an instance of false cultural recall. (This is, as Michael Coyne has shown is *The Crowded Prairie* (1997), a somewhat simplistic and falsified picture. Although television Western serials did suffer a decline in popularity at the beginning of the 1960s, 'nineteen were on the air' (Coyne 1997: 106) on American networks in 1962, and there were still a dozen by the end of the decade.) The 'two words', Sputnik, are seen to be the point of rupture for the innocent world of the Western and the fatal arrival of the space age (and space toys), or the end of the 'innocence' of the 1950s and the beginning of the upheavals of the 1960s. For the Kennedy election programme, 1957 was a key year because it 'exposed' the administration of Eisenhower — who was himself known as a reader of paperback Westerns — as old and weak, unsuited to the challenges of the New Frontier. The departure of Eisenhower is mirrored in Hollywood movie Westerns of the 1960s and after, which increasingly articulate a sense of belatedness or superannuation. These 'Old Age' Westerns that we considered in the last chapter, such as Sam Peckinpah's *Ride the High Country*, John Ford's *The Man Who Shot Liberty Valance* (both 1962), Peckinpah's *The Wild Bunch* (1969), Siegel's *The Shootist* (1976; John Wayne's valedictory performance), and Clint Eastwood's *Unforgiven* (1992) all represent the problems of ageing and superannuation for the Western 'shootist', be it Steve Judd, J. B. Books or William Munny. These men have 'outlived their time', adrift in a modernity in which their skills and attributes have no utility or value, like Stinky Pete's fears for the Round-Up Gang.

In some ways, this superannuation is a response to the ageing stars of the Western itself: Randolph Scott came out of retirement for *Ride the High Country*; *The Shootist* was John Wayne's last film; Clint Eastwood waited nearly a decade after acquiring *Unforgiven* to be old enough to play the role of Munny. Tensions between the values of West and East, frontier and civilization, tend to be organized in these films mainly around the tension between the old(er) man and a younger 'apprentice' who learns to reject the values of violence (such as in *The Shootist*), or between the homosocial bonds between two 'old-timer' gunfighters and a younger man. The same narrative structure also pertains: set on one last ride, the old shootist(s) resolve the narrative through a last stand, in the course of which an old shootist is killed, and ultimately the younger member of the triumvirate rejects the homosocial and violent past. The opportunity to make a 'last stand', to meet their enemies 'head on', symbolizes the necessary exclusion of the Old Men of the West from the new *polis* (as Stinky Pete is excluded from Andy's bedroom), but also their reinscription into myth: they are afforded a nostalgic last 'showdown' in which to demonstrate the frontier masculinity which brought modernity about, but which cannot incorporate them.

The exclusion of the frontiersmen is, in *Ride the High Country*, *The Shootist* and *Unforgiven*, narratively complemented by the rejection of the homosocial Code of Honour by the young men (who are, in the latter two films, acolytes steeped in the mythic narratives of the frontiersmen they look up to). The young must reject the values of the old while nostalgically reinscribing the authority of the frontiersman as a validating father-figure, gone but not forgotten. What modernity can do, of course, is to recode their exclusion as part of the myth of the West, to make the frontiersman a figure of (fraudulent) nostalgia for a (mythic) past when Honour, not law or money, differentiated man from man, group from group. In the narrative of *Toy Story 2*, the ideological underpinnings of the Western cease to correspond to the cultural and social landscape of the 'Space Age' 1960s, a point underscored in the 'history' of *Woody's Round-Up*. The 1950s then become a locus of false nostalgia that renders the pop-cultural artefacts of the time (be-finned automobiles, Woody merchandise, vinyl records) as 'antique' commodities.

Toy Story 2 encodes cultural change as generic change, from the Western to science fiction. The connection between the two genres forms the core of this chapter. What connects them, and the late-1950s/early-1960s, is the frontier; and, embodied in Woody and Buzz, the centrality of the masculine hero. Although the American frontier was declared closed in 1890, as Richard Slotkin has shown in *Gunfighter Nation* (1998) the rhetoric of the frontier has a vital influence over the American imaginary throughout the twentieth century. As we saw in the previous chapter, Turner's 'The Significance of the Frontier in American History' (1893) defined the experience of Americans and the character of American life through the frontier. Turner's mythic narrative of the frontier, however, is not only about the virile American character; it is about American democracy. It is the conditions of frontier life itself, argued Turner, which gave America its quintessentially democratic flavour. For Turner, American character is American democracy, and the typical American character is formed on the frontier. Little wonder, then, in Slotkin's thesis, that the rhetoric of the frontier has been deployed by successive American Presidents to symbolically validate military intervention overseas.

Frederick Turner's conception of the frontier was that it provided a vital space necessary for the continued economic expansion of the United States. The connection between the frontier and *Outer* Space was articulated most powerfully by President John F. Kennedy during and after his election in 1960. As Slotkin argues, in his address to the Democratic Convention in 1960, Kennedy invoked the language of the frontier to 'summon the nation as a whole to undertake (or at least support) a *heroic* engagement in the "long twilight struggle" against Communism and the social and economic forces that engender it' (Slotkin 1998: 3). Kennedy said: 'we stand today on the edge of a new frontier – the frontier of the 1960s, a frontier of unknown opportunities and paths, a frontier of unfulfilled hopes and threats' (Slotkin 1998: 3). While Slotkin concentrates on the political tenor of this frontier rhetoric – that it aimed to mobilize the United States towards a condition of war and rationalized the counterinsurgency foreign-policy imperatives of the Kennedy and Johnson administrations – it is Kennedy's inauguration of the Space Race, through his declared intention to place an American man on the moon by the end of the 1960s, that is of importance here.

Kennedy made this declaration in 1961, four years after the launch of the Soviet Sputnik satellite, and three years after the foundation of NASA, the National Aeronautics and Space Administration. Dale Carter, in *The Final Frontier*, has suggested that President Eisenhower, whose original estimate of Sputnik's military value was that it worried him 'not one iota' (Carter 1988: 127), was somewhat bounced into creating NASA by Kennedy's political attack on the so-called 'missile gap' and the symbolic 'victory' of Soviet science and technology in the Space Race signalled by Sputnik's beeps. The rhetoric of the 'New Frontier' tied into a renewal of heroic masculinity in the form of the young, virile, war-hero President: as Slotkin argues, 'Kennedy had considerable success in achieving public credibility as a *hero*' (Slotkin 1998: 498). Kennedy's masculine heroism was closely identified with the Mercury and Apollo manned space programmes of the late-1950s and 1960s, particularly in a series of *Life* magazine profiles and stories.

Very few films have directly portrayed the Apollo space programme. Tom Wolfe's book, filmed by Philip Kaufman, *The Right Stuff* (book 1980, film 1983), concentrates on the earliest American attempts to put a man into space. Both texts conflate the rhetoric of the Western with that of the Kennedy administration to suggest that the astronauts inhabited the kind of aggressive, individualistic masculinity that Frederick Turner proposed to be at the heart of American experience. Wolfe writes:

> The truth was that the fellows had now become the personal symbols not only
> of America's Cold War struggle with the Soviets but also of Kennedy's own
> political comeback. They had become *the* pioneers of the New Frontier. (Wolfe
> 1990: 275)

While seeming to ironize this rhetoric, Wolfe's insistence on centrality of
the 'right stuff' that characterizes the heroic subjectivity of the 'Mercury 7'
indicates a deeper investment in hegemonic constructions of American
masculinity. The conflation of 'astronaut' and 'cowboy' is most evidently
symbolized in the figure of Chuck Yeager, the famous test pilot who
refused to participate in the Mercury programme because he didn't want to
be 'spam in a can'. Before a test flight in the X-1, to try to break the sound
barrier, Yeager takes off on a horse ride with his wife. (In the film, this is
portrayed as part of a bantering sexual game.) Unfortunately, 'he does not
realize that he is not equally gifted in the control of all forms of locomotion.
He and the horse hit a gate, and he goes flying off and lands on his right
side. His side hurts like hell' (Wolfe 1990: 54). Wolfe pitches this episode as
a version of the kind of 'Flying & Drinking and Drinking & Driving' culture
of the test pilots, who see themselves as rebellious figures, their dangerous
job rendering them outside the normative behaviours of servicemen.
Although Yeager's accident threatens to derail the test flight (because his
broken ribs do not allow him the leverage to shut the hatch of the X-1), this
is solved by the use of a sawn-off piece of broom handle: the triumph of
'can-do' over the bureaucratic structures of the Air Force (or NASA).

In Kaufman's film, Yeager (played by Sam Shepard) is portrayed much
more overtly as a horseman. Before the fall, he is seen riding in iconic
Western landscapes, situating him as a Western 'frontiersman'. In one
scene, he rides through the scrub and stumbles across the X-1, which in
Wolfe's words looks like 'a fat orange swallow with white markings' (Wolfe
1990: 55). The rocket plane is being fuelled, the excess boiling off, causing
the plane to start 'steaming and screaming like a teakettle' (Wolfe 1990: 55).
Yeager, on his horse, stands still in contemplation. In the film, the otherness of the X-1 is stressed; it does not belong to the iconography of
the Western landscape, and is a threatening (if not malignant) presence.
It proposes a very different relationship between human and vehicle than
the 'organic' relationship of horse and rider. Inserted into its metal body,
the test pilot becomes mechanized, a very different kind of frontiersman.

The tension between the Western individualist male and the technocratic
imperatives of the space programme recur throughout the film. Yeager's
refusal to participate seems, at first, a statement of independence, but a later
scene in the Edwards Air Force base saloon reveals a rather wistful, even
regretful look on Shepard's face, suggesting that Yeager's 'principled' stand
was in fact a self-defeating one. Unlike Neil Armstrong, who also began as
a test pilot, Yeager places himself outside the national narrative that will
lead to landings on the moon. An excessive individualism here leads to
exclusion. This same opposition can be found in Norman Mailer's writing

on the 1969 Apollo XI moon landing, *Of a Fire on the Moon*. Attending a press conference, Mailer noticed that 'the heart of astronaut talk, like the heart of all bureaucratic talk, was a jargon that could be easily converted to computer programming' (Mailer 1999: 709). The astronauts, gifted and proficient technically and scientifically besides being highly trained athletes, are enclosed within a programme so scientized that it no longer leaves much room for the human. Even more pertinent to the film is what Mailer writes about the idea of the 'team': 'If they were astronauts, they were men who worked for the team, but no man became an astronaut who was not sufficiently exceptional to suspect at times that he might be the best of all' (Mailer 1999: 712). The tension, then, is between being the 'team player' and the individual, the 'representative man' and the 'exceptional' man.

Both Richard Slotkin and Dale Carter use the Emersonian concept of the 'representative man' to consider the role of the heroic within the New Frontier. Slotkin writes that Arthur Schlesinger, Jr, key Kennedy aide and historian in his own right, formulated an argument for the necessity of the Strong Man in a time of geopolitical crisis, a representative hero 'who incarnates the genius of his people and expresses it in ways that the mass of men cannot': 'from the start, democracies have been able to concert their energies and focus their aspirations only as strong individuals embodied and clarified the tendencies of the people' (Slotkin 1998: 502). Kennedy becomes the Strong Man/'representative man', at once typically American and exceptionally qualified to lead. Dale Carter, in turn, suggests that 'the astronauts were "representative men" (to recall Emerson) in a society whose struggle for effective representation and accountability had long since been lost' (Carter 1988: 175). Carter sees the astronauts as (rather troubling) analogues of the President, whose heroic masculinity is confirmed by his association with these exceptional yet ordinary men. In both arguments, the figure of the Strong Man is complemented by the Representative Man: heroic masculinity, in the form of JFK or the astronaut, is an amalgam of both.

Ron Howard's *Apollo 13* (1995) avoids the problems of the 'tediousness' of the successful space mission – generated by NASA's own technocratic presentation of the Apollo programme – by concentrating on triumph generated out of near disaster. Geoff King and Tanya Krzywinska have noted that there is a 'relative absence of films based around real space programmes', mainly because 'the astronauts are ... too deeply immersed in a web of technology, struggling continually to create any kind of space for individual heroics' (King and Krzywinska 2000: 25). Though they are here writing of *The Right Stuff*, their comment is clearly applicable to other films which have too close a proximity to the 'reality' of space travel, such as two I will consider here, Clint Eastwood's *Space Cowboys* (2000) and Brian De Palma's *Mission to Mars* (2000). King and Krzywinska also note that in *Apollo 13*, the only film made about the Apollo programme, it is crisis (the possibility of disaster) which accounts for the film being made at all, as well as the large popular audience for both the original (media) event and the

1995 film. As King suggests, 'Successful space missions are, ironically, all too like some aspects of *2001: A Space Odyssey*: mostly rather dull and tedious and featuring protagonists whose personalities rarely capture the imagination' (King and Krzywinska 2000: 81). *Apollo 13* begins, like De Palma's *Mission to Mars* that we will consider below, with a party. The Apollo astronauts and their families are gathered to watch Armstong's first walk on the moon. These two films – both of which display what Geoff King calls a 'solidly realistic aesthetic in its construction of a flight' (King and Krzywinska 2000: 83) – attempt to humanize the mission from the very beginning, by emphasizing not the technology, but the characters of the astronauts. They too are 'representative men', ordinary but, as astronauts, partaking of an extraordinary endeavour. In the course of *Apollo 13*, as the technology fails and the men must battle to return home, heroism is located (as in *The Right Stuff*) not in the bureaucratic and technocratic structures of NASA, but in the 'can-do' individualism that underlies and eventually countermands it.

Both *The Right Stuff* and *Apollo 13* are also concerned with homosocial bonds between the men; or, rather, the lack of them. Both films, Wolfe's book, and Andrew Smith's *Moondust* (2005), a series of interviews with the 'moonwalkers', emphasize the competitiveness of the astronauts. Each jockeyed, more or less consciously, for a place aboard the first or early flights. Smith's *Moondust* suggests that Buzz Aldrin, the second man to walk on the moon, allowed the bitterness of 'losing' to Armstrong to affect him to such an extent that he refused to take any pictures of his colleague on the Lunar surface: the only image of Armstrong is one he himself took, reflected in Aldrin's helmet visor. Overcoming the aggressive, competitive instincts which drove the men to become astronauts in the first place is prioritized in *Apollo 13*; when the Command Module pilot is 'bumped' from the flight because the NASA doctors fear he will develop measles, his replacement finds it difficult to insert himself into the homosocial network that has formed between the three astronauts of the original crew. The crew of Apollo 13, and the 'bumped' pilot, must work together in the narrative to ensure the safe return of the men, an interesting inversion of the individualistic imperatives of other space fictions.

Eastwood's *Space Cowboys* (2000), which Tim Groves describes as a 'humorous counterpoint to *Unforgiven*' (Groves 2001: par 30), combines elements from both Western and science fiction genres, as its title suggests. The narrative, for example, repeats the 'last stand' or 'last ride' of the post-1962 Old Age Westerns. The film begins in 1958, just prior to the institution of NASA. Two pilots, Frank Corvin (Clint Eastwood) and Hawk Hawkins (Tommy Lee Jones), are part of Team Daedalus, who test (to destruction) X-15-type rocket planes. Clearly modelled on *The Right Stuff*, Corvin and Hawkins are Chuck Yeager-type 'cowboys', individualistic pioneers who do not sit easily within the bureaucratic and administrative confines of their careers. After crashing yet another rocket plane, they are summoned to a press conference by their manager Bob Gerson (James

Cromwell), where they are told that the programme is being taken over by the newly created NASA, and their piloting skills replaced by automation and chimpanzees. Corvin and Hawkins see this as a personal betrayal, a feeling the audience is invited to share: there is no sense here of the wider political arena in which the NASA decision was taken. The key opposition, which will pertain throughout the rest of the film, is between the bureaucratic imperatives of NASA and the individualistic, maverick masculinity of the members of the re-formed, superannuated Team Daedalus (who also include James Garner as Tank Sullivan and Donald Sutherland as Jerry O'Neill).

As the title of the film suggests, *Space Cowboys* attempts to weld the figures of Cowboy and Space Ranger, Strong Man and Representative Man together, nostalgically revisiting the superannuated Old Westerner and reinserting old-time, heroic masculinity into the contemporary science fiction film (and, by extension, the NASA space programme). Tommy Lee Jones even wears a Stetson in early scenes to emphasize the point. Aware that unreconstructed heroic masculinity may seem somewhat antiquated if presented unambiguously, *Space Cowboys* allows the audience the pleasures of male heroism while gently satirizing itself in the (out of) shapes of the four pensioner-age astronauts, and softening the negative possibilities of the 'maverick' by emphasizing a team ethos. Corvin is goaded by the astronaut Ethan and his former boss, Bob Gerson, as 'not being a team player'; it is Corvin's character trajectory that he should prove his responsibilities to his team-mates, two of whom reciprocate by staying with him on the crippled shuttle's return to Earth.

Team Daedalus certainly does have the 'right stuff': the film's scenario even has NASA's popularity amongst Americans massively enhanced by the presence of the four 'old timers'. *Space Cowboys* encodes a nostalgia for Kennedy-era New Frontiers, but here they are the preserve of twilight cowboys who recognize their opportunity and know what to do when they get there. Throughout the film, Team Daedalus are contrasted with the technocratic insider, the (young) NASA astronaut Ethan. Although Team Daedalus are 'mavericks', once in space they become the models of professionalism. It is Ethan, the 'brown-nosing' 'organization man', who contravenes orders and puts the whole mission in jeopardy, at the same time destroying himself. In *Space Cowboys*, the homosocial 'team' ethos articulates greater social responsibility than the bureaucratic imperatives of the NASA insider.

As Tim Groves notes, *Space Cowboys* draws heavily upon *The Right Stuff* for its imagery and the portrayal of Team Daedalus (2001: par. 26); the same is also true of Michael Bay's *Armageddon* (1998), which seems a clear (if unacknowledged) precursor of Eastwood's film. Like Team Daedalus, the roughneck oilmen of *Armageddon* are called upon to save the world when NASA is proved unable to come up with a means to do so. Near the beginning of *Armageddon*, NASA mission leader Dan Truman (Billy Bob Thornton), having witnessed the destruction of an orbiting Space Shuttle in a catastrophic meteorite shower, is told that an asteroid 'the size of Texas' is heading towards earth, a 'global killer' that will wipe out all life. 'For 30 years they've been questioning the need for NASA, now we're gonna show them,' he says. What happens is the reverse; as in *Space Cowboys*, the bureaucratic structure of NASA is incapable of dealing with the crisis, and must turn to the kind of heroic, maverick masculinity hitherto excluded from the programme. As Geoff King notes, this opposition reveals a curious and problematic underside to the rhetoric of the frontier:

> One option for the film is to cast NASA as the 'bad' bureaucracy to which the 'good' guys are opposed ... . NASA appears to be part of a network of potentially sinister state forces, the favourite demons of the contemporary frontier tradition. (King and Krzywinska 2000: 85)

One can also find the representation of NASA as a sinister state force in *Capricorn One* (1977), a connection between the space fictions studied here and the conspiracy thrillers of the 1970s. This film recapitulates the 'moon hoax' conspiracy theories which have circulated since the end of the Apollo programme in 1972: that the moon landings were staged. In *Capricorn One*, it is a Mars landing that NASA wants to fake, but this is exposed through the 'heroic' activites of the astronauts themselves and an investigative journalist.

Crisis is key to the narratives of *Space Cowboys* and *Armageddon*, for it necessitates the reintroduction of the element of the 'right stuff', the heroic pioneering masculinity that is supposed to characterize the early test pilots rather than the NASA-enclosed astronauts. Like *Space Cowboys*, *Armageddon* playfully satirizes itself, sweetening the pill of heroic masculinity. When they are kitted out in orange flight suits (in a slow-motion shot which parodies the 'Mercury 7' of *The Right Stuff*), the roughneck crew converge on Colonel Sharp, the NASA pilot who will take them into space. Looking at their antics, he cries, 'talk about the wrong stuff!' The roughnecks of *Armageddon* display a similar team ethos to the veterans of *Space Cowboys*. Once NASA identifies Harry Stamper (Bruce Willis) as the best oil-driller in the world, he tells them: 'I'm only the best because I work with the best', and demands that his team must be taken up into space with him. Stamper's surrogate son, A. J. (Ben Affleck), is positioned similarly to the 'acolyte' or apprentice figures of the Old Age Westerns; like Heck Longtree or the Schofield Kid, he must learn that success comes through teamwork and mutual responsibility, rather than quasi-heroic individualism (which may end in disaster). The team, and in particular the father-figure Harry, must learn to accept and deploy A. J.'s 'cowboy' individualism, rather than punishing it or excluding it.

Even more than *Space Cowboys*, *Armageddon* encodes nostalgia for the strong leadership of the Kennedy-era New Frontier (relocated to space, the Final Frontier). Just as the roughnecks/Team Daedalus become the Strong Men/Representative Men of America, the United States must perform the same role in world affairs. In *Armageddon*, this is made explicit in the rhetoric of the address the President of the United States makes to a global audience before the launch: 'I speak to you ... as a citizen of humanity,' he declares. 'The dreams of an entire planet are focused tonight on those fourteen brave souls travelling into the heavens', all of whom seem to be Americans. As they watch the events unfolding, 'the consciousness of the planet is unified'. Here, then, America represents the earth, and the President represents himself as a 'citizen of humanity'. As Norman Mailer noted in *Of a Fire on the Moon*, Neil Armstrong used the very same rhetoric in his conversation with President Nixon from the Moon's surface: ' "It's a great honour and a privilege", Armstrong went on, "to be representing not only the United States but men of peace of all nations" ' (Mailer 1999: 759). America becomes both the Strong Man and the representative Man of the Earth, also echoing Armstrong's famous declaration, 'A small step for [a] man, one giant leap for mankind.' It is American exceptionalism, and American heroism, which will save the Earth; it is also, in both *Space Cowboys* and *Armageddon*, an act of sacrifice.

Before they take off on their mission, A. J. and Harry Stamper's daughter Grace (Liv Tyler) kiss beneath the launch platform of Apollo I. For a few seconds, the camera lingers on a plaque which reads: 'In Memory of those who made the ultimate sacrifice so others could reach for the stars. AD ASTRA PER ASPERA. A rough road leads to the stars. God Speed to the crew of Apollo I.' Apollo I was the first major tragedy and loss of life for NASA: a fire in the capsule cost the lives of the astronauts Gus Grissom, Ed White and Roger Chaffee in 1967. The history of the space programme is, then, one of sacrifice: 'A rough road leads to the stars.' Later NASA programmes have also incurred the deaths of astronauts, particularly two disasters involving the Space Shuttles that are the recognizable templates for the vehicles in *Space Cowboys* and *Armageddon*. As Dale Carter has argued, sacrifice has been a recurrent motif in the discourse of the space programme from its earliest inception. When Sputnik orbited the earth, *Life* magazine's editorial demanded 'a national renunciation of trivialities and a solemn dedication to serious purpose' (Carter 1988: 122). The need for sacrifice is found in *Space Cowboys* and *Armageddon*, as well as in Brian De Palma's *Mission to Mars* (2000), a film that extrapolates from the Apollo programme.

To destroy the 'global killer' asteroid in *Armageddon*, Harry Stamper sacrifices himself while sending his surrogate son A. J. back to wed his own daughter. In *Mission to Mars*, which blends NASA shuttle and 'big suit' imagery with *2001: A Space Odyssey*-style mysticism, mission commander Woody (Tim Robbins) sacrifices himself to save his wife and other fellow astronauts when their ship suffers a catastrophic failure while entering Mars orbit. (His name is surely coincidence, but a telling one: like Buzz, Hamm, Mr Potato Head *et al.*, commander Woody and his crew are on a rescue mission.) His team ethos and sacrifice eventually enables his colleagues to survive, while one heads off into the stars aboard an 'alien' craft. In *Space Cowboys*, it is Hawk Hawkins who sacrifices himself, strapping himself onto the satellite and pointing himself at the Moon. Tim Groves notes that *Space*

Cowboys contrasts with *Armageddon* here, as Tommy Lee Jones (as Hawkins) is 'appreciably younger' than Eastwood (Groves 2001: par. 29). However, this is a matter of degree, as Team Daedalus are all 'old timers'. Here we can see connections to the rhetoric of Heinlein's *Starship Troopers*, that we considered in Chapter 1. As David Seed notes, the case for citizenship proposed by Heinlein's tutor Dubois 'puts the case for heroic sacrifice .... Military service is thus presented as an idealised form of citizenship' (Seed 1999: 37). The astronaut then becomes another version of the 'citizen-soldier' that I discussed at the beginning of this book, whose subjectivity is so bound up with the nation-state that he is willing to lay down his life (heroically) for it.

For the astronauts to 'pay any price, bear any burden' to save the Earth (or one another) reveals the indebtedness of these films to not only New Frontier rhetoric, but that of the Cold War. The Cold War makes several explicit appearances in both *Space Cowboys* and *Armageddon*. In *Space Cowboys*, the satellite IKON, which Corvin and crew are called back to repair, baffles NASA experts because it is 'obsolete technology', 'a relic of the Cold War'. Initially believed to be a communications satellite, IKON is revealed to be an orbital weapons platform, its ICBMs targeted at major North American cities. This recalls not only President Reagan's SDI project, but also the fears made manifest by Sputnik's launch: Eisenhower's Secretary of Defense, Charles Wilson, reassured the American public that 'nobody is going to drop anything down on you from a satellite while you are sleeping, so don't start to worry about it' (Carter 1988: 128). In *Armageddon*, the 'Cold War relic' is the manned Russian satellite at which the shuttles dock. Emphasizing American technological superiority, the space station malfunctions and blows up, but the Russian Cosmonaut is saved and helps the roughnecks complete their mission. More importantly, on their return to Earth in the surviving shuttle, the pilot Colonel Sharp brings them in to land at the Kennedy Space Center in Florida. 'Kennedy, we see you, and you never looked so good,' he says, which would remain an unremarkable piece of dialogue except for the preceding shot. There, children play safely in the street in front of a faded poster of JFK, on which is inscribed the slogan: 'PEACE – HOPE – LIFE'. 'Kennedy, we see you': for *Armageddon*, the New Frontier nostalgically becomes the place of symbolic social, cultural or global regeneration, where the Space Race represents not an American endeavour, but a human one.

When Hawkins straps himself to IKON (nuclear missiles revealed for all to see), the film encodes another Cold War intertext: *Dr Strangelove* (1964), a rather strange and ironic reference at this point, considering Kubrick's absurdist undermining of the rhetoric of Mutually Assured Destruction and *Dr Strangelove*'s apocalyptic ending. The same reference is made by *Armageddon*, albeit more explicitly. When suffering from 'space dementia', the 'genius' roughneck (played by Steve Buscemi) climbs astride the nuclear device that is meant to split the asteroid, shouting: 'Yee-hah! Ride 'em cowboy!' When he does not get the right response, he explains: 'I was doing that guy from the movie, y'know, Slim Pickens, where he rides it all the way in ...' *Armageddon* (like *Dr Strangelove*) explicitly parodies the massive phallicism of the heroic masculinity encoded in Cold War/New Frontier discourse, a phallicism (perhaps unsurprisingly) picked up by Norman Mailer in 1970: 'if one studies the morphology of rockets [the inescapable answer] is that man worships his phallus' (Mailer 1999: 720). *Space Cowboys*, it seems, does not undercut its heroism quite so mercilessly. Although he is strapped to the IKON weapons platform (called a 'six-gun' by Eastwood), like *Armageddon* parodying phallic heroism, Hawk's sacrifice is also a fulfilment of his dearest wish: to finally go to the Moon. In the final shot of the film, Hawk sits, in his 'big suit', on the Moon's surface, facing back to an Earth reflected in his polarized suit visor, as 'Fly Me to the Moon' plays on the soundtrack, somewhat lightening the motif of heroic sacrifice. What this final image also does is to re-encode the Right Stuff-era test pilots as displaced (and frustrated) Apollo astronauts; in *Space Cowboys*, Hawk and Team Daedalus finally get to complete their 'true' mission. Like Steve Judd or J. B. Books, Hawk Hawkins and Harry Stamper can step off the stage, their heroic masculinity having outlived its time, but bringing a better world into being.

To conclude, we will turn briefly to *the* fiction of the Final Frontier, one that began in the Apollo era. This is, of course, *Star Trek*, broadcast over three seasons from 1966 to 1969. *Star Trek* remains a massively popular phenomenon nearly 40 years after its inception, long outlasting the public taste for 'real' space programmes. In the world of *Star Trek*, the Federation can be read as a kind of Greater NASA, which embodies what James Earl Webb, the Administrator of NASA from 1961 to 1968, believed were its guiding principles. As Dale Carter summarizes:

> The large-scale integration of men and machinery, of invention and production ... comprised both a practical mechanism for the creation of an efficient, benevolent, and liberating social system and a formal paradigm for the rational administration of the resulting society. (Carter 1988: 199)

The future in *Star Trek* has been variously characterized as militaristic, imperialistic or even utopian. It is described by Carter as an 'American-led multinational corps of missionaries ... spreading peace by enterprise' (Carter 1988: 201), while Richard Slotkin calls the typical *Star Trek* narrative a 'tale of individual action (typically a captivity/rescue) [that] is presented as the key to a world-historical (or cosmic-historical) struggle between darkness and light' (Slotkin 1998: 635). As an extension of the NASA paradigm, the starship *Enterprise* surely becomes, in Thomas M. Disch's phrase, 'an office disguised as the Future' (Disch 1998: 101), the triumph of heroic administration.

The adventures of Captain Kirk (an analogue of the heroic Apollo astronaut) suffer the same tension between being the Strong Man and the Representative Man: *Star Trek* seems to encode a virile, heroic masculinity within the rigid hierarchy of the Federation, through which macro-political conflicts can be resolved. The most explicit version of this in the original television series is the episode 'Arena', first broadcast in 1967, which explicitly presents itself as a Cold War parable. Discovering that the human colony of Cestus III has been subject to a massacre (which has implicit shades of the Western frontier outpost), Kirk reads this act as a hostile prelude to invasion: 'It's a matter of policy', the hawkish Kirk tells the dove-like Spock, who counsels caution and negotiation; 'out here we're the only policeman around.' (This somewhat compromises the famous opening rhetoric of the show: 'To seek out new worlds, new civilizations, to boldly go where no one has gone before': exploration rather than policing.) Chasing the 'Gorn' ship into unknown territory, both captains are removed by a super-advanced species and placed on a deserted planet, where physical combat will determine the winner. The advanced beings, the Metrones, indulge themselves in a form of conflict resolution; it is, however, only when Kirk realizes that the Gorn may have read the Cestus III colony as itself an invasion, that he is able to show mercy to his defeated alien foe. 'We can talk,' he tells the opposing captain, 'maybe reach an agreement'. For this display of 'civilized' attributes, the Metrones spare both crews. In 'Arena', détente is preferable to conflict, and even the heroic Cold Warrior, Kirk, must bow to the precedence of a negotiated settlement.

In *Star Trek VI: The Undiscovered Country* (1991), the last film made by the 'original' crew, conflict (this time with the Klingon Empire) is again brought to an end. The Cold War analogy is even more explicit: 'In space, all warriors are Cold Warriors.' When the Klingon diplomat is assassinated, suspicion falls on Kirk, who finds it hard to abandon his Cold War hatreds: 'How on Earth can history get past people like me?' he asks. Unfortunately, Kirk's antagonist is General Chang (Christopher Plummer), who engineers a show trial in which Kirk and Doctor McCoy are found guilty of murder; his motive is that he does not want the war to end or for détente to take place, for fear of loss of prestige or power. Once again, ideological tensions are resolved in combat, and eventually Kirk and crew engage Chang's ship and destroy him.

Star Trek VI is patterned on the Old Age Westerns, battling the inevitable onset of superannuation, finally exercising violent means to bring violence to an end. Spock asks Kirk: 'Is it possible that you and I have grown so old, so inflexible, that we have outlived our usefulness?' Having completed their final mission, like Steve Judd, J. B. Books, Hawk Hawkins and Harry Stamper, they step off the stage; or rather, fly the *Enterprise* into the sun. Asked where they are heading, Kirk replies: 'second star to the right, and straight on 'til morning.' Early in *Space Cowboys*, when Corvin is trying to persuade Hawk to rejoin Team Daedalus, they are told: 'when are the two of you going to grow up and stop acting like little boys?'; and Jay Leno, in a short cameo appearance as himself, says about the Team, 'No matter what age men are, they never change.' However, the key line is given by Hawk to the attractive young female engineer he romances before the mission: 'Did you ever meet a kid who wouldn't grow up?' he says of himself, and by extension all of Team Daedalus. In fulfilling Hawk's desire, *Space Cowboys* returns him (and the other members of the Team) to the dreams of youth; in its fantasy rewriting of the script of superannuation, *Space Cowboys* makes its old men (like Buzz and Woody) forever young. *Star Trek VI: The Undiscovered Country* affords its superannuated Cold Warriors a final voyage into undying legend. The myth underlying both films, and the return of old men to the New Frontier, to the 'hopes and threats' of the late-1950s and early-1960s, is, curiously enough, that of Peter Pan.

Star Trek VI was in production as the fall of the Berlin Wall changed the political and cultural landscape, making its end-of-the-Cold War scenario particularly pertinent. The other films considered in this chapter were all released, or were in production, during President Clinton's second term. Clinton's administration, while not deploying New Frontier mythology, did, however, inherit the counterinsurgency imperatives of the Kennedy/ Johnson administrations, and sent American troops to Somalia and Kosovo. The New Frontier nostalgia of *Armageddon* and *Space Cowboys* does, then, perhaps sit well in the culture of the decade. Richard Slotkin's thesis, that the rhetoric of the New Frontier articulated an ideological programme of the heroic President, strong leadership at home and intervention abroad, does not quite explain the recurrent motif of the old age hero, nor the necessity of sacrifice. However, in articulating the sentiment 'Kennedy, we see you, and you never looked so good', *Armageddon* portrays the loss of the heroic leader, the one who is strong in times of crisis. (Despite his rhetoric of unity, the President in *Armageddon* is weak. It is the sacrificed hero, Harry Stamper, who saves the world.) In the films under discussion, this strength may not be found in young astronauts, such as Ethan in *Space Cowboys*, but in those associated with the time of Cold War 'hopes and threats'. The motif of old age, imported from the post-1962 Hollywood Western, indicates not the 'dying of the light' for the masculine hero, but the necessity for the Cold Warrior to be forever young.

Bibliography

Abbott, M. E. (2002), *The Street Was Mine: White Masculinity in Hardboiled Fiction and Film Noir*. Basingstoke and New York: Palgrave Macmillan.

Allsop, K. (1958), *The Angry Decade: A Survey of the Cultural Revolt of the Nineteen-Fifties*. London: Peter Owen.

Althusser, L. (1971), 'Ideology and State Ideological Apparatuses', in *Lenin and Philosophy and other essays*. Trans. B. Brewster. London: NLB, pp. 123–73.

Amis, K. (1954), *Lucky Jim* (1953). London: Gollancz.

Amis, K. (1961), *New Maps of Hell*. London: Gollancz.

Anderson, S. (1996), 'A City Called Heaven: Black Enchantment and Despair in Los Angeles', in *The City: Los Angeles and Urban Theory at the End of the Twentieth Century*, A. C. Scott and E. Soja (eds). Berkeley, Los Angeles and London: University of California Press, pp. 336–64.

Atkins, J. (1984), *The British Spy Novel: Styles in Treachery*. London: John Calder.

Barley, T. (1986), *Taking Sides: The Fiction of John Le Carré*. Milton Keynes and Philadelphia: Open University Press.

Barthes, R. (1973), *Mythologies*. London: Paladin.

Bazin, A. (1971), 'The Evolution of the Western' (1955), in *What is Cinema? volume II*, H. Gray (ed.). Berkeley, Los Angeles and London: University of California Press, pp. 149–57.

Beard, W. (2000), *Persistence of Double Vision: Essays on Clint Eastwood*. Edmonton: The University of Alberta Press.

Bellour, R. (2002) *The Analysis of Film*, C. Penley (ed.). Bloomington: Indiana University Press.

Bennett, T. and Woollacott, J. (1990), 'Figures of Bond', in *Popular Fiction: Technology, Ideology, Production, Reading*, T. Bennett (ed.). London: Routledge, pp. 425–43.

Berger, J. (1972), *Ways of Seeing*. Harmondsworth: BBC/Penguin.

Beynon, J. (2002), *Masculinities and Culture*. Buckingham and Philadelphia: Open University Press.

Bingham, D. (1994), *Acting Male: Masculinities in the Films of James Stewart, Jack Nicholson and Clint Eastwood*. New Brunswick, NJ: Rutgers University Press.

Biskind, P. (2001), *Seeing Is Believing: Or How Hollywood Taught Us to Stop Worrying and Love the Fifties*. London: Bloomsbury.

Black, J. (2001), *The Politics of James Bond: From Fleming's Novels to the Big Screen*. Westport, CT: Praeger.

Bobbitt, P. (2003), *The Shield of Achilles: War, Peace and the Course of History*. London: Penguin.

Braine, J. (1991), *Room at the Top* (1957). London: Mandarin.

Brod, H. (1995), 'Masculinity as Masquerade', in *The Masculine Masquerade: Masculinity and Representation*, A. Perchuk and H. Posner (eds). Cambridge, MA and London: MIT Press, pp. 13–19.

Brookeman, C. (1984), *American Culture and Society since the 1930s*. London and Basingstoke: Macmillan.

Brown, R. (1994), 'Postmodern Americas in the Fiction of Angela Carter, Martin Amis and Ian McEwan', in *Forked Tongues: Comparing Twentieth-century British and American literature*, A. Massa and A. Stead (eds). London and New York: Longman.

Bukatman, S. (1993), *Terminal Identity: The Virtual Subject in Postmodern Science Fiction*. Durham and London: Duke University Press.

Burnham, J. (1972), *The Managerial Revolution: What is Happening in the World* (1941). Westport, CT: Greenwood Press.

Buscombe, E. (ed.) (1993), *The BFI Companion to the Western* (2nd edn). London: BFI.

Buscombe, E. (2004), *Unforgiven*. London: BFI.

Butler, J. (1990), *Gender Trouble: Feminism and the Subversion of Identity*. London and New York: Routledge.

Carroll, N. (1998), 'The Professional Western: South of the Border', in *Back in the Saddle Again: New Essays on the Western*, E. Buscombe and R. E. Pearson (eds). London: BFI, pp. 46–62.

Carter, D. (1988), *The Final Frontier: The Rise and Fall of the American Rocket State*. London and New York: Verso.

Caughie, J., A. Kuhn, M. Merck and B. Creed (eds) (1992), *The Sexual Subject: A Screen Reader in Sexuality*. London and New York: Routledge.

Cawelti, J. G. and Rosenberg, B. A. (1987), *The Spy Story*. Chicago and London: University of Chicago Press.

Church Gibson, P. (2004), 'Queer looks, male gazes, taut torsos and designer labels', in *The Trouble With Men: Masculinities in European and Hollywood Cinema*, P. Powrie, A. Davies and B. Babington (eds). London: Wallflower.

Clover, C. J. (1992), *Men, Women and Chainsaws: Gender in the Modern Horror Film*. London: BFI.

Cobley, P. (2000), *The American Thriller: Generic Innovation and Social Change in the 1970s*. Basingstoke: Palgrave.

Coe, J. (1990), 'In a Tunnel called Love', *Guardian*, 10 May, 22.

Cohan, S. (1995), 'The Spy in the Grey Flannel Suit: Gender Performance and the Representation of Masculinity in *North by Northwest*', in *The Masculine Masquerade: Masculinity and Representation*, A. Perchuk and H. Posner (eds), Cambridge, MA and London: MIT Press, pp. 43–62.

Cohan, S. (1997), *Masked Men: Masculinity and Movies in the Fifties*. Bloomington and Indianapolis: Indiana University Press.

Cohan, S. and R. Hark (eds) (1993), *Screening the Male*, London: Routledge.

Cohen, E. A. (2001), 'Twilight of the Citizen Soldier', *Parameters*, Summer, 21 pars. www.findarticles.com/p/articles/mi_m0IBR/is_2_31/ai_76496206/print

Cohen, J. (1997), 'James Ellroy, Los Angeles and the Spectacular Crisis of Masculinity', in *Criminal Proceedings: The Contemporary American Crime Novel*, P. Messent (ed.). London and Chicago: Pluto Press, pp. 168–86.

Condon, R. (1960), *The Manchurian Candidate*. New York: New American Library.

Corber, R. J. (1993), *In the Name of National Security: Hitchcock, Homophobia, and the Political Construction of Gender in Postwar America*. Durham and London: Duke University Press.

Corkin, S. (2004), *Cowboys as Cold Warriors: The Western and U.S. History*. Philadelphia: Temple University Press.

Coyne, M. (1997), *The Crowded Prairie: American National Identity in the Hollywood Western*. London and New York: I. B. Tauris.

Dargis, M. (2003), *LA Confidential*. London: BFI.

Davies, J. and C. R. Smith (1997), *Gender, Ethnicity and Sexuality in Contemporary American Film*. Edinburgh: Keele University Press.

Davis, M. (1996), 'How Eden Lost its Garden: A Political History of the Los Angeles Landscape', in *The City: Los Angeles and Urban Theory at the End of the Twentieth Century*, A. C. Scott and E. Soja (eds). Berkeley, Los Angeles and London: University of California Press, pp. 160–85.

Davis, M. (1998), *City of Quartz: Excavating the Future in Los Angeles* (1990). London: Pimlico.

Deighton, L. (1984) *Berlin Game* (1983). London: Panther.

Deighton, L. (2001), *Funeral in Berlin* (1964). London: Flamingo.

Denning, M. (1987), *Cover Stories: Narrative and Ideology in the British Spy Thriller*. London and New York: Routledge and Kegan Paul.

Didion, J. (2001), *Slouching Towards Bethlehem* (1968). London: Flamingo.

Disch, T. M. (1998), *The Dreams Our Stuff is Made Of: How Science Fiction Conquered the World*. New York and London: The Free Press.

Dollimore, J. (1991), *Sexual Dissidence: Augustine to Wilde, Freud to Foucault*. Oxford: Clarendon Press.

Dolman, E. C. (1997), 'Military, democracy, and the State in Robert A. Heinlein's *Starship Troopers*', in *Political Science Fiction*, D. M. Hassler and C. Wilcox (eds). Columbia, SC: University of South Carolina Press, pp. 196–213.

Dyer, R. (1997), *White*. London: Routledge.

Dyer, R. (1999), *Seven*. London: BFI.

Edwards, T. (1996), 'Pump Up the Postmodern: Images of Menswear and Masculinity in Contemporary Society'. *Discussion Papers in Sociology*, University of Leicester, March.

Ehrenreich, B. (1983), *The Hearts of Men: American Dreams and the Flight from Commitment*. London: Pluto Press.

Ellis, B. E. (1991), *American Psycho*. New York: Vintage.

Ellroy, J. (1990), *The Big Nowhere* (1988). London: Arrow.

Ellroy, J. (1993a), *The Black Dahlia* (1987). London: Arrow.

Ellroy, J. (1993b), *White Jazz* (1992). London: Arrow.

Ellroy, J. (1994), *LA Confidential* (1990). London: Arrow.

Ellroy, J. (1995), *American Tabloid*. London: Arrow.

Ellroy, J. (2001), *The Cold Six Thousand*. London: Century.

Erlich, R. D. (1981), 'A Womb with a View: Domesticating the Fantastic in Pohl and Kornbuth's *Gladiator-at-Law*', *Foundation* 23, October, pp. 31–9.

Faludi, S. (1999), *Stiffed: The Betrayal of Modern Man*. London: Vintage.

Farber, S. (1994), 'Peckinpah's Return', in *Doing It Right: The Best Criticism of Sam Peckinpah's* The Wild Bunch, M. Bliss (ed.). Carbondale and Edwardsville: Southern Illinois University Press, pp. 31–45.

Fiedler, L. (1967), *Love and Death in the American Novel*. London: Jonathan Cape.

Fleming, I. (2002), *Octopussy and the Living Daylights*. London: Penguin.

Fleming, I. (2004), *From Russia with Love* (1957). London: Penguin.

Foucault, M. (1990), *The History of Sexuality. Volume 1: An Introduction*. Trans. R. Hurley. Harmondsworth: Penguin.

Foucault, M. (1991), *Discipline and Punish: The Birth of the Prison* (1975). Trans. A. Sheridan. Harmondsworth: Penguin.

French, K. (ed.) (1996), *Screen Violence*. London: Bloomsbury.

French, P. (2005), *Westerns*, (Revised edition). London: Carcanet.

Friday, K. (2003), ' "A Generation Without Misery": *Fight Club*, Masculinity, and the Historical Symptom', *Postmodern Culture* 13 (3), May, 38 pars. Acccessed 6 April 2004: www.iath.Virginia.edu/pmc/text-only/issue.503/13.3friday.txt

Fulton, V. (1994), 'An Other Frontier: Voyaging West with Mark Twain and *Star Trek*'s Imperial Subject', *Postmodern Culture* 4 (3), May, 24 pars. Accessed 6 April 2004: www.iath.Virginia.edu/pmc/text-only/issue.594/fulton-v.594

Gallafent, E. (1994), *Clint Eastwood: Filmmaker and Star*. New York: Continuum.

Giroux, H. A. (2001), *Breaking in to the Movies: Film and the Culture of Politics*. Oxford: Blackwell.

Gledhill, C. (1980), '*Klute* 2: feminism and *Klute*', in *Women in Film Noir*, E. A. Kaplan (ed.). London: BFI, pp. 122–8.

Greene, G. (1978), *The Human Factor*. London: The Bodley Head.

Greene, G. (1980), *Ways of Escape*. London: The Bodley Head.

Groves, T. (2001), ' "We all have it coming, Kid": Clint Eastwood and the Dying of the Light', in *Senses of Cinema: An Online Film Journal Devoted to the Serious and Eclectic Discussion of Cinema*, 12, Feb–Mar, 31 pars. Accessed 23 March 2004: www.sensesofcinema.com/contents/01/12/unforgiven.html

Hassler, D. M. (1997), 'Swift, Pohl and Kornbluth: Publicists Anatomize Newness', in *Political Science Fiction*, D. M. Hassler and C. Wilcox (eds). Columbia, SC: University of South Carolina Press, pp. 18–25.

Hayles, N. K. (1991), 'The Borders of Madness', *Science Fiction Studies* 18 (55), Nov, pp. 321–3.

Heinlein, R. A. (1970), *Starship Troopers* (1959). London: New English Library.

Hill, J. (1986), *Sex, Class and Realism: British Cinema 1956–1963*. London: BFI.

Hilton, C. (2001), *The Wall: The People's Story*. Stroud: Sutton.

Hoberman, J. (2003), *The Dream Life: Movies, Media and the Mythology of the Sixties*. New York and London: The New Press.

Hoch, P. (1979), *White Hero, Black Beast: Racism, Sexism and the Mask of Masculinity*. London: Pluto.

Hofstadter, R. (1966), *The Paranoid Style in American Politics and Other Essays*. London: Jonathan Cape.

Hoggart, R. (1958), *The Uses of Literacy* (1957). Harmondsworth: Penguin.

Homberger, E. (1986), *John Le Carré*. London and New York: Methuen.

Huber, C. (2001), 'Andromeda Heights', *Senses of Cinema: An Online Film Journal Devoted to the Serious and Eclectic Discussion of Cinema*, 12, Feb–Mar, 12 pars. Accessed 23 March 2004: www.sensesofcinema.com/contents/01/12/ andromeda.html

Hunter, I. Q. (1999), 'From SF to sci-fi: Paul Verhoeven's *Starship Troopers*', in *Writing and Cinema*, J. Bignell (ed.). Harlow: Longman, pp. 179–92.

Huxley, A. (1994), *Brave New World Revisited*. London: Flamingo.

James, D. (2003), '"A boy stepped out": migrancy, visuality, and the mapping of masculinities in later fiction by Ian McEwan', in *Textual Practice* 17 (1), pp. 81–100.

Jameson, F. (1991), *Postmodernism, or, The Cultural Logic of Late Capitalism*. London: Verso.

Jameson, F. (1992), *The Geopolitical Aesthetic: Cinema and Space in the World System*. London: BFI.

Jeffords, S. (1994), *Hard Bodies: Hollywood Masculinity in the Reagan Era*. New Brunswick, NJ: Rutgers University Press.

Jenks, C. (1996), 'Hetero-Architecture and the L.A. School', in *The City: Los Angeles and Urban Theory at the End of the Twentieth Century*, A. C. Scott and E. Soja (eds). Berkeley, Los Angeles and London: University of California Press, pp. 47–75.

Johnson, B. S. (1973), *All Bull: The National Servicemen*. London: Allison and Busby.

Johnstone, I. (1981), *The Man with No Name*. London: Plexus.

Jones, D. (1990), 'The Great Game/The Spy Fiction of Len Deighton', in *Spy Thrillers: From Buchan to Le Carré*, Clive Bloom (ed.). Basingstoke: Macmillan, pp. 100–12.

Kadri, S. (2005), *The Trial: A History from Socrates to O. J. Simpson*. London: HarperCollins.

Kael, P. (1997), 'Killing Time', in *Screen Violence*, K. French (ed.). London: Bloomsbury, pp. 171–8.

Karsten, P. (1966), 'The American Democratic Citizen Soldier: Triumph or Disaster?', in *Military Affairs*, 30 (1), Spring, pp. 34–40.

Kartsen, P. (2001), 'The US Citizen-Soldier's Past, Present and Likely Future', *Parameters*, Summer, 28 pars. www.findarticles.com/p/articles/mi_m0IBR/is_2_ 31/ai_76496209/print

Kaveney, R. (2005), *From Alien to The Matrix: Reading Science Fiction Film*. London and New York: I. B. Tauris.

King, G. and T. Krzywinska (2000), *Science Fiction Cinema: From Outerspace to Cyberspace*. London: Wallflower.

Kinkead, E. (1959), *In Every War But One*. New York: Norton.

Kipling, R. (1994), *Kim* (1901). London: Penguin.

Kitses, J. (2004), *Horizons West: Directing the Western from John Ford to Clint Eastwood* (Revised edn). London: BFI.

Kitses, J. and G. Rickman (1998), *The Western Reader*. New York: Limelight.

Knight, P. (2001), *Conspiracy Culture: From the Kennedy Assassination to The X-Files*. London and New York: Routledge.

Le Carré, J. (1983), *Tinker, Tailor, Soldier, Spy* (1974). London: Pan.

Le Carré, J. (1999), *The Spy Who Came in from the Cold* (1963). London: Sceptre.

Lee, M. A. and B. Shlain (2002), *Acid Dreams: The Complete Social History of LSD, The CIA, The Sixties, and Beyond.* London: Pan.

Lev, P. (1986), *American Films of the 70s: Conflicting Visions.* Austin, TX: University of Texas Press.

Lyotard, J.-F. (1984), *The Postmodern Condition: A Report On Knowledge.* Trans. G. Bennington and B. Massumi. Manchester: Manchester University Press.

MacKinnon, K. (1997), *Uneasy Pleasures: The Male As Erotic Object.* London: Cygnus Arts.

MacKinnon, K. (1999), 'After Mulvey: Male Erotic Objectification', in *The Body's Perilous Pleasures: Dangerous Desires and Contemporary Culture,* M. Aaron (ed.). Edinburgh: Edinburgh University Press, pp. 13–29.

Mailer, N. (1968), 'The White Negro' (1957), in *Advertisements for Myself* (1961). London: Panther. pp. 269–89.

Mailer, N. (1999a), *Of a Fire on the Moon* (1970). London: Weidenfeld and Nicholson.

Mailer, N. (1999b), *The Time of Our Time.* London: Abacus.

Marcus, G. (2002), *The Manchurian Candidate.* London: BFI.

McCracken, S. (1998), *Pulp: Reading Popular Fiction.* Manchester: Manchester University Press.

McEwan, I. (1998), *Black Dogs* (1992). London: Vintage.

McEwan, I. (2001), *The Innocent* (1990). London: Vintage.

Middleton, P. (1992), *The Inward Gaze: Masculinity and Subjectivity In Modern Culture.* London and New York: Routledge.

Miller, A. (1988), *Timebends: A Life.* London: Methuen.

Mills, C. W. (1956), *The Power Elite.* London, Oxford and New York: Oxford University Press.

Mitchell, L. C. (1996), *Westerns: Making the Man in Fiction and Film.* Chicago and London: University of Chicago Press.

Morrison, J. (2001), 'Narration and Unease in Ian McEwan's Later Fiction', *Critique* 42 (3), Spring, pp. 253–68.

Mosley, W. (1996), *The Walter Mosley Omnibus: Devil in a Blue Dress, A Red Death, White Butterfly.* London: Picador.

Moylan, T. (1979), 'Gladiator-at-Law', *Survey of Science Fiction Literature,* vol. 2, F. N. Magill (ed.). Englewood Cliffs: Salem Press, pp. 894–7.

Mulvey, L. (1992), 'Visual Pleasure and Narrative Cinema' (1975), reprinted in *The Sexual Subject: A Screen Reader in Sexuality,* J. Caughie, A. Kuhn, M. Merck and B. Creed (eds). London and New York: Routledge, pp. 22–34.

Mulvey, L. (1993), 'Afterthoughts on "Visual Pleasure and Narrative Cinema" inspired by King Vidor's *Duel in the Sun* (1946)' (1983), in *Contemporary Film Theory,* A. Easthope (ed.). London and New York: Longman, pp. 125–34.

Murphet, J. (2001), *Literature and Race in Los Angeles.* Cambridge: Cambridge University Press.

Neale, S. (1993), 'Masculinity as Spectacle: reflections on men and mainstream cinema' (1983), in *Screening the Male: Exploring Masculinities in Hollywood Cinema,* S. Cohan and I. R. Hark (eds). London and New York: Routledge, pp. 9–20.

Neale, S. (2000), *Genre and Hollywood*. London and New York: Routledge.

Osborne, J. (1957), *Look Back in Anger* (1956). London: Faber.

Palladino, P. and T. Young (2003), 'Fight Club and the World Trade Center: On Metaphor, Scale and the Spatio-temporal (Dis)location of Violence', *Journal for Cultural Research* 7 (3), April, pp. 195–218.

Peek, W. C. (2003), 'The Romance of Competence: rethinking masculinity in the Western', *Journal of Popular Film and Television*, 30 (4), Winter, 46 pars. Accessed 23 March 2004: www.findarticles.com/cf_dls/m0412/4_30/97629463/print.jhtml

Penley, C. (1997), *NASA/Trek: Popular Science and Sex in America*. London: Verso.

Pilkington, E. (1992), 'Berlin Mon Amour', *Guardian*, 13 June, 29.

Pohl, F. and C. Kornbluth (1960a), *The Space Merchants* (1953). London: Digit.

Pohl, F. and C. Kornbluth (1960b), *Search the Sky* (1953). London: Digit.

Pohl, F. and C. Kornbluth (1973), *Gladiator-at-Law* (1955). London: Gollancz.

Pohl, F. and C. Kornbluth (1986), *The Merchants' War* (1984). New York: St Martin's.

Prowe, D. (1996), 'The making of *ein Berliner*: Kennedy, Brandt, and the origins of Détente Policy in Germany', in *From the Berlin Museum to the Berlin Wall: Essays on the Cultural and Political History of Modern Germany*, D. Wetzel (ed.). Westport, CT and London: Praeger, pp. 169–89.

Riesman, D. (1950), *The Lonely Crowd: A Study of the Changing American Character*. New Haven and London: Yale University Press.

Royle, T. (2002), *National Service: The Best Years of Their Lives*. London: Andre Deutsch.

Rubin, G. (1975), 'The Traffic in Women: Notes on the "Political Economy" of Sex', in *Toward an Anthropology of Women*. R. R. Reiter (ed.). New York and London: Monthly Review Press, pp. 157–210.

Ryan, K. (1994), *Ian McEwan*. Plymouth: Northcote.

Said, E. W. (1993), *Culture and Imperialism*. London: Chatto and Windus.

Sardar, Z. (2002), 'Introduction', in *Aliens R Us: The Other in Science Fiction*, Z. Sardar and S. Cubitt (eds). London: Pluto, pp. 1–17.

Saunders, J. (2001), *The Western Genre: From Lordsburg to Big Whiskey*. London: Wallflower.

Savran, D. (1998), *Taking It Like A Man: White Masculinity, Masochism, and Contemporary American Culture*. Princeton, NJ and Chichester: Princeton University Press.

Schatz, T. (1981), *Hollywood Genres: Formulas, Filmmaking, and the Studio System*. Boston: McGraw-Hill.

Schoene-Harwood, B. (2000), *Writing Men: Literary Masculinities from Frankenstein to the New Man*. Edinburgh: Edinburgh University Press.

Sedgwick, E. K. (1985), *Between Men: English Literature and Male Homosocial Desire*. New York: Columbia University Press.

Seed, D. (1999), *American Science Fiction and the Cold War: Literature and Film*. Edinburgh: Edinburgh University Press.

Segal, L. (1997), *Slow Motion: Changing Masculinities, Changing Men*. London: Virago.

Sharrett, C. (1999), 'Peckinpah the Radical: The Politics of *The Wild Bunch*', in *Sam Peckinpah's The Wild Bunch*, M. Bliss (ed.). Cambridge: Cambridge University Press, pp. 79–104.

Shaw, D. B. (2003), 'Making Starship Troopers', *Bad Subjects* 63, April, 18 pars. http://bad.eserver.org/issues/2003/63/shaw.html

Shippey, T. (2000), 'Starship Troopers, Galactic heroes, Mercenary Princes: the Military and Its Discontents in Science Fiction', in *Histories of the Future: Studies in Fact, Fantasy and Science Fiction*, A. Sandison and R. Dingley (eds). Basingstoke: Palgrave, pp. 168–83.

Siegel, D. (1993), *A Siegel Film*. London: Faber.

Sillitoe, A. (1958), *Saturday Night and Sunday Morning*. London: W. H. Allen.

Silverman, K. (1992), *Male Subjectivity at the Margins*. New York and London: Routledge.

Slotkin, R. (1973), *Regeneration Through Violence*. Middletown, CT: Wesleyan University Press.

Slotkin, R. (1998), *Gunfighter Nation: The Myth of the Frontier in Twentieth-Century America*. Norman: University of Oklahoma Press.

Smith, A. (2005), *Moondust: In Search Of The Men Who Fell To Earth*. London: Bloomsbury.

Smith, H. N. (1970), *Virgin Land: The American West as Symbol and Myth* (1950). Cambridge, MA and London: University of Massachusetts.

Smith, P. (1993), *Clint Eastwood: A Cultural Production*. London and Minneapolis: University of Minnesota Press.

Smith, W. (2001), 'Conspiracy, corporate culture and criticism', in *The Age of Anxiety: Conspiracy Theory and the Human Sciences*, J. Parish and M. Parker (eds). Oxford: Blackwell/The Sociological Review, pp. 153–65.

Soja, E. W. (1989), *Postmodern Geographies: The Reassertion of Space in Critical Social Theory*. London and New York: Verso.

Soja, E. and A. C. Scott (1996), 'Introduction to Los Angeles: City and Region', in *The City: Los Angeles and Urban Theory at the End of the Twentieth Century*. A. C. Scott and E. Soja (eds). Berkeley, Los Angeles and London: University of California Press, pp. 1–21.

Solnit, R. (2000), *Hollow City: The Siege of San Francisco and the Crisis of American Urbanism*. London and New York: Verso.

Spark, A. (1990), 'The Art of Future War: *Starship Troopers*, *The Forever War* and Vietnam', *Essays and Studies* 43, pp. 133–65.

Spicer, A. (2003), *Typical Men: The Representation of Masculinity in Popular British Cinema*. London and New York: I. B. Tauris.

Straw, W. (1997), 'Urban Confidential: the Lurid City of the 1950s', in *The Cinematic City*, D. B. Clarke (ed.). London and New York: Routledge, pp. 110–28.

Tasker, Y. (1993), *Spectacular Bodies: Gender, Genre and the Action Cinema*. London and New York: Routledge.

Taubin, A. (1999), 'So Good It Hurts', *Sight and Sound*, November, pp. 16–18.

Terkel, S. (1998), *My American Century*. London: Phoenix.

Theweleit, K. (1987), *Male Fantasies, Vol. I: Women, Floods, Bodies, History*. Trans. S. Conway, E. Carter and C. Turner. Cambridge: Polity.

Theweleit, K. (1989), *Male Fantasies Vol. II: Male Bodies: Psychoanalysing the White Terror*. Trans. C. Turner and E. Carter, with S. Conway. Cambridge: Polity.

Turner, F. J. (1963), *The Significance of the Frontier in American History*, H. P. Simonsen (ed.). New York: Frederick Ungar.

Vidal, G. (1994a), 'President and Mrs U.S. Grant', *United States: Essays 1952–1992*. London: Abacus, pp. 708–22.

Vidal, G. (1994b), 'The Four Generations of the Adams Family', *United States: Essays 1952–1992*. London: Abacus, pp. 644–63.

Vidal, G. (1994c), 'Homage to Daniel Shays', *United States: Essays 1952–1992*. London: Abacus, pp. 906–18.

Vidal, G. (1994d), 'The National Security State', *United States: Essays 1952–1992*. London: Abacus, pp. 1017–28.

Vidal, G. (1996), *Palimpsest: A Memoir*. London: Abacus.

Vidal, G. (1999), 'The Birds and the Bees', in *The Essential Gore Vidal*, F. Kaplan (ed.). London: Little, Brown, pp. 721–5.

Walker, J. (2001), 'Introduction: Westerns Through History', in *Westerns: Films Through History*, J. Walker (ed.). New York and London: Routledge, pp. 1–24.

Westwood, S. (1996), ' "Feckless fathers": masculinities and the British state', in *Understanding Masculinities: Social Relations and Cultural Arenas*, M. Mac an Ghaill (ed.). Buckingham and Philadelphia: Open University Press, pp. 21–34.

Whitehall, G. (2003), 'The Problem of the "World and Beyond": Encountering "the Other" in Science Fiction', in *To Seek Out New Worlds: Science Fiction and World Politics*, J. Weldes (ed.). New York and Basingstoke: Palgrave, pp. 169–93.

Whyte, W. H. (1956), *The Organization Man* (1955). New York: Simon and Schuster.

Willeman, P. (1999), 'Anthony Mann: Looking at the Male', in *The Western Reader*, J. Kitses and G. Rickman (eds). New York: Limelight, pp. 209–12.

Wolfe, T. (1990), *The Right Stuff* (1980). London: Picador.

Worland, R. and E. Countryman (1998), 'The New American Historiography and the Emergence of the New American Westerns', in *Back in the Saddle Again: New Essays on the Western*, E. Buscombe and R. E. Pearson (eds). London: BFI, pp. 182–96.

Wrathall, J. (2001), review of *LA Confidential*, in *Film/Literature/Heritage: A Sight and Sound Reader*, G. Vincendeau (ed.). London: BFI.

Wright, W. (1975), *Sixguns and Society: A Structural Study of the Western*. Berkeley and London: University of California Press.

List of films cited

A Fistful of Dollars. Dir. Sergio Leone. 1963.
Alamo, The. Dir. John Wayne. 1960.
All the President's Men. Dir. Alan J. Pakula. 1976.
American Beauty. Dir. Sam Mendes. 1999.
American Psycho. Dir. Mary Harron. 1999.
Apollo 13. Dir. Ron Howard. 1995.
Armageddon. Dir. Michael Bay. 1998.
Bend of the River. Dir. Anthony Mann. 1952.

Big Heat, The. Dir. Fritz Lang. 1953.
Big Sleep, The. Dir. Howard Hawks. 1946.
Big Trail, The. Dir. Raoul Walsh. 1930.
Blue Dahlia, The. Dir. George Marshall. 1946.
Buffalo Bill and the Indians. Dir. Robert Altman. 1976.
Bullitt. Dir. Peter Yates. 1968.
Butch Cassidy and the Sundance Kid. Dir. George Roy Hill. 1969.
Capricorn One. Dir. Peter Hyams. 1977.
Cheyenne Autumn. Dir. John Ford. 1964.
Chinatown. Dir. Roman Polanski. 1974.
Conversation, The. Dir. Francis Ford Coppola. 1974.
Coogan's Bluff. Dir. Don Siegel. 1968.
Cool Hand Luke. Dir. Stuart Rosenberg. 1967.
Covered Wagon, The. Dir. James Cruze. 1923.
Death Wish. Dir. Michael Winner. 1974.
Detective, The. Dir. Irvin Kershner. 1968.
Dirty Harry. Dir. Don Siegel. 1971.
Dr Strangelove. Dir. Stanley Kubrick. 1964.
Easy Rider. Dir. Dennis Hopper. 1969.
El Dorado. Dir. Howard Hawks. 1966.
Enforcer, The. Dir. James Fargo. 1976.
Falling Down. Dir. Joel Schumacher. 1991.
Fight Club. Dir. David Fincher. 1999.
For a Few Dollars More. Dir. Sergio Leone. 1964.
French Connection, The. Dir. William Friedkin. 1971.
From Russia with Love. Dir. Terence Young. 1963.
Game, The. Dir. David Fincher. 1997.
Gauntlet, The. Dir. Clint Eastwood. 1977.
GoldenEye. Dir. Martin Campbell. 1995.
Good, the Bad and the Ugly, The. Dir. Sergio Leone. 1966.
Halloween. Dir. John Carpenter. 1978.
High Plains Drifter. Dir. Clint Eastwood. 1972.
Hondo. Dir. John Farrow. 1953.
How The West Was Won. Dir. John Ford. 1962.
Hud. Dir. Martin Ritt. 1963.
In a Lonely Place. Dir. Nicholas Ray. 1950.
Klute. Dir. Alan J. Pakula. 1971.
LA Confidential. Dir. Curtis Hanson. 1997.
Living Daylights, The. Dir. John Glen. 1987.
Magnificient Seven, The. Dir. John Sturges. 1960.
Magnum Force. Dir. Ted Post. 1973.
Man Who Shot Liberty Valance, The. Dir. John Ford. 1962
Manchurian Candidate, The. Dir. John Frankenheimer. 1962.
Midnight Cowboy. Dir John Schlesinger. 1969.
Mission to Mars. Dir. Brian De Palma. 2000.
My Darling Clementine. Dir. John Ford. 1946.

Naked Spur, The. Dir. Anthony Mann. 1952.
North by Northwest. Dir. Alfred Hitchcock. 1959.
Open Range. Dir. Kevin Costner. 2004.
Pale Rider. Dir. Clint Eastwood. 1984.
Parallax View, The. Dir. Alan J. Pakula. 1974.
Peeping Tom. Dir. Michael Powell, 1960.
Professionals, The. Dir. Richard Brooks. 1966.
Psycho. Dir. Alfred Hitchcock. 1960.
Rear Window. Dir. Alfred Hitchcock. 1954.
Red River. Dir. Howard Hawks. 1948.
Ride the High Country. Dir. Sam Peckinpah. 1962.
Right Stuff, The. Dir. Philip Kaufman. 1983.
Rio Bravo. Dir. Howard Hawks. 1959.
Saving Private Ryan. Dir. Steven Spielberg. 1998.
Searchers, The. Dir. John Ford. 1956.
Seven. Dir. David Fincher. 1995.
Shane. Dir. George Stevens. 1953.
Shootist, The. Dir. Don Siegel. 1976.
Space Cowboys. Dir. Clint Eastwood. 2000.
Star Trek VI: The Undiscovered Country. Dir. Nicholas Meyer. 1991.
Star Trek: 'Arena'. Dir. Joseph Pevney. Broadcast 19 January 1967.
Starship Troopers. Dir. Paul Verhoeven. 1997.
Taxi Driver. Dir. Martin Scorsese. 1976.
Texas Chainsaw Massacre, The. Dir. Tobe Hooper. 1974.
This Gun for Hire. Dir. Frank Tuttle, 1942.
Toy Story. Dir. John Lasseter. 1995.
Toy Story 2. Dir. John Lasseter. 1999.
Unforgiven. Dir. Clint Eastwood. 1992.
Vertigo. Dir. Alfred Hitchcock. 1958.
Wall Street. Dir. Oliver Stone. 1986.
Wild Bunch, The. Dir. Sam Peckinpah. 1969.

Index

Lightning Source UK Ltd.
Milton Keynes UK
UKOW030612170212

187467UK00002B/15/P